Instructor's Resource Manual
and
Test Bank

to accompany

The Humanistic Tradition
Books 1 through 6
Volumes I and II

Fourth Edition

Gloria K. Fiero

Prepared by
Paul Antal
Regis University, Denver
and
Gloria K. Fiero

McGraw
Hill

Boston   Burr Ridge, IL   Dubuque, IA   Madison, WI   New York   San Francisco   St. Louis
Bangkok   Bogotá   Caracas   Kuala Lumpur   Lisbon   London   Madrid   Mexico City
Milan   Montreal   New Delhi   Santiago   Seoul   Singapore   Sydney   Taipei   Toronto

McGraw-Hill Higher Education

A Division of The McGraw-Hill Companies

Instructor's Manual and Test Bank to accompany
THE HUMANISTIC TRADITION
Gloria K. Fiero

Published by McGraw-Hill, an imprint of the McGraw-Hill Companies, Inc., 1221 Avenue of the Americas, New York, NY 10020. Copyright © 2002, 1998, 1994, 1990 by the McGraw-Hill Companies, Inc.

2 3 4 5 6 7 8 9 0 QSR/QSR 0 9 8 7 6 5 4 3 2

ISBN 0-07-238844-7

www.mhhe.com

Contents

BOOK 1

THE FIRST CIVILIZATIONS AND THE CLASSICAL LEGACY

BOOK 2

MEDIEVAL EUROPE AND THE WORLD BEYOND

BOOK 3

THE EUROPEAN RENAISSANCE, THE REFORMATION, AND GLOBAL ENCOUNTER

BOOK 4

FAITH, REASON, AND POWER IN THE EARLY MODERN WORLD

BOOK 5

ROMANTICISM, REALISM, AND THE NINETEENTH-CENTURY WORLD

BOOK 6

MODERNISM, GLOBALISM, AND THE INFORMATION AGE

Preface

A Note to Instructors

The key to successful classroom use of *The Humanistic Tradition* is **selectivity.** Students are usually assigned to read whole chapters, and some may also be required to read primary sources that supplement the abridged readings in the textbook. However, the classroom should be the stage for a selective treatment of the materials in the chapter. Concentration on the text, context, and subtext of a single major example or set of examples should prompt students to apply a similar analysis to other aspects of the chapter. Selectivity also works to free instructors from the futile effort to "teach everything" in a highly circumscribed time period, and to "rotate" the choice of texts from one semester to the next. *The Humanistic Tradition* is designed to emphasize themes that cut across geographic boundaries; themes whose universal significance invite students to evaluate and compare rather than simply memorize and repeat lists of names and places. Achieving global cultural literacy is the general goal.

Using the Instructor's Manual

This manual is intended to help both experienced and beginning humanities instructors to obtain the maximum benefit from *The Humanistic Tradition.*

How the manual is organized. Each chapter of the manual has the following parts:
A **Summary** of the thematic focus of the text chapter.
An **Outline** for preparing lectures, or for use as a checklist of topics to be covered, followed by a **Pronunciation Guide.**
Key Terms and **Key Images** are the equivalent of terms the instructor might put on the board for special emphasis, as well as slides and text illustrations central to the concerns of the chapter.
Study Questions, divided into *Factual* and *Challenge*, may be used for written assignments, test essay questions, and topics for discussion, as well as topics for independent research.
Strategies for discussion/lecture are suggestions for organizing the material of the chapter for presentation in class and stimulating thought and discussion on some of the larger implications of the issues raised.
Audiovisuals and McGraw-Hill resources to complement those on the website: www.mhhe.com/fiero.
Sample test questions at the end of each chapter of the manual.

Discussion/lecture strategies. These are designed as suggestions for presenting selected materials in class. Although many variations are possible, this manual presumes a format that includes

1. A short written assignment to be completed before class—a "micro-theme" on an important topic, often in connection with a Factual or Challenge Question, whose purpose is to stimulate students to begin thinking of broad issues raised in the chapter
2. A lecture or slide presentation providing background information
3. Suggestions for focused lecturing or for leading discussions on selected issues and texts. These suggestions include questions that have no definitive, limited answer, but challenge participants to express a viewpoint and support it with evidence from their reading, viewing, or listening.

Some assumptions underlie the framing of these strategies. The first is that no specialized, discipline-oriented point of view is adopted—or recommended. The humanities instructor and student should ask of human artifacts whatever questions bear on **general human concerns**. What does it mean to be a human? What is the relationship with fellow humans, with the environment, with God? What is the relative importance of body, feelings, imagination, reason in the human makeup? Specialized comments, whether from the instructor's particular discipline or from "specialists" and scholars, generally impress the beginning student and, therefore, stultify participation and inquiry, on the grounds that he or she lacks the requisite prior training.

The question of how someone new to humanities instruction is to approach these materials without special preparation points to a second assumption: that **a comparative approach** will be used whenever possible. Students typically feel at sea when asked to give a reaction to a Byzantine icon, for example, yet they prove quite capable of comparing that image to a second one in a different style, or from a different period or culture. Here the thematic and topical emphasis of *The Humanistic Tradition* will prove very helpful, as will the numerous cross references in the volumes.

A third assumption is that the instructor will try to relate documents remote in time, or culturally distant, to the lives of the students. A simple opening question might be "What from the heritage of _____ is present in your life?" The text provides many such suggestions, and students will offer others, from the math of Mesopotamia to the food of Italy, to the beliefs of the major religious traditions. Providing a contemporary perspective can take many forms, including negative ones, such as the difficulty of relating Arabic or Indian music to current taste. The reaction, "It's hard to listen to" can become the inquiry, "What do you imagine a Hindu or a Muslim hears when American popular music comes over the radio?" Another technique for **making remote historical artifacts alive** today is to ask the class members to place themselves in the period, for instance, in front of the Louvre or the palace at Versailles: imagine it is the seventeenth century; are you a peasant? a visiting aristocrat? can you go into this palace? what does the size and style of the building tell you about those in power?

As both instructors and students become comfortable with a nonspecialized, "amateur" status in humanistic studies, a larger goal will have been achieved: what appeared a deficit at the start will prove a strength, as all participants become involved inquirers, adding multiple perspectives to our views of humanity and culture.

Using the Student Study Guide

Instructors may wish to familiarize themselves with the two-volume Student Study Guide prepared by Gloria K. Fiero. This guide, available for purchase, provides students with chapter by chapter learning goals; an outline of each chapter; key names, terms, and dates; multiple choice questions and essay questions designed to test both the general knowledge and the creative imagination of the student. A section entitled "Making Connections" asks students to probe the relevance of the material in the chapter to their own lives. Included also are map quizzes and bonus information, such as diagrams showing types of Greek vases, musical scales, and categories of musical instruments. The Student Study Guide includes models for an innovative learning technique known as "clustering."[1] Clustering is a technique that encourages students to focus on key words and phrases that prompt ideas and associations. In contrast with linear modes of organizing information, the clustering process, which uses the "windows-style" graphics of some software programs, is spatial and holistic. You may wish to assign these worksheets (or other exercises in the Guide) prior to class discussion. The pages of the Student Study Guide are perforated so that these and other assignments may be removed and submitted in class.

---

[1] Gabriele L. Rico. *Writing the Natural Way.* New York: St. Martin's Press, 1983; see also G. L. Rico and M. F. Claggett. *Balancing the Hemispheres: Brain Research and the Teaching of Writing.* Berkeley: University of California, 1980.

About MicroTest

The sample test questions at the end of each chapter are available on MicroTest III, a powerful but easy-to-use test-generating program by Chariot Software Group. MicroTest is available for DOS, Windows, and Macintosh personal computers. With MicroTest, you can easily view and select the test item file questions, then print a test and answer key. You can customize questions, headings, and instructions, you can add or import questions of your own, and you can print your test in a choice of fonts allowed by your printer.

Please consult your local McGraw-Hill representative for policies, prices, and availability of all ancillaries.

The Classical Legacy

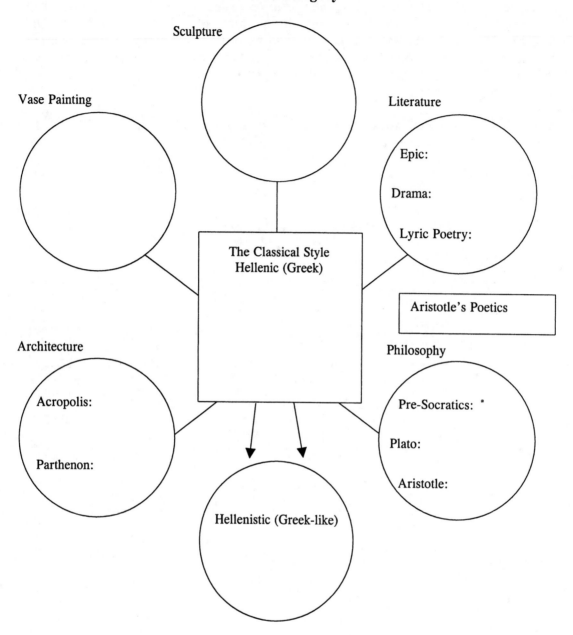

Sculpture

Vase Painting

Literature

Epic:

Drama:

Lyric Poetry:

The Classical Style
Hellenic (Greek)

Aristotle's Poetics

Architecture

Acropolis:

Parthenon:

Philosophy

Pre-Socratics:

Plato:

Aristotle:

Hellenistic (Greek-like)

Nineteenth-Century Romanticism

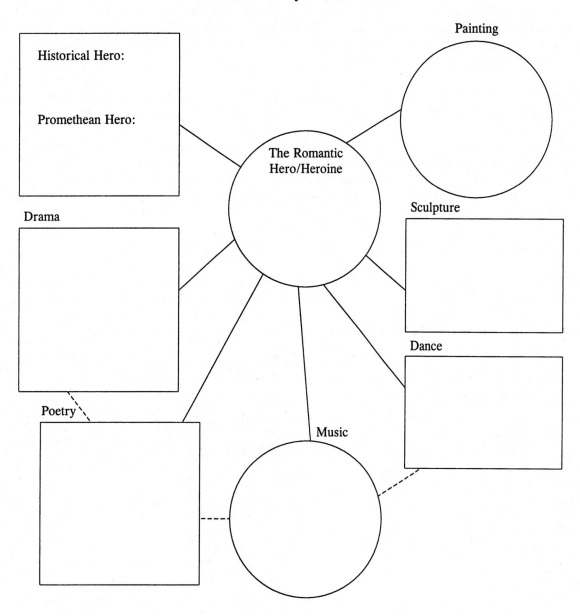

About the Audiovisual Resource Listings

The Video/CD-ROM section in each chapter of the IM has been updated to include many new videos on topics featured in *The Humanistic Tradition,* fourth edition. Some products may be out-of-print and unavailable from a known distributor. However, most of these videos are still staples in university humanities libraries and can be found there.

A variety of multimedia products along with brief descriptions are listed for each chapter. The CD-ROMs can be purchased by calling the multimedia vendors, many of whom have email and/or Web sites.

The Web sites listed here are only the tip of the iceberg. With the explosion of information on the Web, new sites are cropping up daily. Instructors and students can find new Web sites easily by typing key words into any search engines such as Alta Vista, Lycos, and Yahoo. Because the nature of the Web is change, Web sites also disappear quickly. An effort was made to select Web sites which appeared to have lasting qualities.

General Audiovisual Resources

The addresses for the media companies who publish the films, videos, and CD-ROMs cited in this manual, usually in an abbreviated form, are listed below. In addition to the up-to-date catalogs that may be obtained from writing or calling these companies, instructors in search of audiovisual resources should consult *The Video Source Book*, 25th edition, 2001 (Detroit: Gale Group)

AE
ARTS & ENTERTAINMENT HOME VIDEO
(History Channel & Biography)
http://store.aetv.com/html/h01.jhtml
Phone: 888-423-1212

AZ
AMAZON
Amazon.com

BLACKWOOD PRODUCTIONS
BLACKWOOD PRODUCTIONS
251 W. 57th Street
New York, NY 10019
212-247-4710

CAROUSEL
CAROUSEL FILM & VIDEO
260 5th Ave. #905
New York, NY 10019
1-800-683-1660

CORONET
CORONET/MTI Film & Video
4350 Equity Drive
P.O. Box 2649
Columbus, OH 43216
1-800-777-8100

CPB
CORPORATION FOR PUBLIC
BROADCASTING
901 E Street NW
Washington, DC 20004-2037
1-800-LEARNER

CRM
CRM/MCGRAW-HILL FILMS
2215 Faraday Ave.
Carlsbad, CA 92008
1-800-421-0833

CREES
Materials from the documentary lending library are available for two-week checkout by instructors in the US and Canada for classroom use and curriculum development. The user is responsible for paying postage and postal insurance for the return of the video. To check out a video or for further information, please submit an online request or contact Mary Dakin, CREES Assistant Director, at (650) 723-3562 or mdakin@stanford.edu.
http://www.stanford.edu/dept/CREES/videolib.html

EBBC
ENCYCLOPEDIA BRITANNICA
EDUCATIONAL CORP.
310 S. Michigan Ave.
Chicago, IL 60604
1-800-323-1229
britannica.com

EVN
EDUCATIONAL VIDEO NETWORK
1401 19th Street
Huntsville, TX 77340
1-800-762-0060

FFH
FILMS FOR THE HUMANITIES &
SCIENCES
P.O. Box 2053
Princeton, NJ 08543-2053
Phone: 800-257-5126
Fax: 609-275-3767
www.films.com

HTG
HUMANITIES TO GO
1500 N. Delaware St.
Indianapolis, IN 46202-2419
Phone: 317.638.1500 or
1.800.675.8897, ext. 128
Lending Video Library—initial membership
fee required
www.inc4u.org/htg.htm

IFB
INTERNATIONAL FILM BUREAU
332 S. Michigan Ave.
Chicago, IL 60604-4382
512-427-4545

IM
INSIGHT MEDIA
2162 Broadway
New York, NY 10024
10-800-233-9910

IU
INDIANA UNIVERSITY
Instructional Support Services
Bloomington, IN 47405-5908
1-800-552-8620
issmedia@indiana.edu

MMA
METROPOLITAN MUSEUM OF ART
1000 5th Ave.
New York, NY 10028
212-535-7710

MYSTIC
MYSTIC FIRE VIDEO
524 Broadway #604
New York, NY 10012
1-800-64-LEARN

NETCHE
NETCHE
1800 N. 33 rd Street
Lincoln, NE 68503
402-472-3611
www.netche.unl.edu

NOVA
NOVA
967 Broadway
New York, NY 10007

PBS
PBS.ORG
PBS Home Video,
P.O. Box 751089
Charlotte, NC 28275
Call 877-PBS-SHOP

PH
PHAIDON
Phaidon Press Inc.
7195 Grayson Road
Harrisburg, PA 17111
Phone: 877 PHAIDON (toll free)
Fax: 877 742 4370 (toll free)
Customer Service: ussales@phaidon.com
http://www.phaidon.com

RMI
RMI MEDIA PRODUCTIONS, INC
1365 N. Winchester
Olathe, KS 66061
1-800-745-5480

TLF
TIME-LIFE VIDEO AND TELEVISION
1450 E. Parham Rd.
Richmond, VA 23280
1-800-621-7026

UC
UNIVERSITY OF CALIFORNIA
Extension Media Center
2000 Center Street
4th floor
Berkley, CA 94720
510-642-0460

UEUWIS
UNIVERSITY OF WISCONSIN-
EXTENSION
Bureau of AV Instruction
1327 University Ave.
Madison, WI 53701

UMNAV
UNIVERSITY OF MINNESOTA
Media Distribution
Box 734 Mayo Memorial Building
420 Delaware St. SE
Minneapolis, MN 55455
612-624-7306

VC
THE VIDEO CATALOG
700 Westgate Drive
St. Paul, MN 55114
1-800-733-6656

VM
VIDEO MONUMENTS
P.O. Box 5743
Berkley, CA 94705
510-549-1922

WEBC
GROUP W. PRODUCTIONS, INC.
Westinghouse Broadcasting
240 W. 44th Street
New York, NY 10036

Multimedia Resources

Below is contact information for the multimedia companies who publish products listed in this manual.

Anglia Multimedia
info@angmulti.demon.co.uk
http://www.anglia.co.uk

Beijing Tinguan Electronic
Science and Technology
wangxxin@public.bta.net.cn
http://ele.ceiec.com.cn/company/
eyinguan.html

Cambridge University Press
information@cup.com.ac.uk
http://www.cup.cam.ac.uk

Chadwyck-Healy, Inc.
1101 King Street
Alexandria, VA 22314
800-752-0515
contact@chadwyck.fr
http://www.chadwyck.com

CLEARVUE
6465 North Avondale Avenue
Chicago, IL 60631-1996
800-CLEARVU (253-2788)
http://www.clearvue.com

Digital Collections Inc.
1301 Marina Village Parkway
Alameda, CA 94501
800-449-6220
sales@digital-collections.com
http://www.digital-collections.com

ECS
Electronic Courseware Systems, Inc.
1210 Lancaster Drive
Champaign, IL 61821
217-359-7099
800-832-4965

EEME Interactive
emmeusa@aol.com
http://www.emme.com

Endless SA
prudhomme@interpac.be

Future Publishers
future@future-publishers.com.lb
http://www.future-publishers.com.lb/

Grolier Interactive
213-797-3530
http://www.grolier.com

Intellimation
intellifm@aol.com

Interplay Company
800-969-4263

Lambrakis Research Foundation
iml@iml.ath.forthnet.gr
http://www.lrf.gr

Logos Research Systems
715 SE Fidalgo Avenue
Oak Harbor, WA 98277-4049
360-679-6575
info@logos.com
http://www.logos.com

Mediasat Group
Guzman El Bueno, 133
Madrid, 28003 Spain
+ 34 153 38818
http://www.mediasat.it/

Mediatime Sri
Via Udine No. 15
33050 Pavia di Udine (UD)
Italy

Mille Médias
390 Quietwood Drive
San Rafael, CA 94903
415-507-9524
syrinxusa@aol.com

Montparness Multimedia
grand-chavin@itw.fr

Oxford University Press
2001 Evans Road
Cary, NC 27513
800-445-9714
caldwelj@oup.co.uk
ep.help@oup.co.uk

Philips Interactive Multimedia
188 Tottenham Ct Rd
London W1P 9LE, UK
+44 171 9 113000

Primary Source Media
12 Lunar Drive
Woodbridge, CT 06525
800-444-0799
sales@psmedia.co.uk
http://www.thomson.com/psmedia.html

Queue Inc.
338 Commerce Drive
Fairfield, CT 06432
800-232-2224
sales@mail.queueinc.com
queueinc@aol.com
http://www.queueinc.com

Réunion des Musées Nationaux
reumunat@iway.fr

SoftKey International
Heritage House
21 Inner Park Road
Wimbledon Common
London, SW196ED, UK
+44 181 2464000
http://www.softkey.com/

Take 2 Interactive Software
575 Broadway
New York, NY 10012
212-941-2988

Thomas S. Klise Company
PO Box 317
Waterford, CT 06385
860-442-4449
klise@klise.com
http://www.klise.com

Time Warner Electronic Publishing
http://www.pathfinder.com/twep

World Library Inc.
800-443-0238

Zane Interactive Publishing
PO Box 2075
Dallas, TX 75207
800-460-0444
customer@zane.com
http://www.zane.com

General Music Resources

Two CDs are available to accompany *The Humanistic Tradition*. CD I corresponds to the Music Listening Selections discussed in Books 1–3 and CD II to the music in Books 4–6. Each selection on the CDs is discussed in the text and includes a voice introduction for easier location.

For music of individual composers, electronic music, and special collections, the best single resource is the most current edition of *Opus* (also known as *Schwann Opus*), available at any large store or from Schwann Publications, 1280 Santa Anita Court, Woodland, CA 95776, 1-800-792-9447.

For non-Western music (including Asian, Islamic, and Native American), see the large collection of cassettes available from Folkways, now

Smithsonian/Folkways Recordings
Center for Folklife and Cultural Heritage
Smithsonian Institution
750 9th Street, N.W. Suite 4100
Washington, D.C. 20560-0953
202-275-1143

McGraw-Hill Music Resources:

The Development of Western Music, 3e, by K. Marie Stolba,
Volumes I and II CDs or cassettes offer a chronological presentation of the sweep of Western music and its composers, beginning with the music of antiquity and proceeding to the 20th century.

Music: An Appreciation, 7e, by Roger Kamien
Basic Set of 8 CDs or cassettes
Brief Set of 4 CDs or cassettes
Western musical styles from Middle Ages to the present, including jazz and rock, as well as non-Western music.

The World of Music, 5e, by David Willoughby
5 CD set includes a diverse range of listening examples including folk, spiritual, jazz, pop, and world music, in addition to more traditional Western "art music" selections.

General Slide Resources

A set of 100 slides is available to accompany books 1-6 or Volumes I and II of The Humanistic Tradition. Please contact your local sales representative if you are interested in obtaining the slide set. Universal Color Slide also has a "pick your own" list of slides available. Please contact Universal Color Slide if you are interested.

Universal Color Slide
8450 South Tamiami Trail
Sarasota, FL 34238-2936
Tel: 800-326-1367
Fax: 800-487-0250
www.universalcolorslide.com

Saskia, Ltd.
5 Horizon Lane
Freeport, ME 04032
877-727-5422
www.saskia.com

Davis Art Slides (formerly Rosenthal Art Slides)
50 Portland Street
Worcester, MA 01608
800-533-2847
www.davis-art.com

The Humanistic Tradition Contents: Books 1–6

Sample Syllabi

BOOK 1

The First Civilizations and the Classical Legacy

Introduction **Prehistory and the Birth of Civilization**

Summary

The story of our humanistic tradition begins in the prehistory of the human family as it struggled for survival in an environment it sought to control. Paleolithic people were tribal hunters and gatherers who attempted to control nature by means of stone and bone tools and weapons, and cooperated with natural cycles by moving with the food supply they gathered. Neolithic people sought even greater control over nature by producing crops and domesticating animals. With the birth of civilization (about 4000 B.C.E.) in river valleys from the North Africa to China, urban trading centers cultivated the hallmarks of early civilization, including a written system of record-keeping, bronze technology, wheeled vehicles, and monumental architecture.

Outline	Pronunciation Guide
A. Prehistory	**Australopithicus** [ahws tra low PI thi kus]
1. methods of compilation	*Homo habilis* [how mow HAB ilis]
2. chronology	**Neanderthal** [nee AN der tahl]
B. Paleolithic ("Old Stone Age") culture	**Lascaux** [las KOW]
1. hominids	**Cyclades** [SEYE klah deez]
2. *homo erectus*	**cuneiform** [kyoo NEE I form]
3. *homo sapiens*	**Willendorf** [VILL en dorf]
a. tools and weapons	**Sumer** [SOO mer]
b. visual record	**stele** [STAY LAY}
C. Neolithic ("New Stone Age") culture	
1. food production	
2. tools and crafts	
3. visual record	
a. new awareness of seasonal change	
b. post and lintel construction	
4. birth of cities	
a. the first urban communities	**Pronunciation Key:** (*Note: Use this key for all subsequent chapters.*) a*pp*le, *pl*ay, **ah** (altar), *e*gg, *k*ee*p*, *inch*, **eye**, *gl*ow, *b*oo*z*e, ou*tf*it, *bul*k, **u** in *b*oo*k*, *single*, *shin*, *ch*apter, *j*ust; *z*ebra, *zh*ivago (vision), *canyon*.
b. specialization of labor	
c. metallurgy/bronze technology	
d. writing: origins and function	
D. Myth and the quest for beginnings	

Key terms: hominids, *homo habilis, homo sapiens,* sympathetic magic, gathering and hunting, dolmen, megaliths, agriculture, Paleolithic, Neolithic, civilization, pictographs, metallurgy, B.C.E./C.E., animism, myth.

Key Images	
Hall of Bulls, Lascaux	Neolithic house at Hassuna
Venus of Willendorf	Painted Beaker from Susa
Stonehenge	King of Lagash Limestone stele

Study Questions

Factual

1. Describe the primary characteristics of Paleolithic and Neolithic cultures, citing similarities and differences.
2. Why did early people originate forms of sacrifice and rituals?
3. Distinguish between hominid, *homo habilis,* and *homo sapiens.*
4. Give a rough description of the sequence of tool making. What does each tool add to human control over nature?
5. What was the relative span of time occupied by *homo sapiens* in the life of the species *homo*?
6. What is the Rosetta Stone? Why was its discovery so significant?
7. What makes the Neolithic Age "revolutionary?"
8. In Reading 1.1, what do "preparations for the hunt" mean to the Pygmies? How do they differ from those of a modern hunter?
9. Put into your own words the term *sympathetic magic.*
10. What do all the "creation myths" in the introduction have in common?

Challenge

1. The reconstruction of prehistory depends on "documents," such as tools made of durable materials like stone. How might this basis of evidence distort our view of cultures remote in time? What aspects of early human life have left no records?
2. The earliest tools were made of perishable materials (baskets, fabric, digging sticks). Describe their function and importance to the community.
3. When asked what distinguishes existing hunter/gatherers from urban societies, one feature Margaret Mead singled out was that the former could not imagine learning anything from a book. Have we personally learned what is most important to living from books?
4. Give a general description of the new tool kit required by an agricultural society. How did these tools extend control over nature?
5. Survey the art in the introduction: How are people and nature depicted? Do you see any significant changes in the art that comes from the transition to urban life?
6. What circumstances contributed to the development of writing? What purpose did it serve? Did the entire population master this new technique?
7. Make two lists describing "art" as conceived and executed by early humans and how we think of "museum art." Include (a) who makes it, (b) for what reason, (c) who owns it, (d) where it is displayed, (e) what it is made out of.

8. Research the tribes of people still living by hunting and gathering: describe the environment in which they live.
9. What other creation myths can you uncover? How do they compare with those in the introduction? What role does the union of male and female deities play in some creation myths?

Strategies for Discussion/Lecture

1. As preparation for class, students can be asked to write a mini-theme based on Factual #1 or a brief essay comparing art works from the time before cities (Figures 0.1–0.14) and in the first cities (Figures 0.15–0.20). The lecturer can follow up with a presentation of slides stressing the transition from the gathering/hunting culture to life in agricultural villages and cities.

    An effort should be made to impart a sense of the relative time involved in these two stages, roughly a million years of mobile collecting of food from the land, followed by about 5,000 years of settled life based on agriculture, or a ratio of 1:200 (a proportional time line on the board, an analogy of one volume alongside a shelf of 200 books, etc.).
2. Some time should be spent with the term "sympathetic magic" as basic to ritual, both ancient and modern. What is the relationship between ritual and myth? The word *mythos* is defined by some anthropologists as the "spoken part of the ritual"; why is this so? Do we still celebrate rituals of seasonal change? Rites of passage in our individual lives? How do these contribute to our well-being? To our sense of "control" over time and nature?
3. What can we reliably assume about the roles males and females might have played in prehistoric culture? Keep in mind Challenge Question 1, regarding the physical record: have we lost the physical evidence of important human activities in the remotest times? A brief lecture might even take the form of a "thought experiment" like this: "Let us imagine that writing and musical notation/recordings do not exist; what effect would that have on the survival into the future of what we consider our present-day culture?"
4. It is often said that the need for survival and security were the driving forces of humankind's earliest development, during which time the ideal self consisted in fertility for women and physical prowess for men. Only slowly did the community and community values come to play a dominant role. This theme might be carried through the treatment of Chapters 1 through 7 of this textbook.

Introduction Audiovisual Resources

Video/CD-ROM Sources

ARCHEOLOLOGY: Quoting the Past (1987)   **UC**

THE CAVES OF ALTAMIRA
    A tour of Altamira and the magnificent cave paintings. 26 min. **FFH**

IRAQ: Cradle of Civilization 60 min., color 1991 **IM**

OUT OF THE PAST
    Series of eight one-hour programs. Examines physical evidence of ancient societies along with contemporary cultures to give insights into the evolution of humankind and societies. **CPB**

PREHISTORIC MAN IN EUROPE 43 min., color **IFB**

PREHISTORIC MONUMENTS IN EUROPE 43 min., color **FFH**

STONEHENGE
A look at the questions surrounding Stonehenge and at its meaning throughout history. 28 min. **FFH**

Sample Test Questions for the Introduction

Select the letter of the choice that BEST answers the question.

1. In estimating the importance of religion and the afterlife for humankind, archeological evidence suggests that humans have been concerned about immortality since
   a. the beginning of the human race.
   b. Neolithic culture of approximately 8,000 B.C.E.
   c. Neanderthal culture
   d. 4,000 B.C.E. when cities were first founded.
   Ans: c

2. In light of the total amount of time humans have existed, it is fair to say that, so far, the most successful adaptation of humankind to the environment has been the life of
   a. cities.
   b. ranchers.
   c. hunters and gatherers.
   d. city-states.
   Ans: c

3. According to recent findings, the first people who lived a settled village life based on agriculture were
   a. the tribes along the Nile in Africa
   b. the settlers in what is modern Israel and Iraq.
   c. the Aztecs.
   d. the Persians.
   Ans: b

4. Which of the following best defines the term *prehistory?*
   a. the study of fossil remains
   b. the measurement of atoms in the earth's strata
   c. the study of history before written records
   d. the discussion of living habits of early humans
   Ans: c

5. Which of the following sequences illustrates the chronology of early human toolmaking?
   a. Neolithic, Paleolithic, Iron Age
   b. Paleolithic, Neolithic, Iron Age
   c. Iron Age, Paleolithic, Neolithic
   d. Neolithic, Iron Age, Paleolithic
   Ans: b

6. Farming first became the human family's principal occupation in the
   a. Paleolithic Age.
   b. Neolithic Age.
   c. Iron Age.
   Ans: b

7. The development of an extensive array of tools and weapons occurred during the hunting/gathering phase of the
   a. Paleolithic Age.
   b. Neolithic Age.
   c. Iron Age.
   Ans: a

8. The Ice Age, involving at least four glacial advances, occurred at the same time as the
   a. Paleolithic Age.
   b. Neolithic Age.
   c. Iron Age.
   Ans: a

9. Which label designates the people or genus and species that left burial evidence reflecting concerns about the possibility of life after death?
   a. *homo sapiens*
   b. *homo habilis*
   c. *homo erectus*
   d. Australopithicus
   Ans: a

10. Early people engaged in a ritualistic performance of the hunt in the hope that
    a. their hunting skills would be developed.
    b. their status in the band would be enhanced.
    c. their subsequent hunt would be successful.
    d. a child would be born to their family.
    Ans: c

11. The birth of civilization began with
    a. a slow process of urban growth.
    b. the appearance of complex religious institutions.
    c. the first examples of sculpture.
    d. the distinction between an elite and a peasant population.
    Ans: a

12. The first urban civilizations all appeared
    a. in mountain valleys.
    b. on high plateaus.
    c. along the sides of lakes.
    d. on river banks.
    Ans: d

13. The thousands of clay tablets found in Sumer indicate that most early writing was used in the field of
    a. religion.
    b. literature.
    c. autobiography.
    d. accounting.
    Ans: d

14. As far as can be determined, the purpose behind erecting Stonehenge shows a compelling interest in what field on the part of early inhabitants of England?
    a. domestication of animals
    b. astronomy
    c. chemistry
    d. theology
    Ans: b

15. Looking at Stonehenge as purely a building challenge, the ruins suggest that the builders
    a. possessed cranes and the block and tackle.
    b. could mine stone but not shape it.
    c. could shape stone but not transport it.
    d. commanded large numbers of disciplined laborers.
    Ans: d

16. The development of agriculture had as a consequence the equalization of the economic roles of the sexes.
    Ans: F

Open Book

17. Fiero, Figure 0.3, Venus of Willendorf. The artist who executed this piece probably exaggerated the breasts and abdomen because
    a. artistic technique in those times was crude.
    b. the model who posed for the sculptor looked like this.
    c. the piece is atypical and probably the work of an unskilled amateur.
    d. the artist wanted to show a symbol of fertility, not an individual.
    Ans: d

Chapter **1** **Egypt: Gods, Rulers, and the Social Order**

Summary

Among ancient civilizations, nature and the natural geography influenced the formation and character of religious belief. In Egypt, the Nile river and a constant climate encouraged the development of a host of benevolent nature deities and the promise of a life that continued after death. The sun and the Nile were the two principal figures in the spiritual life of ancient Egypt. A theocratic ruler assumed the authority and eminence of the sun god and joined that god after death. Served by a huge bureaucracy, more than twenty ruling dynasties maintained a course of stability and unity for well over 2000 years. Egypt's monumental pyramids and temples, filled with artifacts for the deceased and ornamented with frescoes and relief carvings, leave an astonishing record of one of the most enduring of humankind's first civilizations.

Outline	Pronunciation Guide

A. The Gods of Ancient Egypt
    1.   effects of the environment
    2.   worship of Aten, symbol of life force
    3.   worship of Osiris, symbol of rebirth
B. The Rulers of Ancient Egypt
    1.   union of upper and lower Egypt
    2.   dynasties and the role of the pharaoh
    3.   Akhenaton and reform
C. Egypt's Cult of the Dead
    1.   the pharaoh and the sun-god
    2.   burial practices
        a.   the pyramids
        b.   The Book of the Dead
D. Egypt and the Social Order
    1.   the social hierarchy
    2.   the role of women
E. The Arts in Ancient Egypt
    1.   literature
    2.   sculpture and painting
    3.   temple architecture
    4.   music
	Aten [AH ten]
	Osiris [ow SI ris]
	visier [vee SIR]
	hieroglyph [HEYE row glif]
	Akhenaton [ak NAH ton]
	Nefertiti [ne fur TEE tee]
	Nubia [NOO bya]
	papyrus [pe PEYE rus]

Key Terms: polytheism, Gift of the Nile, dynasty, theocratic monarchy, hieroglyphs, pyramid building, mummy, Book of the Dead, fresco, canon, lyric poetry

Key Images	Palette of Narmer
	Head of Nefertiti
Great Pyramids of Gizeh; Sphinx	Weighing of the Heart, Book of the Dead
Coffin of Tutankhamen	Statue of Mycerinus and his Queen

Study Questions

Factual
1. What natural forces were considered sacred in Egyptian society?
2. How did Egyptian geography and topography affect the area's history and religious life?
3. The "Hymn to the Aten" (Reading 1.3) praises the sun for a variety of features? What are these?
4. What themes are depicted on the Palette of Narmer (Figure 1.3)?
5. Where were the pyramids erected? Why? Why did later dynasties abandon this burial site?
6. What is the "Book of the Dead?"
7. What was the main thrust of Akhenaton's reforms? Why did they fail?
8. Briefly describe ancient Egypt's social order; what role did women play in this order?

Challenge
1. Why is the building of the pyramids considered a "primitive act of faith"?
2. Assess the role of tradition in Egyptian culture and history. To what extent did the traditional order operate to give stability to Egyptian culture?
3. How did Egyptians prepare the body of the pharaoh for burial? Why were these procedures undertaken?
4. Why, in your view, do mummies and mummification remain a subject of fascination in our own time?
5. What was the function of the "canon" in Egyptian art?
6. What themes were depicted in the frescoes and carvings of Egyptian tombs?
7. What themes dominate Egyptian lyric poetry? What can be said of the "speakers" in each poem (Reading 1.4)?
8. Who controlled Egypt's great temples? How did the temples function in daily life?
9. Research the technology of pyramid and temple building. How did they differ from those of the culture that constructed Stonehenge?
10. What roles did slaves play in Egyptian life? How did individuals fall into the status of slaves?

Strategies for Discussion/Lecture

1. Any of the first three Factual questions might be assigned ahead as mini-themes, preparatory to lecture and/or discussion. Slides work well here but are not essential.
2. The written texts can be coordinated with trends in art and architecture. Using Figure 1.13 (Scene of Fowling) as an example, ask students to relate the details of this representation of the Pharaoh to what they have read about his status in Egyptian society.

3. It is said that women assumed an elevated position in Egyptian society. Ask students to use the figures in the chapter that give evidence of the relationships between males and females; how do these images of women differ from those in the introduction?
4. The chapter invites discussion concerning a theme that runs throughout these chapters: the formulation of an "immortality ideology," that is, a clearly defined picture of life after death. Establish the nature of this ideology among the ancient Egyptians, and use this for comparative purposes in chapters 2, 3, 4, 8, and 9.

Chapter 1 Audiovisual Resources

Video/CD-ROM Sources

ANCIENT CIVILIZATIONS
Mighty civilizations rise again! Through computer reconstructions, original location footage, and interviews with leading historians, study the glorious achievements of the past. Visit ancient Egypt, Greece, Rome, and Pompeii. Witness the fall of the Aztec and Maya empires, meet Egypt's visionary ruler Cleopatra, and tour the Seven Wonders of the Ancient World. 405 minutes on 6 tapes **PBS**

ANCIENT EGYPT, TLF

ANCIENT EGYPT: Digging Up Her Rich Past. 51 min., color **TLF**

ANCIENT LIVES (Series) (1985) **FFH**
An Artist's Life
The Deserted Village 27 min., color
Dreams and Rituals 29 min., color
Temple Priests and Civil Servants 25 min., color
The Valley of the Kings 29 min., color
Village of the Craftmen 23 min., color

EXPLORING THE EGYPTIAN PYRAMIDS
This documentary solves the mystery behind the pyramids of Egypt's construction, and explains their significance to the ancient culture that built them. Original BBC broadcast title: *The Oldest Wonder.* 50 min. **FFH**

THE GREAT PHARAOHS OF EGYPT
Stunning footage from Egypt's legendary ruins and a first-ever look inside a newly discovered tomb make this the ultimate examination of the fabled pharaohs. 200 min.; 4 videos **AE**

LEGACY - Vol. #4: Egypt - The Habit of Civilization (1991)
DIRECTOR: SPRY-LEVERTON, PETER 57 min., color, sound **PBS**

MUMMIES AND THE WONDERS OF ANCIENT EGYPT
The rich, seductive world of ancient Egypt beckons you back in time, to a land where giant pyramids were a gateway to the afterlife and a king's ransom could buy an elaborate 70-day process that would guarantee your body immortality. Renowned Egyptologists and the latest computer technology join forces to unlock the secrets of the Pyramids and the Sphinx, decipher long-secret hieroglyphs and explore the glittering sepulcher of the legendary King Tut. You'll even get an inside look at the

recently discovered KV-5, believed to be the family tomb of Ramses the Great. Titles are: *Great Pyramids*, *The Sphinx*, *Hieroglyphs*, and *King Tut*. **PBS**

PYRAMID (1988)
  DIRECTOR: MACAULAY, DAVID 58 min., color **PBS**

SECRETS OF THE PHARAOHS
  For nearly 3,000 years, ancient Egypt was the greatest civilization on Earth. But what the modern world knows about ancient Egyptian culture has been pieced together from surprisingly little hard information. Many mysteries remain. In the last few years, it has become possible to decipher a vast source of information from the Egyptian dead. Thanks to new scientific techniques, Egyptian mummies have begun revealing secrets of their lost world. This three-part series brings these revelations to viewers. Liev Schreiber narrates. 180 minutes on 3 tapes **PBS**

TREASURES OF EGYPT
  The keys to the pyramids are yours in this three-video set from the National Geographic Society. *Egypt: Quest for Eternity* explores the great temples of Luxor and Karnak, enters elaborately decorated tombs in the Land of the Dead, and joins Egyptologists as they unravel the riddles of this country's buried past. In *Mysteries of Egypt*, travel back more than 4,000 years with film star Omar Sharif to the building of the Great Pyramids of Giza. Through the magic of large-format cinematography, you'll soar over the Nile, cross the deathly quiet Valley of the Kings, and peer inside the shadowy chamber of King Tut's tomb. Finally, *Egypt: Secrets of the Pharaohs* explains the ancient royal ritual of mummification, how the pyramids were built, and the puzzle of Khufu's underground ship. A breathtaking journey into the past! 180 minutes on 3 tapes **PBS**

TUT: The Boy King 55 min., color **VC**

UNDER WRAPS: An Autopsy of Three Egyptian Mummies (1998)
  30 min., color **Astarte Resources**; GPO Box 920;Canberra; ACT 2601; Australia

Web Resources

A list of Egyptian rulers—http://www.touregypt.net/kings.htm

Recent excavations of burial sites near the Pyramids—http://guardians.net/hawass/buildtomb.htm

Excavations at the Great Pyramids and the Sphinx—http://www.pbs.org/wgbh/nova/pyramid/

Internet resources about the Pyramids—http://guardians.net/egypt/pyramids.htm

Internet resources about hieroglyphs and the Egyptian Book of the Dead—
    http://guardians.net/egypt/hiero.htm

Information about mummies—http://www.si.umich.edu/CHICO/mummy

McGraw-Hill Resources

Transparencies: A.21 Ancient Architecture
                  MA.1: Ancient River-Valley Civilizations 8000 B.C.E.–1 B.C.E.

Sample Test Questions for Chapter 1

Select the letter of the choice that BEST answers the question:

1. In their worship of the sun god Aten, the early Egyptians emphasized their
   a   sense of optimism.
   b. preoccupation with evil.
   c. belief in resurrection.
   d. veneration of noble rank.
   Ans: c

2. The Egyptians worshiped Osiris, god of the Nile, who was also associated with
   a   military success.
   b. urban prosperity.
   c. the system of hieroglyphs.
   d. the underworld.
   Ans: d

3. Which of the following is NOT true about the pyramids?
   a   They contained the Pharoah's most valued possessions.
   b. They were embellished with frescoes and hieroglyphs.
   c. They were the tombs of pharaohs throughout Egyptian history.
   d. They were part of an elaborate burial complex.
   Ans: c

4. Which of the following characterizes Egyptian art?
   a. an emphasis on the social elite
   b. a preoccupation with immediacy and realism
   c. a celebration of individual artists
   d. a strong sense of perspective
   Ans: a

5. A belief in the existence of many gods is known as _____.
   Ans: polytheism

6. The first capital city of ancient Egypt was
   a. Narmer.
   b. Gizeh.
   c. Memphis.
   d. Thebes.
   Ans: c

7. Fiero, Figure 1.12: The girl carries on her head a basket filled with
   a. agricultural tools.
   b. food for the deceased.
   c. grain to feed farm animals.
   d. wine for priestly rituals.
   Ans: b

8. Recent excavations near Gizeh suggest that the promise of life after death was
   a. anticipated by all social classes.
   b. reserved for the upper classes.
   c. extended by the pharaoh to his favorites.
   d. offered by priests to their followers.
   Ans: a

9. A principal subject of Egyptian poetry was
   a. warfare.
   b. love.
   c. social mobility.
   d. death.
   Ans: b

10. Generally speaking, in Egyptian art
    a. upper-class people are shown larger than lower-class people.
    b. women are always shown smaller than their consorts.
    c. women are rarely shown in the presence of men.
    d. soldiers are shown the same size as servants.
    Ans: a

11. New Kingdom temples were regularly run and dominated by
    a. pharaohs.
    b. viziers.
    c. priests.
    d. scribes.
    Ans: c

12. The gate that stands at the entry to the Egyptian temple is known as a(n)
    a. sphinx.
    b. pylon.
    c. obelisk.
    d. hypostyle.
    Ans: b

13. Not true of the Egyptian pyramids:
    a. They were built with mortar.
    b. They were built without pulleys.
    c. They were made of limestone and granite.
    d. Copper saws and chisels were employed.
    Ans: a

14. Politically, the greatest challenge to the authority of the pharaoh came from the
    a. invading tribes.
    b. local priests.
    c. army.
    d. royal consort.
    Ans: b

15. Akhenaton's effort to establish monotheism was surely related to his
    a. wish to strengthen his own political authority.
    b. effort to eliminate the influence of Nefertiti.
    c. inherent rejection of polytheism.
    d. attempt to establish a new religion.
    Ans: a

16. In Egyptian society, slaves were usually those
    a. with darker skin colors.
    b. with physical deformities.
    c. who were victims of war.
    d. who were too poor to support themselves.
    Ans: c

17. A ruler who combines political with spiritual power is characterized as a _____ monarch.
    a. theocratic
    b. democratic
    c. autocratic
    d. polycratic
    Ans: a

18. Which of the following was NOT usually part of the pharaoh's responsibility?
    a. appointment of a bureaucracy
    b. mobilization of an army
    c. distribution of private property
    d. issuance of legal decrees
    Ans: c

Chapter **2 Mesopotamia: Gods, Rulers, and the Social Order**

Summary

In contrast with Egypt, the geography of Mesopotamia invited the rise of small city-states (such as Sumer and Babylon), and, eventually, the development of more complex political states and empires (such as that of Assyria and Persia). Harsh natural conditions inspired a pantheon of capricious gods and the epic quest for an unobtainable immortality. While in Egypt, laws remained unwritten for centuries, in ancient Babylon, laws were codified and recorded: Hammurabi's Code reveals a complex social order with strict rules predicated on social status. A unique Mesopotamian people, the Hebrews came to worship a single transcendental Creator-god with whom they established a covenant. The Hebrew people had little hope of personal immortality but affirmed the necessity of faith in one god and obedience to a code of moral conduct, whose rewards would occur on earth. The history of the Hebrews would form a body of Scripture with long-ranging influence, but the Hebrews themselves fell prey to the larger, more powerful empires of Assyria and Persia. All of the small states and empires of Mesopotamia nevertheless shared a unique set of cultural characteristics that included the earliest written efforts to monitor the social and moral order.

Outline	**Pronunciation Guide**

A. The Gods of Mesopotamia
  1. effects of the environment
  2. Sumerian creation myth: *The Babylonian Creation*
  3. the search for immortality:: *The Epic of Gilgamesh*
B. The Rulers of Mesopotamia
  1. Sumer
  2. Babylon
C. The Social Order and the Arts
  1. Hammurabi's Code
  2. the ziggurat
D. Hebrew monotheism
  1. early history of the Hebrews
    a. the covenant
    b. ethical monotheism
  2. the early Hebrew social order
    a. morality and patriarchy
    b. laws added to the Decalogue
  3. the early Hebrew state
    a. the role of the prophets
    b. the Babylonian Captivity and the Book of Job
	Gilgamesh [GIL gah mesh]
	Enkidu [en KEE doo]
	Utnapishtim [ut nah PISH tim]
	Urshanabi [ur shah NAH bee]
	Hammurabi [ham mu RAH bee]
	ziggurat [ZI gu rat]
	Zoroaster [zor oh AZ tah]
	Nebuchadnezzar
	    [ne boo kahd NE zur]
	Chaldaean [kal DEE un]
	pairidaeza [para DAYZ ah]
	Assyria [u SI ree u]
	Ninevah [NI ne vah]

E. The Iron Age	
1. the Hittites	
2. the Assyrian empire	
3. the Persian empire	

Key Terms: epic, ziggurat, written law, *biblia*, Torah, monotheism, covenant, prophet, Iron Age, Babylonian Captivity, empire/imperialism, Near East/Middle East as "western" terms for the area more objectively called "Southwest Asia."

Key Images	
Standard of Ur	Stele of Hammurabi
Statuettes from Abu temple, Tell Asmar	King Ashurnasirpal II Killing Lions (Nimrud)
Ziggurat at Ur	Assyrian Winged, Human-Headed Bull
Head of Sargon	Gold Vessel, Persia

Study Questions

Factual

1. How did Mesopotamian geography and topography affect the area's history and religious life?
2. How did the gods of Mesopotamia differ from those of Egypt? How were they similar?
3. Where was Sumer located? Why was this location advantageous to the birth of civilization?
4. Who was Gilgamesh? What was he searching for and why? How does this epic reflect the ideals of Mesopotamian culture?
5. What was the function of the Mesopotamian ziggurat? How did it differ from the Egyptian pyramid?
6. What types of activities were regulated by Hammurabi's code?
7. What were the unique characteristics of the Hebrew faith after Moses?
8. How do the later laws in Exodus (Reading 1.8b) differ from those in the Decalogue?
9. What is the nature of Jeremiah's warning to the Hebrew people (Reading 1.8c)?
10. What is God's answer (Reading 1.8d) to the question Job asks throughout his suffering: "why me?"
11. What were the major effects of Iron Age technology in Mesopotamia?
12. What aspects of Assyrian life are depicted in the arts of its palaces?

Challenge

1. Compare the creation of human beings in *The Babylonian Creation* and in *Genesis*
2. At the end of Job's trials, God answers his question with another question: "Who are you to inquire about divine justice?" What message does this send regarding the proper human attitude toward the deity?
3. What does Hammurabi's Code tell us about the role of women in ancient Babylon? (Refer to specific clauses in answering.)
4. How does the *Epic of Gilgamesh* fulfill the major characteristics of the literary genre known as "the epic"?
5. Why, in your opinion, are so many of the Ten Commandments (Reading 1.8a) framed in the negative? Are any of these laws conditional? What is the nature of the punishment that god threatens if the laws of the Decalogue are violated (Exodus 20: 5)?
6. Compare Sumerian, Egyptian, and Hebraic ideas of the afterlife.

7. What are the advantages/disadvantages of a community ruled by "the laws of men" as opposed to the rule of written law? Does written law ensure fairness and consistency? Even in a largely illiterate society?

8. How did changing technology affect the history of Mesopotamia? What modern-day states does Mesopotamia comprise? Is the current history of this area also turbulent?

9. Discuss the art of the Assyrians as an expression of political propaganda. Refer to specific figures and the subject matter of the art itself.

10. In what ways did the Persian empire preserve the culture of Mesopotamia? What unique contribution did they make to the humanistic tradition?

Strategies for Discussion/Lecture

1. The argument that "history begins in Sumer" may open a lecture on this first civilization. From there it is a short distance to the Epic of Gilgamesh, which might be the focus of discussion. Assigning Factual question #4 as a mini-theme is good preparation for general discussion. The "immortality ideology" (or lack thereof) may be compared with that of ancient Egyptians and for a discussion of the absence of a clear-cut eschatology among the early Hebrews. The oral origins of the *Epic of Gilgamesh* (and Hebrew Scripture) may be stressed by calling attention to passages marked by repetition and other mnemonic aids.

2. Students love dealing with Hammurabi's Code. Assigning ahead Challenge question #3 forces them to read the code carefully and exercise their powers of analysis in interpreting the clauses. This is also an excellent way to show students how primary sources can be tapped for what they reveal about a culture or time period. A comparison of the Babylonian laws with those of the Hebrews is also fruitful. In which does class matter less?

3. After reading aloud Genesis 1: 26–27, ask the class "Where is the part about Adam's rib?" The lecturer may wish to assign additionally Genesis 2: 7 and 2: 18, 21–25. He/she may also wish to add Genesis 5: 1–2, the third account of creation. How do they differ? Why, when asked, do we tend to remember the second account, in which woman is a subsidiary creation? Currently, with increased sensitivity to the environment so much in evidence, instructors may wish to view Genesis 1 as the foundational passage in the Judeo-Christian world for the human relationship to the rest of nature: humans are to be the masters. There is a growing literature on early exhaustion of land by agriculture that can be used in this connection (see Clive Ponting, *A Green History of the World*, St. Martin's Press, 1992). Is mastery more crucial than cooperation?

4. Another focus for the chapter might be technology and its impact. How did the onset of the Iron Age influence the course of history in Mesopotamia?

Chapter 2 Audiovisual Resources

Video/CD-ROM Sources

ANCIENT CIVILIZATIONS

Mighty civilizations rise again! Through computer reconstructions, original location footage, and interviews with leading historians, study the glorious achievements of the past. Visit ancient Egypt, Greece, Rome, and Pompeii. Witness the fall of the Aztec and Maya empires, meet Egypt's visionary ruler Cleopatra, and tour the Seven Wonders of the Ancient World. 405 min. on 6 tapes **PBS**

ANCIENT MESOPOTAMIA 10 min., color **CORONET**

BELIEFS AND BELIEVERS
Twenty-four one-hour programs offering a comprehensive look at the nature and function of religions and secular beliefs that compromise today's world views; especially see number 4 "Hindusim" and number 8 "Mythic Dimension: Judaism." **CPB**

THE BIBLE AS LITERATURE: PART I—Saga and Story in the Old Testament 24 min., color **EBEC**

THE BIBLE AS LITERATURE: PART II—History, Poetry, and Drama in the Old Testament 24 min., color **EBEC**

JOSEPH CAMPELL AND THE POWER OF MYTH (Series) (1988) **MYSTIC**

THE FIRST STORYTELLERS: Gift of the NILE 29 min., color **TLF**

LEGACY - Vol. #1: Iraq - The Cradle of Civilization (1991)
DIRECTOR: SPRY-LEVERTON, PETER 57 min., color **PBS**

LOST CIVILIZATIONS: Mesopotamia: "Return to Eden" **PBS**

PERSIA: The Sudden Empire 30 min., color **TLF**

MYSTERY OF THE ARK OF THE COVENANT
available at: http://www.inwave.com/~monument/index.html

THE SEARCH FOR THE REAL MT. SINAI
available at: http://www.inwave.com/~monument/index.html

SUMER, BABYLON, ASSYRIA: The Wolf
A look at the collection of antiquities from Sumer, Babylon, and Assyria housed at the British Museum. 26 min. **FFH**

YESTERDAY'S WORLDS: The Missing City Gates 29 min., color **NETCHE**

YESTERDAY'S WORLDS: Treasures from the Land of the Bible 29 min., color **NETCHE**

Web Resources

Information on Jewish history—http://www.fordham.edu.halsall/jewish/jewishsbook/html

Resources about Mesopotamia—http://www.mrdowling.com/603mesopotamia.html

History and resources about Mesopotamia—http://www.fordham.edu/halsall/ancient/asbook03.html

History and resources about the Hittites—http://members.bellatlantic.net/~vze33gpz/hittite-ref.html

Sample Test Questions for Chapter 2

Select the letter of the choice that BEST answers the question:

1. Which one of the following can NOT be considered part of the legacy of Sumer?
   a. the brewing of beer
   b. mathematics on base 60
   c. the worship of one god
   d. building stepped pyramids
   Ans: c

2. *The Epic of Gilgamesh* involves a
   a. search for immortality.
   b. conflict within class structure.
   c. challenge to polytheism.
   d. summary of previous epic poems.
   Ans: a

3. Mesopotamian culture is dominated by the theme of
   a. human perfection.
   b. adventure.
   c. female dominance.
   d. human vulnerability.
   Ans: d

4. Hammurabi codified the laws of
   a. Babylon and its surrounding territories.
   b. Sumer and its surrounding territories.
   c. the Hebrews and other tribal Mesopotamians.
   d. Ur, Lagash, and Nimrud.
   Ans: a

5. Comparing the laws of Hammurabi with those of the Decalogue, we find that the latter
   a. apply only to the Hebrews.
   b. deal with only individual infractions of the law.
   c. do not specify consequences for their violation.
   d. include all of the above.
   Ans: c

6. In the Hebrew Bible, the relationship between humans and the natural environment is best characterized as
   a. cooperation with the environment.
   b. mastery over the environment.
   c. a struggle against the environment.
   d. natural environment first, humans second.
   Ans: b

7. In the Hebrew Bible, there are two accounts of the creation of females. In the first, woman is created
    a. from the rib of man.
    b. before man.
    c. with man in the image of God.
    d. with man but in an image inferior to man's.
    Ans: c

8. Which of the following best describes how the God of the Hebrews punishes the sin of worshiping other gods?
    a. He punishes the sinner in Hell.
    b. He punishes the sinner in this life on earth.
    c. He leaves it to the priests to punish the sinner.
    d. He punishes the sinner and his family for generations.
    Ans: d

9. Which of the following is the best description of what Job learns at the end of the story?
    a. Job learns why he has been made to suffer so much.
    b. Job learns that he has no business questioning why God acts as he does.
    c. Job learns that he has suffered unjustly.
    d. Job learns that Satan was behind his suffering.
    Ans: b

10. Hebrew monotheism reflects the theme of
    a. the belief in many gods.
    b. a covenant between human beings and God.
    c. a universe of spontaneous creation.
    d. the unalterable evil of human beings.
    Ans: b

11. Which of the following best characterizes the prophet Jeremiah's message?
    a. an emphasis on material success
    b. the importance of nonviolence
    c. a warning of divine punishment
    d. the promise of agrarian fertility
    Ans: c

12. Like Gilgamesh, Job
    a. seeks divine explanations for human sufferings and death.
    b. triumphs over evil and death.
    c. finds a rational explanation of divine will.
    d. achieves the certainty of Heaven.
    Ans: a

13. The *Epic of Gilgamesh* contains a description of a universal flood, apparently based on the account in Genesis.
    Ans: F

14. For centuries, Mesopotamian politics were influenced by
    a. a stable natural environment.
    b. geographical barriers against invasion.
    c. women in significant bureaucratic posts.
    d. the dominance of local rulers.
    Ans: d

15. The architecture of the Assyrian palaces reflects the rulers' preoccupation with
    a. religion.
    b. war.
    c. fertility.
    d. social stability.
    Ans: b

16. When we compare the laws of Egypt with that of Babylon and the Hebrews, we find that those of Egypt
    a. make no mention of bribes.
    b. were not written down.
    c. punish according to social class.
    d. provide for women's rights.
    Ans: b

17. A central premise of Hebrew law was that the law applied equally to all social classes, except for slaves.
    Ans: T

18. The first five books of the Hebrew Bible are referred to as the _____.
    Ans: Torah

19. Fiero, Figure 2.5 the Standard of Ur. If you dug up this panel, you would date it from the time of cities, based on one of the following characteristics.
    a. the depiction of palace architecture
    b. the representation of specialized labor and classes
    c. the depiction of a female accompanying the harp-player
    d. the depiction of a festive meal
    Ans: b

20. The name Zoroaster is associated with the religious life of
    a. Sumer.
    b. Assyria.
    c. Persia.
    d. Babylon.
    Ans: c

Chapter **3** India and China: Gods, Rulers, and the Social Order

Summary

Emerging somewhat later than Egypt and Sumer, ancient India and China claimed all the hallmarks of the earliest river valley civilizations. The Indus Valley was the scene of a flourishing bronze age culture that fell to invading Aryans, who introduced Sanskrit, the caste system, and cultivated the pantheistic Hinduism that is practiced in India to this day. China's river valleys brought forth an equally impressive civilization governed by kings and priests who revered the natural order and the way of nature. Extensive preparations for deceased rulers suggest a cult of the dead not unlike that of Egypt. Considered sacred, the right to rule was bestowed by the mandate of heaven; China's rulers assumed responsibility for maintaining the will of heaven in the form of a proper moral and social order on earth.

Outline	Pronunciation Guide

A. Ancient India
  1. Indus Valley Civilization
  2. the Vedic Era
    a. Sanscrit
    b. epic poetry
    c. caste system
  3. Hinduism
    a. the *Vedas*
    b. the *Upanishads*
    c. *Bhagavad-Gita*
B. Ancient China
  1. Shang Dynasty
  2. Zhou dynasty: the Mandate of Heaven
  3. the natural order
    a. *The Book of Songs*
    b. *Yin/yang*
  4. the Dao and Daoism
	Mohenjo-daro [mow hen ow DAH row]
	Vedas [VAY dahs]
	Brahman [BRAH mahn]
	Atman [AHT mahn]
	nirvana [nir VAH nah]
	Bhagavad-Gita [BUG ah vad GEE tah]
	Mahabharata [ma hah BAH rah tah]
	Dao [DAH ow]
	qi [KEY}
	Shi jing [shee CHEEN]
	I jing [ee CHEEN]
	Zhou [SHOO]
	Lao Zi [LAH ow tzee]

Key Terms: caste, Brahman/Atman, *nirvana*, Wheel of Rebirth, Mandate of Heaven, *li, chi,* Dao, *yin* and *yang*, the way of nature.

Key Images	
Bearded Man, Mohenjo-daro *Dancing girl*, Mohenjo-daro *Ceremonial vessel*, Shang dynasty	*Jade Disk*, Zhou dynasty *Standing Bronze Figure*, Shang dynasty

Study Questions

Factual
1. Where and when did the earliest civilization in India emerge?
2. What were the distinctive features of Indus Valley civilization?
3. What features did the Aryans introduce into India?
4, Define *pantheism*. How does this belief differ from monotheism and polytheism?
5. What was the subject matter of India's earliest epics?
6. Explain these words: Brahman; Atman; nirvana; reincarnation.
7. Briefly describe Krishna's message to Arjuna in the *Bhagavad-Gita* (Reading 1.8).
8. Explain: *qi*; *yin/yang*; Mandate of Heaven.
9. What were some of the grave goods found in Shang imperial tombs?
10. What is the main theme of the *Dao de jing*?

Challenge
1. How did the Indus Valley civilization differ from the early civilizations of Egypt and Mesopotamia?
2. How did Hinduism differ from the religious beliefs and practice of the early Hebrews?
3. Apply the word *holism* to a brief discussion of ancient India and ancient China.
4. Explain the concept of hierarchy as it applied to power and leadership in the ancient world.
   Are there any distinct differences between the operation of this concept as it applies in ancient Egypt and in ancient China or India?
5. The caste system is usually associated with the history of India. Did similar systems of social stratification exist in ancient Egypt, Babylon, and China?
6.. Slavery was a fact of the ancient world. Investigate and compare the ways in which people became slaves in ancient Egypt, Mesopotamia, India, and China.
7. Did early Chinese culture share the antimaterialistic position of Hinduism? Offer evidence to support your answer.
8. How does wit and paradox operate in the poetry of the *Dao de jing*? (The complete *Dao* is available in numerous paperback versions.)
9. Why was jade considered a sacred medium among the Chinese? What properties did the Chinese ascribe to jade?
10. Divination (or augury) played a large role in ancient life; research to discover the significance of divination in other ancient cultures.

Strategies for Discussion/Lecture

1. The chapter is best presented in the context established by the previous two chapters. What did the ancient civilizations of India and China share with those of Egypt and Mesopotamia? The hallmarks of civilization are fairly similar, though East Asian bronze techniques seem to have been more sophisticated than those in Egypt. How did the Aryan invasions affect the Indus Valley civilization? What do we know about pre-Shang China? From there the focus should be on the pantheistic nature of early Hinduism. Chinese burial practices may be compared with those of Egypt; the social hierarchy and the natural order may also be treated in comparison with ancient Egypt, especially as the authority of the ruler plays such an important part in both cultures.
2. Assigning Challenge question #3 as an essay to be prepared prior to class pushes students to deal analytically with the materials in the chapter and often leads to lively discussion. The current popularity with "holistic" medicine, meditation, and other eastern concepts should be mentioned here.

3. Visual aids are often difficult to locate for lecturing on India and China, but slides of Shang and Zhou jade and bronze articles are usually available. There are, additionally, a number of museum catalogues from various exhibitions of Chinese art recently uncovered and displayed in this country. One of the best is *The Golden Age of Chinese Archeology: Celebrated Discoveries from the People's Republic of China*, edited by Xiaoneng Yang (Yale University Press, 2000).

Chapter 3 Audiovisual Resources

Video/CD-ROM Sources

ANCIENT CIVILIZATIONS
Mighty civilizations rise again! Through computer reconstructions, original location footage, and interviews with leading historians, study the glorious achievements of the past. Visit ancient Egypt, Greece, Rome, and Pompeii. Witness the fall of the Aztec and Maya empires, meet Egypt's visionary ruler Cleopatra, and tour the Seven Wonders of the Ancient World. 405 min. on 6 tapes **PBS**

DISCOVERING CHINA
available through: http://www.edvidnet.com/default.html

FIVE MILLENNIA OF CHINESE ART: A SPIRITUAL JOURNEY—ON CD-ROM
This elegant CD-ROM replicates the experience of touring the Chi-Shan Garden and the museum's four floors of galleries. Windows only. **FFH**

LEGACY - Vol. #2: India - The Empire of the Spirit (1991)
DIRECTOR: SPRY-LEVERTON, PETER 57 min., color **PBS**

LEGACY - Vol. #3: China - The Mandate of Heaven (1991)
DIRECTOR: SPRY-LEVERTON, PETER 57 min., color **PBS**

ORIGINS OF INDIA'S HINDU CIVILIZATION
available through: http://www.edvidnet.com/default.html

Web Resources

Life at Mohenjo-daro and Indus Valley civilization—http://www.wnn.or.jp/wnn-asia/moenjo_e/moenjo_e.html

Rise and fall of the Indus civilization—http://www.harappa.com/har/har3.html

Sanskrit documents—http://www.hscc.net/sanskrit/doc_1_title.html

Hindu resources online—http://www.hindu.org/

Hindu resources online—http://hindunet.org

Hindu resources online—http://www.hinduism.co.za/

Information related to Taoism—http://www.easternreligions.com/tframe.html

Information related to Taoism—http://www.taorestore.org/intro.html

Information related to Taoism—http://www.tao.org/

McGraw-Hill Resources

Transparencies: MA.1 Ancient River-Valley Civilizations 8000 B.C.E.–1 B.C.E.

Sample Test Questions for Chapter 3

Select the letter of the choice that BEST answers the question:

1. Indus Valley civilization was notable for all except which of the following:
   a. river valley location
   b. expertise in bronze-casting
   c. urban life
   d. elaborate tomb burials
   Ans: d

2. The Sanskrit word *karma* means
   a. deed.
   b. law.
   c. god.
   d. duty.
   Ans: a

3. The *Dancing Girl* pictured in Figure 3.2 is evidence of ancient India's achievements in
   a. portraiture.
   b. wood-carving.
   c. bronze-casting.
   d. stone-carving.
   Ans: c

4. India's oldest known devotional texts are the
   a. *Vedas.*
   b. *Upanishads.*
   c. *Mahabharata.*
   d. *Ramayana.*
   Ans: a

5. The belief known as pantheism holds that
   a. nothing but human beings is sacred.
   b. everything in nature is sacred.
   c. everything except human beings is sacred.
   d. there are neither gods nor spirits.
   Ans: b

6. "Free from fear, free from anger,/ Free from the things of desire" is, according to the *Bhagavad-Gita*, the condition of
   a. fools.
   b. gods.
   c. illumined individuals.
   d. deceased human beings.
   Ans: c

7. Unlike Egypt, the earliest tribal chiefs in China did not proclaim to be divine.
   Ans: F

8. Fiero, Figure 3.8, Inscribed Oracle Bone. In China's earliest period, the interpretation of these inscribed bones was entrusted to
   a. a special group of priests.
   b. tribal elders.
   c. women.
   d. the rulers.
   Ans: a

9. China's oldest written text is unusual in that it contains no creation myths or stories of gods. It is called
   a. *Shi jing.*
   b. *I jing.*
   c. *Dao de jing.*
   d. *yin/yang.*
   Ans: b

10. In the text, the Dao is said to be ineffable. This means
    a. that it cannot be destroyed.
    b. that it is impossible to understand.
    c. that it is invisible.
    d. that it cannot be described in words.
    Ans: d

11. Daoism and meditation are compatible because the adherent to Daoism seeks
    a. material success.
    b. individual insight.
    c. communal benefits.
    d. family harmony.
    Ans: b

12. The power given by the gods to the Chinese rulers was called the _____.
    Ans: Mandate of Heaven

13. Not true of the religious culture of early China:
    a. Local spirits were associated with natural forces.
    b. Deceased ancestors were highly revered.
    c. A supreme Being was honored.
    d. Reincarnation was considered likely.
    Ans: d

14. The head and body of the deceased Chinese ruler was often shrouded in
    a. gold.
    b. jade.
    c. silk.
    d. ivory.
    Ans: b

15. In the earliest texts of both India and China, veneration is displayed for
    a. vegetation and natural elements.
    b. human beings and human life.
    c. a monotheistic deity.
    d. totemic animals.
    Ans: a

Chapter **4 Greece: Humanism and the Speculative Leap**

Summary

This chapter treats the development of Hellenic civilization from its Aegean (Minoan/Mycenaean) roots to the end of the Golden Age. Its primary focus is on the centrality of humanism and individualism in the Greek city-state (Athens in particular) and on the relationship between the self and society. These ideas are illustrated by means of three principal selections: the *Iliad,* Pericles' *Funeral Speech,* and Sophocles' *Antigone.* These works offer various perceptions of the shift from earlier beliefs that the destinies of human beings lay in the hands of the gods to the classical notion that humans shape their own destinies. The second portion of this chapter deals with the rise and development of Greek philosophy, the so-called "speculative leap" from supernatural to natural, rational explanations of the unknown. Pre-Socratic philosophers (Thales, Democritus, Pythagoras) are examined, followed by more extensive treatment of the humanist philosophers, Socrates, Plato, and Aristotle. The Pre-Socratics tried to determine the basic stuff of nature and the ground of being. The Sophists and the humanistic philosophers, Socrates, Plato, and Aristotle, moved beyond natural physics to seek metaphysical truths concerning the nature of knowledge (how we know what we know) and the meaning of virtue and the good life.

Outline	Pronunciation Guide
A. Bronze Age (Aegean) civilizations	**Aegean** [ay GEE un]
1. Minoan culture	**Knossos** [NAH sus]
2. Mycenae	**Mycenaean** [meye su NEE un]
B. The Heroic Age	**Dionysus** [dei ow NEYE sus]
1. Homer and the *Iliad*	**Poseidon** [pow SEI dun]
2. the Greek gods	**Aphrodite** [af row DEYE tee]
C. The rise of the *Polis*	**Herodotus** [he RAH du tus]
1. the Greek *polis*	**Thucydides** [thoo SI di deez]
2. the Persian wars	**Pericles** [PER i kleez]
D. Athens and the Golden Age	**Aeschylus** [ES ku lus]
1. the evolution of democracy	**Sophocles** [SOF u kleez]
2. Pericles' view of Athenian society	**Euripides** [yoo RI pi deez]
3. the Olympic games	**Aristophanes** [aris TOF uneez]
4. Greek drama	**Antigone** [an TI gu nee]
a. origins and development	**Ismene** [iz MAY ne]
b. Sophocles' *Antigone*	**Teiresias** [teye REE see us]
c. Aristotle on tragedy	**Socrates** [SAHK ru teez]

E. Greek philosophy
  1. Naturalist philosophy: pre-Socratics
    a   Thales; Heraclitus
    b. Leucippus; Democritus
    c. Pythagoras; Hippocrates
  2. Humanist philosophy
    a. the Sophists
    b. Socrates
      (1) Socratic method
      (2) the nature of virtue
      (3) the *Crito*
    c. Plato
      (1) the Theory of Forms
      (2) the just society (*The Republic*)
    d. Aristotle
      (1) the empirical method
      (2) the science of logic
      (3) the golden mean
	Crito [KREYE tow]
	Ionia [ei OW nee ah]
	Miletus [meye LEE tus]
	Thales [THAY leez]
	Leucippus [loo SI pus]
	Democritus [de MAH kri tus]
	Pythagoras [pi THA gow rus]
	Protagoras [prow TA gow rus]
	Heraclitus [her ah KLEYE tus]
	Hippocrates [hip PAHK rah teez]
	Sophist [SAHF ist]
	Glaucon [GLAHW kun]
	Nichomachean
	   [NI kow mah KEE un]
	syllogism [SIL low ji zum]
	eudaimonia [yoo deye mow NEE ah]
	arete [ar e TAY]

Key Terms: epic, oligarchy, democracy, humanism, individualism, tragedy, comedy, protagonist, antagonist, dialectic, oligarchy, *polis,* Olympic games, pre-Socratics, atoms, *psyche,* dialectical method, Theory of Forms, the life of virtue, empirical method, syllogism, Golden Mean.

Key Images Minoan priestess with snakes Palace of Minos, Knossos Contest of Two Warriors, Attic Black-Figure Amphora	 Lion Gate, Mycenae Theater of Epidaurus Portrait Bust of Socrates

Study Questions

Factual

1. How did the geography of the Aegean influence the civilizations that grew up there?
2. How does Achilles differ from Gilgamesh as an epic hero? Is Achilles as concerned about life after death?
3. Describe and evaluate Athenian democracy.
4. Who was Pericles? What is the theme of the *Funeral Speech?* In what ways does Pericles find Athens unique? What does Pericles mean when he says, "Athens is the school of Hellas"?
5. Why is the fifth century B.C.E. in Athens referred to as a Golden Age?
6. What was the basis of the conflict between Antigone and Creon?
7. How many people die in *Antigone?* What causes these deaths?
8. What, according to Thales, was the single, unifying substance of nature? Why, in his view, was this so?
9. Who was Crito? What arguments does Socrates give Crito for refusing to escape from prison?
10. What is the "dialectical method"?

11. Define *allegory* in your own words. Explain the main elements of the allegory in the excerpt from the *Republic.*
12. According to Plato, who should rule society? Why?
13. In Aristotle's view, which is more important, the individual or the state? What did Aristotle mean by saying, "Man is a political animal"?

Challenge
1. In the interchange between Achilles and Priam (Reading 1.11), what aspects are especially "human"? Describe in your own words the personality of Achilles.
2. The Homeric warrior seems to be obsessed with honor and reputation; to what extent is the *Iliad* the reflection of a man's world?
3. To avow poverty is no disgrace, says Pericles in the *Funeral Speech*; "The true disgrace is in doing nothing to avoid it." Comment and apply to contemporary society.
4. Contrast Athenian and Spartan (Lacedaemonian) culture as presented in Pericles' *Funeral Speech.* Research further to compare further the two city-states.
5. In Greek plays, violent action never takes place on stage. Why do you think the Greeks avoided displaying violence? What did they achieve by this? What, by contrast, is the function and purpose of contemporary violence in television and film?
6. Whom do you consider the "tragic figure" in Sophocles' *Antigone:* Antigone or Creon? Why? Who is the protagonist, who the antagonist?
7. Paraphrase the message of the Chorus of *Antigone* (page 81, lines 275–289). How does this choral passage bear on the action of the play?
8. Socrates argued that the unexamined life was not worth living. Would you agree? Are there any major advantages to living life "unexamined"?
9. Aristotle explains that happiness is a pleasure of the mind. Would you agree? Comment on the role of happiness in your own life and how you might advise a loved one to go about pursuing happiness.
10. Which aspects of the Olympic games have survived into our own time?
11. According to Aristotle, what are the three principal types of lives humans can choose to lead? What, according to Aristotle, is humankind's unique virtue? What is the Golden Mean?

Strategies for Discussion/Lecture

1. The chapter demands a minimum of three class periods (the model syllabi on page xxix of this Instructor's Manual suggest two full weeks). The focus might be divided into (1) an introductory class that deals with the context: the rise of the Greek city-states from within the Aegean world. The main documents here would be the *Iliad* and Pericles' *Funeral Speech.* Assigning a mini-theme, such as Factual question #2 or 4 will prepare students for discussion; (2) Greek drama with the focus on *Antigone*, preceded by a mini-theme assignment such as Challenge question #5; (3) Greek philosophy, preceded by a mini-theme assignment such as Factual question #9 or 11, or Challenge question #10, depending on where the lecturer wishes to focus class discussion.
2. As an opening gambit for a treatment of the *Iliad* or the *Crito*, the lecturer might center on this theme: "To the Greeks, moral value lay in proper action, even if the consequence of that action meant death." The personalities of Achilles and Socrates inevitably present themselves as examples.
3. *Antigone* is a central text in the chapter, and most of the themes of this section can be summed up in reading and discussion. Central issues: the law of man versus the law of god; male power versus female power; the rights of the individual versus the requirements of the state; the demands of family versus the demands of the community. In addition to Challenge question #5, one might pursue investigation of the other characters in the play. One might ask, for instance: "Imagine this play

without Ismene: does she help to put Antigone in relief?" Some argue that the play is the tragedy of both Creon and Antigone. It is true that although she dies, she becomes immortal by her action, whereas Creon ends up in a kind of personal desert, that is without family. The meaning of the word *tragedy* (as generally understood versus as a literary genre) will be crucial here, as is Aristotle's description (Reading 1.14).

4. Greek philosophy: Be sure students feel comfortable with the phrase *the speculative leap* by comparing how the ancient Egyptians, Sumerians, and Hebrews might have explained a sudden violent windstorm, versus how the Greek naturalists might have explained this phenomenon. (It is important to remind students that the latter were not average Greeks-in-the-street.) A second distinction must be made between naturalist and humanist philosophy, the shift from **what** to **how** one knows. Thorough treatment may require an hour on the *Republic* and an hour on the *Nichomachean Ethics*. The commonplace statement that "All Western philosophy is but a footnote to Plato" points to the value of spending this time—if it is available. Pre-assigned mini-themes are extremely helpful to prepare for class discussion. The lecturer will want to make sure the students understand all the elements of the Allegory of the Cave and then focus on its major themes: Plato's conviction that there *are* ultimate realities, non-relative absolutes; his notion that education is a process of conversion; his political view that political power is best vested in people who do not seek it. Other "prompts" for discussion: How do Plato and Aristotle define the good? What does Plato mean when he says that enlightenment is a "conversion of the soul"? Given Plato's view of education, what would a good teacher be like?

5. The analysis of the role of reason in acquiring virtue is one of the finest accomplishments in all of Aristotle's teaching, something like a masterpiece of intellectual art. Students, however, can be asked if the semi-technical "mean with respect to the individual" can be reduced to two old Greek folk maxims: "nothing too much," and "know yourself." How do we find out what is "too much" (liquor, arsenic, anger, compassion) in general and "too much" for us as individuals? If consensus is reached that no amount of poison and a moderate amount of everything else (discovered through individual trial and error) leads to happiness, students will understand the subtle blend of absolute and relative in Aristotle's ethical thought.

Chapter 4 Audiovisual Resources

Video/CD-ROM Sources

THE AEGEAN AGE 14 min., color **CORONET**

AESCHYLUS:
Orestia
Agamemnon 90 min., color
Choephori 70 min., color
Eumenides 70 min., color **FFH**

ANCIENT CIVILIZATIONS
Mighty civilizations rise again! Through computer reconstructions, original location footage, and interviews with leading historians, study the glorious achievements of the past. Visit ancient Egypt, Greece, Rome, and Pompeii. Witness the fall of the Aztec and Maya empires, meet Egypt's visionary ruler Cleopatra, and tour the Seven Wonders of the Ancient World. 405 minutes on 6 tapes **PBS**

ARISTOTLE'S ETHICS—The Theory of Happiness 30 min., color **EBEC**

ASCENT OF MAN: The Music of The Spheres 52 min., color **TLF**

ATHENS: The Golden Age 30 min., color **EBEC**

JOSEPH CAMPELL AND THE POWER OF MYTH (Series) (1988) **MYSTIC**

CLASSICAL AGE FFH

DEATH OF SOCRATES (1968) 45 min., B&W **TLF**

EURIPIDES: *Medea* 90 min., color **FFH**

THE GLORY THAT WAS GREECE: The Age of Civil War (on the Persian Wars) 36 min., B&W
TLF

THE GLORY THAT WAS GREECE: The Age of Minos 36 min., B&W **TLF**

THE GREEK BEGINNING (1980) **FFH**

GREEK EPIC 40 min., color **FFH**

THE GREEK MYTHS PART 1 and PART 2 54 min., color **EBEC**

THE GREEKS: CRUCIBLE OF CIVILIZATION
Classical Greece of the fourth and fifth centuries, B.C. This magnificent civilization laid the
foundations for modern science, politics, warfare, and philosophy, and produced some of the most
breathtaking art and architecture the world has ever known. Through the eyes and words of the great
heroes of ancient Greece, this dazzling production charts the rise, triumph, and eventual decline of
the world's first democracy. Now, through dramatic storytelling and state-of-the-art computer
animation, you witness history, art, and government with giants like Pericles, Socrates, Plato, and
Aristotle. 150 minutes on 2 tapes **PBS**

THE GREEKS: A Journey in Space and Time; The Minds of Men Series **FFH**

IPHIGENIA 127 min., color **FFH**

OEDIPUS THE KING (SERIES)
    Oedipus Rex: Man and God
    Age of Sophocles
    The Character of Oedipus
    The Recovery of Oedipus EBBC

PERSEUS A CD-ROM with text and images, an interactive multimedia resource for Macintosh
computers, dealing with the culture of fifth century B.C.E. ancient Greece. **CPB**

PLATO'S APOLOGY—The Life and Teachings of Socrates 30 min., color **EBEC**

THE ROLE OF THEATER IN ANCIENT GREECE 26 min., color **FFH**

SOPHOCLES: THE THEBAN PLAYS

    Oedipus the King 120 min., color

    Oedipus at Colonus 120 min., color

    Antigone, this film is ideal for use with Chapter 4. Based on an up-to-date translation, the play is performed by an all-star cast: Juliet Stevenson, John Shrapnel, and John Gielgud. 120 min., color **FFH**

THUCYDIDES: *THE PELOPONNESIAN WARS* **and PLATO:** *ALCIBIADES I*

    In this adaptation of the Thucydides and Plato texts, members of the Royal National Theatre and the Royal Shakespeare Company conduct viewers through the story of the Peloponnesian War. Produced by BBC Television and the Greek Collection. **FFH**

THE TRIAL OF SOCRATES, Man and the State Series, BFA, Educational Media (1971) 30 min., color **PHOENIX**

Trojan Women (1971) 111 min., color **FFH**

Web Resources

Ancient Olympic Games—http://www.perseus.tufts.edu/Olympics

Minoan history and culture—http://www.dilos.com/region/crete/min_cul.html

Pictures of Minoan cultural relics—http://jade.ccccd.edu/andrade/worldlitl2332/slidesofminoan.html

Images of Mycenae—http://jade.ccccd.edu/andrade/worldlitl2332/slidesofmycenae.html

History of Mycenae—http://www.dilos.com/region/pelopon/mycenae.html

History and resources related to Greek drama—http://www.watson.org/rivendell/dramagreek.html

Selected works of Socrates—http://socrates.clarke.edu/

Biographical information and resources about Socrates—http://www.philosophypages.com/ph/socr.htm

Biographical information about Plato—http://www.rit.edu/~flwstv/plato.html

Online lectures about Aristotle and ethics—http://ethics.acusd.edu/aristotle.html

Biographical information and resources related to Aristotle—
    http://www.utm.edu/research/iep/a/aristotle.html

McGraw-Hill Resources

Transparencies: MA.2 Greece 3000–3030 B.C.E.

Sample Test Questions for Chapter 4

Select the letter of the choice that BEST answers the question:

1. The hallmarks of the classical legacy are
   a. political harmony and social order.
   b. advances in religious speculation.
   c. humanism and individualism.
   d. class equity and individual rights.
   Ans: c

2. What distinguishes the Greeks from other civilizations is their
   a. deep concern for the quality of human life.
   b. fatalism about human destiny.
   c. attempts to correct economic injustice.
   d. preoccupation with religion.
   Ans: a

3. Located on the island of Crete, the earliest Greek society was that of the
   a. Hellenes.
   b. Minoans.
   c. Mycenaeans.
   d. Tyrannians.
   Ans: b

4. Which of the following is NOT true of Greek deities?
   a. They are associated with natural forces.
   b. They intervene in human affairs.
   c. They proclaim guidelines for religious belief.
   d. They are capricious and quarrelsome.
   Ans: c

5. In the selection from the *Iliad* in the textbook (Reading 1.11), we see Achilles
   a. extend courtesy to his enemy.
   b. confirm his right to have withdrawn from battle.
   c. glorify war and combat.
   d. refusing to accept his fate.
   Ans: a

6. That the *Iliad* was improvised orally and not written down is shown by
   a. the many lapses in plot structure.
   b. Homer's blindness.
   c. Homer's use of repeated metric formulae.
   d. the lack of visual realism.
   Ans: c

7. A participatory democracy is one in which
    a. all citizens have the right to take part in governmental deliberations.
    b. all inhabitants have the right to vote.
    c. women are accorded equal legal status with men.
    d. all interest groups participate through their elected representatives.
    Ans: a

8. The excerpt from Pericles' *Funeral Speech* shows that when Pericles made the speech, Athens was
    a. smaller than Sparta.
    b. a democratic city-state.
    c. a near copy of the Persian Empire.
    d. an oligarchy.
    Ans: b

9. Which one of the following statements is the *fullest* description of what causes the tragic events of *Antigone?*
    a. Creon has a problem with women.
    b. Creon knows nothing about government and gets advice too late.
    c. Antigone is stronger than Creon.
    d. Creon follows a rigid policy in a situation calling for flexibility.
    Ans: d

10. Creon's exchange with his son, Haemon, suggests that the Athenian audience of the time would have been sensitive to which one of the following issues.
    a. Creon's refusal to listen to family advice
    b. Creon's rejection of advice from the Theban populus
    c. Haemon's support of his fiancée
    d. Haemon's standing up to his father
    Ans: b

11. The death of Creon's wife, Eurydice, near the end of the play
    a. comes as a complete surprise.
    b. is a result of her part in Antigone's illegal act.
    c. is a result of her plotting with her son, Haemon.
    d. follows logically from the plan she made with Ismene.
    Ans: a

12. The performance of Greek drama was always accompanied by music and dance.
    Ans: T

13. Like the *Epic of Gilgamesh,* the *Iliad* and the *Odyssey* were passed orally from generation to generation.
    Ans: T

14. Plato was a staunch proponent of Athenian democracy.
    Ans: F

15. It is fair to say that, on the whole, Homer's *Iliad* seems to glorify war without qualification.
    Ans: F

16. Pericles' opinion of Homer in his *Funeral Speech* shows a growing skepticism about the authority of the older poets.
    Ans: T

17. In order to persuade Crito that he cannot break the law, Socrates portrays the laws as
    a. voted by a majority.
    b. the equivalent of Socrates' parents.
    c. supremely powerful, god-like creatures.
    d. impersonal forces.
    Ans: b

18. The philosopher Heraclitus had a decisive influence on Socrates. His name is associated with the notion
    a. that all things are made up of atoms.
    b. that all things are in a state of flux and change.
    c. that all things are made up of earth, air, fire, and water.
    d. that the so-called real world is an illusion.
    Ans: b

19. Ultimately, Socrates might be likened to Achilles and Antigone, in that like her
    a. he stood up to his father.
    b. he never fought for the city.
    c. he defended his brothers.
    d. he preferred death to dishonor.
    Ans: d

20. The belief of Plato that mathematics should serve as the standard of certainty and clarity for all knowledge shows the influence of
    a. Aristotle.
    b. Pericles.
    c. Pythagoras.
    d. Heraclitus.
    Ans: c

21. In the "Allegory of the Cave," the ultimate goal of the thinker is to come into contact with
    a. the ultimately true.
    b. mathematical forms.
    c. logical categories.
    d. the good.
    Ans: d

22. For Plato, the realm of the purely intelligible contains objects of knowledge that we grasp
    a. with a combination of mind and imagination.
    b. by means of mind alone.
    c. by the imaginative use of the senses.
    d. by constructing pictures of them on a suitable medium, like paper.
    Ans: b

23. For Socrates, the fact that the soul knows things that it could not possibly learn from sense experience is a sign
    a. that the soul must have existed before its present life.
    b. that the soul is "the place of forms."
    c. that the soul is made up of parts.
    d. that the soul is made by God.
    Ans: a

24. Looked at as an ethical document, the "Allegory of the Cave" tends to the following conclusion:
    a. Virtue is knowledge.
    b. Virtue is training.
    c. Virtue is found by finding the absolute mean in actions.
    d. Virtue is found by finding the mean relative to ourselves.
    Ans: a

25. Aristotle's ethical teachings can be reduced to two basic maxims of traditional Greek folk wisdom:
    a. Love yourself and love your neighbor the same way.
    b. Suppress desire and seek inner peace.
    c. Know the good and teach it to your fellow humans.
    d. Do nothing in excess and know yourself.
    Ans: d

26. In Aristotle's *Ethics*, the statement that "the object of our enquiry is not to know the nature of virtue but to become virtuous" clearly puts Aristotle at odds with his teacher.
    Ans: T

27. Elements of the "Allegory of the Cave." For each numbered question, choose the letter of the choice that BEST matches:
    1. The chained prisoners
    2. The sun
    3. The ascent to the upper world
    4. The shadows on the wall
    a. Objects of sense-perception
    b. The journey of the soul to the realm of the intelligible
    c. The psyche tied to the bodily senses
    d. The light of the good
    Ans: 1.c, 2.d, 3.b, 4.a

Chapter 5 The Classical Style in the Arts

Summary

Two hallmarks of the classical style are order and proportion, qualities that reflect the Hellenic assumption that the arts of humankind (architecture, sculpture, painting, literature, and music) mirror the state of nature. Attention to the life of the individual in the world gives classical art a humanistic character, but the Greek emphasis on the objective presentation of phenomena (realism) is tempered by the will to render a more perfect image of nature (idealism) in accordance with universal laws of proportion and harmony. The spirit of the classical style (as illustrated in vase paintings, the Parthenon, and Golden Age sculpture, as well as in lyric poetry, drama, and music) rests on the belief that aesthetic principles have objective and measurable value. The classical style dominated the art of the Greek Golden Age. During the Hellenistic era, in the territories conquered by Alexander the Great, that style moved in the direction of expressive realism and dramatic monumentality.

Outline	Pronunciation Guide
A. The classical style 1. order and proportion 2. humanism, realism, and idealism 3. black- and red-figured vase painting B. Evolution of the classical style 1. archaic sculpture 2. classical sculpture 3. the Parthenon 4. the Greek orders 5. the sculpture of the Parthenon C. The classical style in poetry 1. Sappho 2. Pindar D. The classical style in music and dance E. Diffusion of the classical style 1. Alexander and the Hellenistic world 2. principle schools of thought 3. the arts	**Vitruvius** [vi TROO vee us] *kouros* [KOO ros] *contrapposto* [kon trah POWS tow] *Doryphorus* [dow RIF o rus] **Polyclitus** [pol ee KLEYE tus] *cire-perdu* [SIR per DOO] **Ictinus** [ik TEE nus] **Callicrates** [kal li KRAH teez] **Acropolis** [a KRAH pow lis] **tholos** [THOW lahs] **metope** [ME tow pee] **Panathenaic** [PAN ath ah NAY ik] **Parthenon** [PAHR the nahn] **Phidias** [FID ee ahs] **Elgin** [EL jin] **Sappho** [SAF fow] *kithara* [KITH ah rah] *aulos* [AHW lahs] **Pergamon** [PEHR gah mon] **Stoicism** [STOW i si zum] **Epicurean** [ep i kyu REE un] **Laocoön** [lay OK ow on] **Diogenes** [deye AH ju nees]

Key Terms: archaic, classical, Hellenic/Hellenistic, Doric, Ionic, Corinthian orders, rationalism, humanism, idealism vs. realism, *contrapposto*, kouros/kore, Nike, optical refinements, modes (music), Doctrine of Ethos.

Key Images	
Calf-Bearer *Anavyssos Kouros* Polycleitus, *Doryphorus* (copy) Zeus (or Poseidon) Myron, *Discobolus* (copy) *Kore from Chios*	Praxiteles, *Aphrodite of Cnidos* (copy) Acropolis, Athens Parthenon Panathenaic Frieze *Nike of Samothrace* *Laocoön and His Sons* *Altar of Zeus*

Study Questions

Factual
1. What, according to Vitruvius, is the basis for architectural design?
2. Define these terms and give examples (from figures in this chapter): "humanism," "realism," "idealism."
3. How do Figures 5.10 (*Discobolus*) and 5.11 (*Zeus*) differ from the four that precede it in this chapter?
4. Why did Greek artists depict the human figure in the nude?
5. How does the Parthenon exemplify the classical style?
6. What are the basic characteristics of Sappho's poetry?
7. Into what parts of the world did Alexander carry the classical style?
8. Describe in your own words: Skepticism, Stoicism, Epicureanism.
9. What figures in the sciences graced the Hellenistic era?
10. Describe the differences between classical and Hellenistic sculpture. What is carried over from classicism to the Hellenistic period?

Challenge
1. Making reference to works of art illustrated in this chapter, give specific examples of symmetry, geometric clarity, and proportion in classical art.
2. Compare Greek statues of the female nude to earlier examples of women in ancient society. What is similar; what is different?
3. What features in the female nude did Greek sculptors find attractive? Are the breasts large or small; the hips wide or narrow? Can you draw any associations between the form of the nude and the roles women might have played in society?
4. Apply this statement to selected figures in the text: "In the development of the classical style, the Greek quest for fidelity to nature was balanced by a tendency to idealize." How, specifically, did the Greeks idealize nature?
5. Pericles (Chapter 4) says of Athenian achievements, "There are mighty monuments of our power which will make us the wonder of this and succeeding ages." In what ways might the Parthenon fit this description? Might the temple also be described as a victory monument?
6. Explain how the subject matter of the Parthenon sculpture illustrates the major concerns and values of Athens in the time of Pericles.
7. Evaluate the Greek "doctrine of ethos"; do you think music influences human conduct? Do certain kinds of music generate distinct kinds of behavior or feelings? Relate these considerations to current efforts to monitor and censor some styles of popular music.

8. Examine the sexual dimension of Sappho's poetry; are these lyrics explicitly about one gender or another?

9. Find examples of Neoclassical architecture in your community. In light of the fact that the originals would have been temples to Greek gods, what impact do you think this style was intended to have on our own life?

10. Put into your own words a description or definition of the word *classic* and the term *classical style*.

Strategies for Discussion/Lecture

1. The introduction to the classical style emphasizes the underlying theory of mathematical proportions. You may wish to test Vitruvius' declaration (Reading 1.18) that the male foot is to the height of a man in the ratio of 1:6, by asking students to come to class having divided their height by the length of their bare foot. The outcome is usually a rough average of 1:6 for men and 1:8 for women (i.e., the Doric and Ionic proportions). The very act of averaging (and taking account of American mixed physical types) brings out the ideal, mathematical aspect of systems of proportion.

   The lecturer may wish to carry this initial exercise on proportion over to a study of the Parthenon as exemplary of Hellenic esthetic, civic, and moral ideals, using the site and orientation of the temple, its sculpture, and its optical refinements. The lecture/discussion can attempt to give detailed answers to a number of the Factual and Challenge questions.

2. In a slide presentation or using the text illustrations, the sequence of figures in Chapter 4, Minoan and Mycenaean, might be used to preface the development of the classical style. The fish and floral motifs in the queen's quarters at Knossos will not survive in classical Greece: the use of elaborate border ornaments (see the amphora pictured in Figure 4.7) gives way to an almost obsessive concern with the human figure. Use slides or Figures 4.7, 5.4–5.13, 5.21–5.24, 5.26–5.27 to emphasize the *humanistic* focus of Greek art; show the "progress" from Archaic to High Classical male nude sculpture as an example of increasing *realism*; use the *Discobolus* and the *Zeus* as examples of the artist's choice to represent the ideal moment of the action, and extend discussion of *idealism* by asking students: How old are these figures? In what physical condition? How do their physiques compare with your own?

3. If the images presented range from Cycladic sculpture through the Hellenistic period, the predominance of the nude male citizen, athlete, and soldier will be apparent in the high classical period. How, by comparison, are women represented? Ask students if they find the nude statuary of the Greeks seductive; if not, why not? How might Sappho have responded to the dominance of male imagery in Greek society? What do the poems of Pindar and Sappho relate concerning gender in Hellenic culture?

4. In all of the above strategies, the lecturer will want to help students define the word *classic* (as enduring and first-rate), and of the phrase *classical style*, as it applies to these materials. A comparison of Hellenic and Hellenistic art is helpful here: In what ways did the latter diverge from "classical" principles? Why have there been so many classical revivals in Western history (introduce the term *Neoclassic*). Finally, ask students which works of art (including film), literature, and music might become classics (and why so?).

Video/CD-ROM Sources

ALEXANDER THE GREAT AND THE HELLENISTIC AGE 14 min., color **CORONET**

ANCIENT GREEK ART AND ARCHITECTURE
    available through: http://www.edvidnet.com/default.html

ATHENS: The Golden Age EBEC

THE CLASSICAL IDEAL 60 min., color **CPB**

THE GREEK TEMPLE, Museum Without Wall Series 53 min., color **KVC**

IN THE FOOTSTEPS OF ALEXANDER THE GREAT
    Begin a journey of epic proportions with Michael Wood as he travels from Macedonia in Northern
    Greece to India, retelling one of the world's greatest stories. Divided into four parts, "The Speaking
    Tree" examines Alexander's childhood, "Son of God" traces the invasion of Persia and Alexander's
    conquest of the Persian Empire, "The Road to Samarkand" follows Alexander's move to Afghanistan,
    and "To the End of the Earth" sees Alexander invade India, conquering local rulers and ranging as
    far as the Beas River before his long-suffering, exhausted troops refuse to go any further. Unable to
    go on, wounded in mind and body, Alexander returns to Persia. 240 minutes on 2 tapes **PBS**

MONUMENTS OF ANCIENT GREECE
    available through: http://www.edvidnet.com/default.html

THE SEARCH FOR ALEXANDER THE GREAT
    The Young Lion
    The Young Conqueror
    Lord of Asia
    The Last March   each segment 60 min., color **TLF**

YOU ARE THERE: The Triumph of Alexander the Great 26 min., B&W **MCHF**

Music Resources

The History of Music in Sound, Volume 1, RCA.
2000 Years of Music, Folkway Records.

Web Resources

Shrine of the Goddess Athena—http://www.goddess-athena.org

Information about Sappho—http://www.sappho.com/poetry/historical/sappho.html

Oxford University's Ashmolean Museum (Greek sculpture)—
    http://www.ashmol.ox.uk/ash/departments/cast-gallery/

A companion site to the PBS documentary *In the Footsteps of Alexander the Great*—
   http://www.pbs.org/mpt/alexander/

McGraw-Hill Resources

Music Listening Selection: CD I
   I–1 "Seiklos Song"
Transparencies: A.15 Sculpture Process: Subtractive Carving
                A.22 Greek Orders of Columns
                A.23 Parthenon and Acropolis
                MA.2 Greece 3000–3030 B.C.E.

Sample Test Questions for Chapter 5

Select the letter of the choice that BEST answers the question:

1. The principles of Greek art and architecture are most closely associated with the mathematical
    assumptions of the philosopher
    a. Pythagoras.
    b. Leucippus.
    c. Heraclitus.
    d. Socrates.
    Ans: a

2. The notion of symmetry is defined as the
    a. relationship between architectural order and its sculpture.
    b. post and lintel method.
    c. harmonious relation between the whole and its parts.
    d. harmony between the subject of art and its design.
    Ans: c

3. Greek art reflects a preoccupation with
    a. religion and its rituals.
    b. characters from tragedy and comedy.
    c. politicians and philosophers.
    d. human activity and the human form.
    Ans: d

4. The Greek temple typically
    a. blended civic and religious functions.
    b. protected the priests from the rest of the population.
    c. served as a public theater.
    d. housed the deceased monarch.
    Ans: a

5. Which of the following architectural orders uses relatively slender and terminate columns with capitals of paired scrolls?
   a. Iambic
   b. Doric
   c. Ionic
   d. Corinthian
   Ans: c

6. The theme of the Parthenon's sculptures may be interpreted as
   a. combat between the Greeks and the Persians.
   b. struggles of the Trojan War.
   c. triumph of rationalism over barbarianism.
   d. conflict between faith and reason.
   Ans: c

7. The technique in classical sculpture by which the weight of the statue is shifted to one foot is called
   a. *contrapposto.*
   b. rotation.
   c. *chiaroscuro.*
   d. burnishing.
   Ans: a

8. In a Doric temple, entasis refers to
   a. the slight bulge in the middle of the column.
   b. the "pillow" between the column and the stylobate.
   c. the solid square piece between the echinus and the entablature.
   d. the slight curvature of the stylobate used to give the impression that it is perfectly level.
   Ans: a

9. Most Greek sculptures still in existence are actually Roman copies of the originals.
   Ans: T

10. The Parthenon was constructed in such a way that almost all the lines of the temple are straight.
    Ans: F

11. The sculptures of the Parthenon were once painted with vivid colors.
    Ans: T

Answer the following with a word or phrase.

12. An architectural system that defines the parts of a building and its decorative mode is a(n)

    _____.
    Ans: order

13. _____ poetry is a form of literary expression intended to be sung rather than read in silence.
    Ans: lyric

14. _____ led a cult dedicated to Aphrodite and attained celebrity as one of the most expressive writers of love poetry.
    Ans: Sappho

15. The failure of the Greek city-states to live in peace prompted Macedonian rulers to dominate the Greek peninsula and ushered in the _____ or "Greek-like" Age.
    Ans: Hellenistic

16. The Macedonian general _____ spread Greek language and culture throughout the Near East and Egypt.
    Ans: Alexander the Great

Open Book

17. Fiero, Figure 5.20. The space in which the statues are placed is called the
    a. abacus.
    b. frieze.
    c. echinus.
    d. tympanum.
    Ans: d

18. Fiero, Figure 5.14, the Parthenon. Given what you know about Greek thought and art, choose the statement that best expresses the general impression the architect wanted to give.
    a. The Parthenon gives the impression that the priestly class was the most important in Athenian society.
    b. It stands for idealism in Plato's sense, since its beauty is entirely mathematical, and no provision is made for human senses.
    c. It embodies both ideal principles in its structure and consideration of the senses in its optical refinements.
    d. It looks like what it is: a bombed out bank, built for security, not beauty.
    Ans: c

19. Fiero, Figure 5.32, *Laocoön and his Sons*. One feature that marks this work as Hellenistic as contrasted with classical is
    a. its turbulence and agitation.
    b. the portrayal of male nudes.
    c. the inclusion of a reptile.
    d. its small size.
    Ans: a

20. Fiero, Figure 5.31, *Nike of Samothrace*. One feature of this statue that is characteristic of the Hellenistic period, as opposed to the classical is
    a. the fact that it is female.
    b. the fact that it is headless.
    c. its size.
    d. its celebration of victory.
    Ans: c

21. The Doctrine of Ethos holds that
    a. There are seven different musical modes.
    b. Music has a moral influence.
    c. All music should be monophonic.
    d. There are fixed patterns of pitch within the octave.
    Ans: b

22. The flute or reed pipe used in ancient Greek was called the _____.
    Ans: aulos

23. The Hellenistic thinker who taught that happiness depended on avoiding all forms of physical excess was _____.
    Ans: Epicurus

24. Hellenistic thinkers surpassed their predecessors in
    a. speculative philosophy.
    b. iron technology.
    c. astronomy and mathematics.
    d. music.
    Ans: c

Chapter 6 Rome: The Rise to Empire

Summary

The Roman Empire was the longest-lasting and most influential empire in Western history. From the earliest times, the Romans were effective in adopting and modifying the cultures of others, such as the Etruscans and the Greeks. In the transition from Republic to Empire, the Roman genius for administration and organization manifested itself in its military; but (it is argued here) *all* aspects of Roman life and culture reflect, to some extent, the spirit of Roman imperialism. Rome's achievements in engineering, law, and architecture unified the vast territories of the empire, while Roman sculpture and various forms of literary expression gave propagandistic voice to the authority and majesty of the new world empire. Though they borrowed heavily from the Greeks, Roman artists developed their own version of the classical style, one that emphasized practical realism and a close attention to illusionistic detail. Similarly, Roman literature reflects a materialistic and practical frame of mind but one that did not lack caustic wit. The Romans preserved and transmitted Greek culture to the West, but they also created new forms of expression in architecture, literature (satire), and law that have survived into our times.

Outline	Pronunciation Guide
A. Rome's history, from republic to empire	*res publica* [RES POOB li kah]
1. origins and early history	**Josephus** [jow SE fus]
2. the Roman Republic	*Pax Romana*
3. Punic wars and the rise of military	[PAHKS row MAH nah]
generals	*latifundia* [la ti FÛN dee ah]
4. the Roman empire	*imperator* [im pe RAH towr]
B. Key aspects of Roman culture	*jus civile* [YÛS si VI lay]
1. law	**Circus Maximus**
2. philosophic thought: Stoicism	[SUR kus MAX i mus]
3. literature	**Maison Carrée** [may ZOWN ka RAY]
a. prose: history, letters, oratory	**Maxentius** [mak SEN shus]
b. poetry: epic, lyric, satire	**Titus** [TEI tus]
c. drama	*trompe l'oeil* [TRAHMP LOY]
4. engineering and architecture	**Octavian** [ok TAY vee un]
5. sculpture	**Tacitus** [TA si tus]
a. art as propaganda	**Ovid** [AH vid]
b. portraiture	**Juvenal** [JOO vu nul]
6. painting	*Aeneid* [ay NEE id]
7. music	**Pantheon** [PAN thee ahn]
	carpe diem [KAHR pay DEE em]

Key Terms: republic, imperialism, plebeians/patricians, *Pax Romana,* jurisprudence, Roman arch and vault, "bread and circuses," basilica, *trompe l'oeil,* stoicism, satire, realism, oratory, pastoral, epistle.

Key Images	
Arch of Titus	Trajan's Column
Colosseum	Roman baths
Pantheon	Maison Carrée
Equestrian Statue of Marcus Aurelius	Augustus of Primaporta
Basilica of Macentius	Pompeii frescoes and mosaics
Pont du Gard	

Study Questions

Factual

1. What three cultures contributed to the formation of Roman culture? What did each contribute?
2. Briefly define these terms: consul, plebeian, tribune, *res publica, imperium, Pax romana.*
3. What does the *Description of the Roman Army* by Josephus (Reading 1.21) tell one about Roman military life?
4. What were the main achievements of Julius Caesar?
5. Place in time the *Pax Romana* and describe the status of the empire at that time.
6. What role did oratory play in Roman life according to Tacitus (Reading 1.24)?
7. What were Rome's main contributions to the field of law?
8. What does Seneca (Reading 1.22) single out as "the greatest source of affliction to humanity"?
9. What does the poet Juvenal not like about life in Rome (Reading 1.27)? How does he use satire to make his point?
10. In what new ways did the Romans use the principle of the arch?
11. Why was portraiture so important in Roman culture?

Challenge

1. What, in your view, were Rome's most important contributions to the humanistic tradition? How did they differ from that of the Greeks?
2. How did Roman architecture serve the practical needs of Roman life? Give specific examples.
3. With regard to the shaping influence of Greek culture upon Roman civilization, comment on the oft-quoted statement, "Captive Greece made Rome captive."
4. It is said that the Pantheon inspired more world architecture than any other classical structure. Can you offer some examples? Begin by looking in your own city, then in Washington, D.C.
5. If you could fly over the city of Rome in imperial times, as in Figure 6. 7, what kinds of buildings would you notice primarily? What does this say about Roman life?
6. How did Roman sculpture differ from that of the Greeks? Give specific examples.
7. What are the principal themes addressed in the poetry of Catullus and Horace?
8. How did Virgil's *Aeneid* differ from the *Iliad*? In what ways is it similar?
9. Making use of the boxed listings of landmarks in science and technology, discuss the main contributions of the Romans to these fields.
10. Juvenal observes that the Romans of his day "suffer the evils of long peace." What does he mean? What ill effects might peacetime bring to a society?
11. In Aristotle's *Nichomachean Ethics*, the investigation of virtue is centered on "the good life." In Seneca's *On Tranquility of Mind*, the counterpart of the Greek "good life" is the *career*. What does this basic orientation tell us about Roman ideals?

12. Cicero wrote, "When the stress of circumstances demands it, we must gird on the sword and prefer death to slavery and disgrace." What image does it present of Roman society at large? Do you share this point of view? Is it one that influenced history?
13. Tacitus wrote, "The more influence a man could wield by his powers of speech, the more readily did he attain to high office [and] gain favor [and] fame." Is this true in our own time? Can you name figures in American political history that prove or disprove this statement? Compare the powers of eloquence of the following political figures: Abraham Lincoln, Ronald Reagan, and George Bush, Junior.

Strategies for Discussion/Lecture

1. The lecturer might want to approach this chapter by defining *imperialism*; how does Roman culture reflect imperialistic ambitions? Students should be able to cite earlier examples of imperialism (Sargon, Cyrus the Great of Persia, Periclean Athens, Alexander the Great). What are the consequences of imperialism? Is there evidence of imperialism in the art and literature provided in the chapter? A lecture-style review of Rome's rise to empire is valuable; students might be assigned beforehand a mini-theme on Factual question #2 to encourage familiarity with terms.
2. A second lecture might address the literary contributions of ancient Rome; students might be assigned ahead a mini-theme, choosing one from Factual questions #6, 7, or 9. The class usually divides in selection fairly evenly, which produces fruitful variety of discussion on essay writing, oratory, and satire. Challenge questions #7 and 8 might be introduced as well in classroom discussion.
3. A third lecture may be devoted to slide presentation of the major monuments of Rome. Challenge question #5 gives students an opportunity to build a picture of Roman values from the details of its cityscape. They will be quick to notice the prominent structures devoted to spectator sports and leisure activities (aqueducts feeding spas). Participatory sports and the call-up citizen army of the small Greek *poleis* left no equivalent architectural remains. Examples that respond to Factual questions #10 and 11 may also be included here.
4. Compare Seneca with Aristotle's *Ethics*. Of Aristotle's "three kinds of lives," which does Seneca stress? Do we get the sense that Seneca writes for active citizens in a political community? Tacitus can also be read for ethical views—not on present Roman life but on the past: oratory was alive in the good old days of the turbulent republic, when one got ahead by effective speech in real deliberative bodies.
5. Students are likely to have seen the film *Gladiator* (2000), and some will want to know how "authentic" the film is and how historically accurate. These queries can be used to prompt research: divide the class into groups to research different aspects of the period to research and compare (to the film version) what they learn. Topics might include: the death of Marcus Aurelius, techniques of gladiatorial combat, the variety of games, women's dress and jewelry, the construction of the Colosseum, etc.

Video/CD-ROM Sources

ANCIENT CIVILIZATIONS
Mighty civilizations rise again! Through computer reconstructions, original location footage, and interviews with leading historians, study the glorious achievements of the past. Visit ancient Egypt, Greece, Rome, and Pompeii. Witness the fall of the Aztec and Maya empires, meet Egypt's visionary ruler Cleopatra, and tour the Seven Wonders of the Ancient World. 405 minutes on 6 tapes **PBS**

ANCIENT ROME (Series) (1998)
DIRECTOR: VERKLAN, LAURA color **AE**

ART OF THE WESTERN WORLD
Program 1: The Classical Ideal & Imperial Stones of Rome HTG

ART OF THE WESTERN WORLD
Program 2: A White Garment of Churches—Romanesque & The Age of Gothic HTG

BURIED CITIES (Pompeii and Herculaneum) 14 min., color IFB

CIVILISATION—Vol. #01: The Frozen World (1970)
DIRECTOR: CLARK, SIR KENNETH 53 min., color **PBS**

DECLINE OF THE ROMAN EMPIRE 14 min., color CORONET

I, CLAUDIUS, EXXONMOBIL MASTERPIECE THEATRE
Winner of four British Academy Awards, an American Emmy, and other awards worldwide, this landmark series follows the history of the Roman Empire and the fortunes of its ruling family from 50 B.C. to A.D. 50. Derek Jacobi portrays wise old Claudius, who relates the fascinating tale of treachery and debauchery, involving emperors and murderers, blackmailers and schemers. Meet Augustus, and his venomous wife Livia, the treacherous Tiberius and the depraved Caligula, who will keep you enthralled in this spellbinding, superbly acted drama. This special collector's edition features scenes omitted from the original broadcast and includes the famed documentary, *The Epic That Never Was*. 780 minutes on 7 tapes **PBS**

ETRURIA AND THE ETRUSCAN WOMAN
Focusing primarily on the art and architecture and the role of women, this computerized resource allows students of ancient civilizations to examine Etruria's culture, religion, and language through its Villanovan, Oriental, Archaic, Classical, and Hellenistic periods. Can be used with both Windows and Macintosh. **FFH**

THE ETRUSCANS
The life of ancient Etruria as depicted in the Etruscan tombs at Tarquinia and Cerveteri. 27 min. **FFH**

HAIL CAESAR
From Julius to Justinian, explore the lives of the legendary leaders of ancient Rome, and the mighty empire they built. 300 min. **AE**

IN DEFENSE OF ROME 16 min., color **MGHF**

IN SEARCH OF HISTORY: ROME'S ETERNAL WONDERS 50 min. **AE**

IN SEARCH OF HISTORY: POMPEII 50 min. **AE**

JOURNEY THROUGH ANCIENT POMPEII
This outstanding program uses Pompeii's abundant archaeological evidence to re-create daily life at the time Mt. Vesuvius erupted. **FFH**

JULIUS CAESAR—Rise of The Roman Empire 22 min., color **EBEC**

THE LEGACY OF ROME 55 min., color **MGHF**

LIFE IN ANCIENT ROME 14 min., color **EBEC**

POMPEII: Daily Life of the Ancient Romans 45 min., color **FFH**

ROMAN CITY
The ancient Romans built cities in the lands they conquered, linking Western Europe, the Middle East, and North Africa into a vast, thriving Empire. By combining documentary footage and animated story sequences, this program examines how these cities helped maintain the Empire and how they shaped people's lives. Host David Macaulay takes you to many ancient sites to explain how various structures were built and how they were used. Through animation, watch the construction of a fictional city in Gaul. 60 minutes on 1 tape **PBS**

ROMAN WAR MACHINE, THE (Series) (1999)
DIRECTOR: GILLAM, MARTIN 200 min., color **AE**

THE ROMANS IFB

THE SPIRIT OF ROME 29 min., color **EBEC**

Web Resources

Etruscan artifacts—http://www.comune.bologna.it/bologna/Musei/Archaeologico/etruschi/en/7_e.htm

Annotated Guide to Internet Resources related to Julius Caesar—http://virgil.org.caesar

Annotated Guide to Internet Resources related to Caesar Augustus—http://virgil.org/augustus

The Virgil Project—http://virgil.classics.upenn.edu

Cicero—http://www.utexas.edu/depts/classics/documents/Cic.html

Pompeii Forum Project—http://jefferson.village.virginia.edu/pompeii

Roman Law resources—http://iuscivile.com

Oxford University's Ashmolean Museum (Roman sculpture)—
http://www.ashmol.ox.ac.uk.ash/departments/cast-gallery/

McGraw-Hill Resources

Transparencies: MA.3 Rome 735 B.C.E.–476 C.E.

Sample Test Questions for Chapter 6

Select the letter of the choice that BEST answers the question:

1. The powerful landowners of ancient Rome made up the _____ class.
   a. Etruscan
   b. equites
   c. plebeian
   d. patrician
   Ans: d

2. The hard-working small farmers of Rome constituted the _____ class.
   a. Etruscan
   b. equites
   c. plebeian
   d. patrician
   Ans: c

3. After 287 B.C.E., the Roman government was _____ in form.
   a. monarchical
   b. democratic
   c. representative
   d. republican
   Ans: d

4. Greek and Roman civilizations differed significantly in the
   a. size of the territory each governed.
   b. nature of their economies.
   c. role of religion in everyday life.
   d. status of slaves.
   Ans: a

5. Which of the following commemorated military victories in Rome?
   a. Pantheon
   b. Colosseum
   c. Circus Maximus
   d. Arch of Titus
   Ans: d

6. The dominant theme of the *Aeneid* is
   a. the triumph of the Romans over the Greeks.
   b. Rome's destiny as a world ruler.
   c. the conflict between conscience and civic duty.
   d. the nature of immortality.
   Ans: b

7. Roman painting reveals a quest for
   a. symbolism.
   b. abstraction.
   c. idealism.
   d. realism.
   Ans: d

8. The story of the origins of Roman civilization is recounted by your text author and by the poet Virgil in his *Aeneid*: these two versions are basically the same.
   Ans: F

9. One of the major Roman contributions to the realm of Western law was in
   a. jurisprudence.
   b. trial law.
   c. the abolition of slavery.
   d. the use of a jury system.
   Ans: a

10. A landmark event in the rise of the Roman Republic was the
    a. *Pax romana.*
    b. assassination of Julius Caesar.
    c. Punic Wars.
    d. alliance between Anthony and Cleopatra.
    Ans: c

11. The poet who modeled love poems on the lyrics of Sappho was _____.
    Ans: Catullus

12. The Latin title given to Octavian by the Roman Senate was _____.
    Ans: *Augustus*

13. The two media employed in the ornamentation of the walls and floors of Roman villas were

    _____.

    Ans: fresco and mosaic

14. The Roman philosophical current closest to the spirit of Horace's "Carpe Diem" (Reading 1.27) is
    a. Epicureanism.
    b. Stoicism.
    c. Neo-Platonism.
    d. Christianity.
    Ans: a

15. Compared to Greek ethical philosophy (as in Aristotle's *Ethics*), Seneca's view of humans (Reading 1.22) is
    a. different in details but the same in essentials.
    b. more spiritually oriented than Greek ethical thought.
    c. chiefly concerned with finding one's place in the system.
    d. far more concerned with amassing wealth.
    Ans: c

16. In his satire "Against Women," (Reading 1.24), Juvenal attributes the vices of his contemporaries to
    a. the collapse of the republic.
    b. Christian influences.
    c. wealth and corruption
    d. the violence of the army
    Ans: c

17. If you could fly over imperial Rome, as in Figure 6. 7, you would see that the most prominent structures are devoted to
    a. sports and leisure activities.
    b. religious buildings.
    c. Christian structures.
    d. government and administration buildings.
    Ans: a

18. Fiero, Figures 6.7 and 6.9. In its architecture, the Colosseum illustrates
    a. Greek post and lintel construction.
    b. Roman structural principles and Greek decoration.
    c. Pure, unadorned Roman style building.
    d. Roman structure and Egyptian decoration.
    Ans: b

19. Fiero, Figures 6.17.and 6.18. One feature of this basilica that marks it as the prototype of the first Christian churches is
    a. the shape of the apse.
    b. the size of the structure.
    c. the Roman arches.
    d. the open roof.
    Ans: a

20. Fiero, Figures 6.11 and 6.14. The views of the these buildings illustrate which of the following orders.
    a. Doric
    b. Corinthian
    c. Etruscan
    d. Ionic
    Ans: b

21. Fiero, Figure 6.13. Thomas Jefferson's adaptation of the Pantheon is close to the Roman original with the exception of one of the following.
    a. The tympanum is treated differently.
    b. Jefferson's building is Ionic, whereas the Pantheon is Corinthian.
    c. In Jefferson's building, the columns rest directly on the stylobate.
    d. Jefferson's building is dedicated to one god and the Pantheon to all the gods.
    Ans: a

22. Fiero, Figure 6.27 (Atrium, House in Pompeii). According to the poet Juvenal, one of the advantages of this kind of house was
    a. that it let in a quantity of daylight.
    b. that you could get a good night's sleep in it.
    c. that it kept you in touch with daily life in the streets.
    d. that it was available to all inhabitants of Rome.
    Ans: b

Summary

China's rise to empire was an extraordinary achievement that in many aspects paralleled the Roman rise to empire. Under the leadership of Qin and Han rulers, China created a lasting presence in East Asia and left an enduring legacy in philosophic thought and in the arts. The teachings of Confucius became a civilizing force in Chinese society, although opposing schools of thought prevailed as well. The richness and variety of China's classical legacy are visible in the Confucian *Analects*, the writing of prose history and lyric poetry, and the arts of sculpture, architecture, and music. Like the Romans, the Chinese were a practical and inventive culture whose broad range of scientific and technological advances outreached those of Rome itself.

Outline	**Pronunciation Guide**

A. Confucius and the classics
     1.   the five Chinese classics
     2.   the Analects
     3.   post-Confucian moral thought
          a.   Mencius
          b.   legalism
B. China's rise to empire
     1.   the Qin dynasty
     2.   the Han dynasty
C. Key aspects of Chinese culture
     1.   literature
          a.   prose: historical narrative
          b.   poetry
          c.   the visual arts and music
          d.   technology
	Confucius [khan FYU shus]
	li [LEE}
	Ssu-ma Ch'ien [soo ma chee EN]
	Shi jing [shee CHEEN]
	Qin [CHIN]
	Mencius [MEN see us]
	Han [HAHN]
	Sima Qian [see ma CHEE en]

Key Terms: Five Chinese Classics, Analects, *li*, legalism, Great Wall, First Emperor, terra-cotta, bronze bells.

Key Images	
Great Wall of China Tomb Model of a House, Eastern Han Dynasty Terra-cotta army, Qin dynasty	Bronze Mirror Back Ceramic Musicians Bronze Bells of Marquis Yi

Study Questions

Factual
1. When is Confucius thought to have lived? Why did he become a central figure in Chinese culture?
2. What subjects are covered in the Five Chinese Classics?
3. Briefly describe the teachings in the Confucian *Analects*. Do they fall in the category of religion, politics, or ethics?
4. How did Mencius view the role of the state?
5. How did Legalism modify Confucian ideals?
6. What were some of the main achievements of the Qin dynasty? The Han dynasty?
7. Why is Han culture called "classical"?
8. Name some of the technological achievements of the Chinese between 300 B.C.E. and 300 C.E.
9. What evidence of Chinese aristocratic life is provided by Han burial artifacts?
10. What similarities can be drawn between the Roman rise to empire and the Chinese rise to empire?

Challenge
1. What are the principal themes to be found in the Confucian *Analects*? Give examples of these by specific numbers from Reading 1.29. What do these teachings suggest about Chinese values? How does this work compare with Aristotle's *Nicomachean Ethics*?
2. Offer an argument in favor of Mencius' view of human nature; then offer one that supports the Legalist viewpoint. Which do you believe is more persuasive? Why?
3. What features of classical Chinese society may be called "practical" and "materialistic"? What features might be called "mystical" and "intuitive"? Give specific examples.
4. Discuss the similarities between the cultures of ancient Rome and China in the areas of technology and engineering. Give specific examples.
5. Most of what we know about the Qin and Han empires comes from their tombs. Most of what we know about Rome comes from its public monuments. What does this reveal about the differences between these two civilizations?
6. What insights into Chinese society and values are revealed in the selection of Chinese poetry (Reading 1.31)? How do these concerns differ from those found in the selection of Roman poems in Chapter 6?
7. What limitations do Western students encounter when they attempt to understand Eastern cultures? Are we able to know as much about ancient China as we do about ancient Rome?
8. Research the Bronze Bells of Marquis Yi of Zeng. Similar sets of bells appear in numerous Chinese graves through the Ming era. What role might these bells have played in Chinese life?
9. In what evidence do we find the principles discussed in Chapter 3, such as the natural order, yin/yang, and the Mandate of Heaven, still operating in the Qin and Han empires? Give specific examples.
10. China's royal tomb burials can be compared with those of Egypt; what similarities exist? What differences?
11. Sima Qian (Reading 1.30) holds that wealth and virtue are interchangeable; would Confucius agree? Why or why not?

Strategies for Discussion/Lecture

1. One obvious theme for lecture would be a comparison between the Qin and Han consolidation of territory and culture and that of the Roman Empire. The "rise to empire" theme can be better confronted by students who have prepared a mini-theme on Factual question #10. A second focus: the significance of this era in Chinese history as a classical age. Here the definition of "classical" may be revisited, with examples drawn from the enduring aspects of Chinese culture: language, the Confucian tradition, techniques in the arts, lyric poetry, and so on.

2. Confucius was a civilizing force in Chinese society. Invite class discussion as to why this has been the case. Then ask students to identify those figures from Greco-Roman culture who have been similarly "civilizing" in Western society and culture. Are we Westerners, as Shelley suggested, "all Greeks"? Are the Chinese "children of the Han"? Some scholars argue that the sixth to fifth centuries B.C.E. constituted an "Axis Age" in which emerged such important figures as Zoroaster, Socrates, Pythagoras, and Confucius. Discussion on the relationship between these figures works as effective review of Chapters 2 through 7.

3. As an effort at synthesizing the materials in the unit "The Classical Legacy," the lecturer might pose a series of questions and ask students to answer them according to how they believe each of the cultures discussed in the unit (Greek, Roman, Chinese) might respond. The class might be divided into Greeks, Romans, and Chinese; each group would have a "say" in responding to such questions as: "What is my attitude toward the gods?" "What are the obligations of a wife?" "Would I want to be a soldier in this society?" "How does one best prepare for death?" "Which is more important, the family or the state?" "What kind of education is most valuable?" "Is freedom essential to the good life?"

4. Research on the Qin and Han dynasty yields a wealth of information from recent archeological discoveries. The actual tomb of the First Emperor has yet to be uncovered, and it is likely that our knowledge of the Qin era will change in time. Nevertheless, students might be encouraged to read further in Sima Qian's *Records of the Grand Historian* and to assess the extent to which Sima's reports are trustworthy. Were they written to glorify the imperial position? Is Sima more objective than, say, Virgil or Livy?

Chapter 7 Audiovisual Resources

Video/CD-ROM Sources

ALONG THE SILK ROAD (1993)
Silk Road is a series of twelve videos that represents the first major co-production between China and the outside world. *Silk Road* was photographed over the course of ten years at a cost of $50 million and contains a sound track by internationally recognized musician Kitaro. It holds the distinction of being the highest-rated documentary series in Japan's broadcasting history, and has been broadcast in over 25 countries. Six more videos were later released as the *Silk Road II*. **Central Mark Media Distributors** http://www.centralparkmedia.com/cpmdbl/search2.cfm

CHINESE ART: TREASURES OF THE NATIONAL PALACE MUSEUM
This program spotlights 20 works of Chinese art seldom ever seen outside of the National Palace Museum. 26 min., color **FFH**

FIVE MILLENNIA OF CHINESE ART: A SPIRITUAL JOURNEY—ON CD-ROM This elegant CD-ROM replicates the experience of touring the Chi-Shan Garden and the museum's four floors of galleries. Windows only. **FFH**

THE IMMORTAL EMPEROR: SHIHUANGDI
Noted historians, archaeologists, and other experts extrapolate from discoveries made in tomb of China's first emperor, Shihuangdi. A BBC Production. 50 min. **FFH**

IN SEARCH OF HISTORY: THE GREAT WALL 50 min. **AE**

SILK ROAD, THE: Series 1 (Series) (1990)
DIRECTOR: SUZUKI, HAJIME *Silk Road* is a series of twelve videos that represents the first major co-production between China and the outside world. Silk Road was photographed over the course of 10 years at a cost of $50 million and contains a sound track by internationally recognized musician Kitaro. It holds the distinction of being the highest-rated documentary series in Japan's broadcasting history, and has been broadcast in over 25 countries. Six more videos were later released as the Silk Road II. 330 min., color **Central Mark Media Distributors**
http://www.centralparkmedia.com/cpmdbl/search2.cfm

Web Resources

Information related to Confucius—http://www.confucius.org/main01.htm#e

Information related to Confucius—http://www.easternreligions.com.cframe.html

Great Wall of China—http://www.walkthewall.com/greatwall/

Construction of the Great Wall—http://www.crystalinks.com/chinawall.html

Images of the Great Wall as seen from space—
http://www.discovery.com/stories/history/greatwall/satphoto.html

Sample Test Questions for Chapter 7

1. Confucius is thought to have been the compiler and editor of
    a. a series of chronicles.
    b. the five Chinese classics.
    c. only the *Book of Songs*.
    d. the *Analects*.
    Ans: b

2. Confucius' teachings reflect the older Chinese notion that
    a. the ruler must be a philosopher-king.
    b. the gods have established the moral order.
    c. the moral order follows from the natural order.
    d. reason is humankind's unique virtue.
    Ans: c

3. The repeated references in the *Analects* to proper behavior of "the gentleman" reflects the importance of
    a. *yin/yang.*
    b. *qi.*
    c. *li.*
    d. *dao.*
    Ans. c

4. Legalists described human nature as
    a. inherently evil
    b. inherently good
    c. waiting to be shaped by experience
    d. torn between conflicting moral forces
    Ans: a

5. The idea that government must rule absolutely is based on the Legalism of
    a. Confucius.
    b. Mencius.
    c. Sima Qian.
    d. Han Fei Zi.
    Ans: d

6. The Great Wall of China was built in order to
    a. discourage invasions from the West.
    b. cut off China from unwanted trade.
    c. encourage agricultural independence in Han China.
    d. discourage Hunnish attacks in the North.
    Ans: d

7. The Great Wall was approximately how long?
    a. 500 miles
    b. 1000 miles
    c. 1500 miles
    d. 3000 miles
    Ans: c

8. A major feature of the Qin dynasty was
    a. the absence of warfare.
    b. standardization of coins, weights, and measures.
    c. the compilation of the five Chinese classics.
    d. all of the above.
    Ans: b

9. The statues of soldiers and horses found in the tomb of the First Emperors were made of
   a. bronze.
   b. iron.
   c. terra-cotta.
   d. lacquered wood.
   Ans: c

10. The Art of War is a Chinese classic that reflects the thinking of
    a. Confucius.
    b. Sima Qian.
    c. Mencius.
    d. the Legalists.
    Ans: d

11. The Chinese resemble the Romans in their concern about recording history.
    Ans: T

12. For the Han era historian, Sima Qian (Reading 1.30), basic human nature
    a. does not change.
    b. can be changed by good government.
    c. can be improved by philosophy.
    d. changes with each generation.
    Ans: a

13. In his *Records of the Grand Historian* (Reading 1.30), Sima Qian provides his view of poverty, namely
    a. that it uplifts the human spirit.
    b. that it inspires humans to improve.
    c. that it may sometimes lead to moral decay.
    d. that it always leads to moral decay.
    Ans: d

14. The Greeks, Romans, and Chinese all produced a wealth of poetry of many types. Of the following four types, the Chinese did NOT produce one:
    a. lyric poetry, sung to music
    b. love poetry
    c. epic poetry
    d. hymns and ritual songs
    Ans: c

15. According to Sima Qian, all members of society, including its thinkers, are motivated by
    a. the desire to be happy.
    b. money.
    c. fear of death.
    d. respect for the ancestors.
    Ans: b

16 In the Chinese *Records of the Grand Historian,* we find the same attitude towards wealth as in the Roman philosopher Seneca.
Ans: F

17. The Chinese resemble the Romans in their concern about recording history.
Ans: T

18. At its height, the Han empire was larger in population than the Roman empire.
Ans: T

19. Most highly valued among the following members of Han society was the
    a.   scholar-official.
    b.   soldier.
    c.   priestess.
    d.   architect.
    Ans: a

Open Book

20. In all of the poems included in Reading 1.31, reference is made to some aspect of
    a.   family life.
    b.   fear of death.
    c.   nature.
    d.   respect for elders.
    Ans: c

21. The visual information available in Fiero, Figures 7.7, 7.8, and 7.8 suggests that music
    a.   played a major role in court life.
    b.   was employed only for court ritual.
    c.   was performed only by men.
    d.   excluded percussion instruments.
    Ans: a

BOOK 2

Medieval Europe and the World Beyond

PART I   The Shaping of the Middle Ages

Chapter **8** A Flowering of Faith: Religious Renewal West and East

Summary

Jesus was born into a world ripe for religious revitalization. The religion of the Roman world was focused on nature and an impersonal civic worship, though many individual Romans turned to mystery cults featuring savior gods and goddesses. While the province of Judea sought freedom from Roman control, the young Jewish preacher, Jesus, called for an abiding faith in God, compassion for one's fellow human beings, and the renunciation of material wealth. The apostle Paul universalized the message of Jesus by preaching to non-Jews and articulating the doctrines of original sin and salvation through faith in the redeeming power of Jesus' death. In India, the teaching of Siddhartha Gautama took hold as early as the fifth century B.C.E., but swept through East Asia in the same centuries that Christianity spread through the West. The Buddha, as Siddartha came to be called, taught compassion, right conduct, and the renunciation of worldly desires. His message, which focused on individual liberation from the cycle of rebirth, brought a reformed version of Hinduism to the masses, even as the words of Jesus expanded on those of Hebrew Scripture.

Outline	Pronunciation Guide

A. Background to Christianity
   1. Roman religion and late philosophies of antiquity
   2. the mystery cults of southwest Asia
   3. heritage of Judaism
B. Jesus and his followers
   1. the message of Jesus
   2. the message of Paul
   3. the spread of Christianity
C. Buddhism
   1. life and message of Siddhartha
   2. spread of Buddhism in India
     a. Hinayana Buddhism
     b. Mahayana Buddhism
   3. spread of Buddhism in China
	Dominus [DOW mee nus]
	Isis [EYE sis]
	Osiris [ow SEYE ris]
	Apuleius [a poo LAY us]
	Mithra, Mithraic [MI thrah, mi THRAY ik]
	Zoroasterian [zow row AHS tree un]
	Sadducees [SAD yoo seez]
	Pharisees [FA ri seez]
	Essenes [ES seenz]
	Messiah [me SEYE ah]
	asceticism [a SET I siz em]
	Torah [TOW rah]
	Siddhartha Gautama
	   [si DAHR thah gahw TAH mah]
	sutras [SOO trahz]
	bhikkhus [BEE kooz]

	Hinayana [hi neye AH nah] **Mahayana** [mah heye AH nah] **nirvana** [nir VAH nah] **Bodhisattvas** [bow dis AHT vahz] **Asoka** [ah SHOW kah] **Pronunciation Key:** (*Note: Use this key for all subsequent chapters.*) *apple*, *play*, **ah** (*altar*), *egg*, *keep*, *inch*, *eye*, *glow*, *booze*, *outfit*, *bulk*, **u** in *book*, *single*, *shin*, *chapter*, *just*, *zebra, zhivago*, (*vision*), *canyon*.

Key Terms: mystery cults, Pharisees, Sadducees, Essenes, asceticism, neo-Platonism, Messiah, Gospels, evangelists, Original Sin, pacifism, grace, *Christos, nirvana*.

Study Questions

Factual

1. What were the most influential belief systems in Rome before the emergence of Christianity?
2. Define briefly: Neoplatonism; Mithraism; mystery cults.
3. Who were the Pharisees, the Sadducees, the Essenes?
4. Describe briefly the Jewish and Near Eastern backgrounds out of which Jesus emerged.
5. What were Paul's main contributions to the formation of Christianity?
6. Isolate those teachings that form the core of Jesus' message (Reading 2.2).
7. Explain in your own words, "The order of the visible universe sets forth the invisible things of God."
8. Do you find anywhere in the sermons of the Buddha a requirement similar to Jesus' statement, "You must be perfect just as your heavenly Father is perfect"?
9. What role did the bodhisattva play in Buddhism?
10. Describe the differences between Mahayana and Hinayana Buddhism.

Challenge

1. How did Roman political and religious traditions encourage or discourage the rise of Christianity?
2. Is it accurate to say, as some do, that Paul was the "co-founder of Christianity"? How so?
3. In what ways were the mystery cults unique? Why were they so popular in the ancient world?
4. Point out specific similarities and differences between the teachings of Jesus and Siddhartha Gautama as reflected in their sermons.
5. Kindness, the value of human life, and the hope for a better future are major themes in the sermons of Christ and Buddha. What assumptions might we make about the quality of life in the time in which these sermons were preached?
6. Is the observance of ritual in itself inferior to inner purity, or does the performance of rites and rituals have its own value in religious practice? Answer as Jesus might have, as Siddhartha might have, and offer your own views.
7. Discuss the differences between Mahayana Buddhism and the original message of the Buddha as reflected in the Buddha's sermons (Reading 2.4).
8. Buddhism asserts that "desire causes pain." Do you agree? How might Jesus have responded to this central tenet of Buddhism?

9. How might Jesus have responded to the following line from the Buddha's sermons: ". . . he in whom self has become extinct . . . will desire neither worldly nor heavenly pleasures." How might the Buddha have responded to the following line from the Sermon on the Mount: "You must . . . be perfect, just as your heavenly Father is perfect."

Strategies for Discussion/Lecture

1. Begin with a short lecture on the historical background (Outline A) to establish the context for key readings. The *Sermon on the Mount*: In what ways does Jesus appear as a critic of the practices of his own religion and that of the non-Jews (see Chapter 6)? Might the same be said for Siddhartha's *Sermon at Benares* (Reading 2.4) with regard to the ritual excesses of yogism and the Vedic cults? Seek the subtext of the *Sermon on the Mount*, Matthew 5: 1–16. If Jesus declares that peacemakers are blessed, might the contemporary standard have been militant and warlike? "Suffering" (and escape from pain) is the focus of many of the thoughts of Jesus and Siddhartha: what might this suggest about the historical origins of Christianity and Buddhism?

2. Jesus focuses on *intention* and inner purity, in contrast to the Hebraic emphasis on *actions* (*e.g.*, "thou shalt, thou shalt not + verb"—See Fiero, Chapter 2, Reading 1.8b). In your view, is "looking at a woman lustfully" the equivalent of committing an act of adultery?

3. *Epistle to the Romans.* Does any portion of this reading suggest that Paul is unwilling to accommodate Jewish law? Seek the *subtext:* what do the verbs that Paul uses in describing God ("saves," "condemns," etc.) suggest? Is Paul's teaching more mystical than that of Jesus (in the Sermon on the Mount)? It is quite useful to assign beforehand a microtheme on Factual question #5 as preparation for class discussion on Paul. Focus on the *key ideas* in Reading 2.3. How does Paul interpret the death of Jesus? Why, in Paul's view, did Jesus die? (Romans 5: 6–12) How, in Paul's view, did sin enter the world? (verses 12–21) Ask students: "Do you agree with Paul that human beings are inherently sinful?"

4. One instructor asks students to prepare answers to Challenge question #4 ahead, then uses the blackboard to list those responses (items that are similar, items that are different) as they are called out by students. An effort may be made to isolate the essential differences in outlook East and West: the absence of any active divinity in Buddhism; the vagueness of Buddhist law; the concept of reincarnation; the idea of extinction or release of the Self versus the Christian concept of salvation. How do Westerners react to the lack of "precise" answers to the "big questions"? Assigning Challenge question #4 helps students to prepare for discussion here.

5. Compare Siddhartha's use of metaphors (*Sermon on Abuse,* Reading 2.4) and Jesus' use of parables. What deeper purposes are served by these literary devices? Why do teachers and gurus often refuse to prescribe or give answers, preferring indirect forms of response? Find analogies with Socrates (Fiero, Chapter 4, Reading 1.16). In your view, what teaching methods are most effective?

Chapter 8 Audiovisuals

Video/CD-ROM Sources

THE BEGINNINGS OF CHRISTIANITY (1991) 25 min., color **IM**

BELIEFS AND BELIEVERS
Twenty-four one-hour programs offering a comprehensive look at the nature and function of religions and secular beliefs that comprise today's worldviews; especially see number 5 "Religious

Experience: Buddhism," number 12 "Ritual Dimensions: Christianity," and number 14 "Doctrinal Dimension: Christianity." **CPB**

BUDDHISM

He was the first American to be ordained as a Tibetan Buddhist monk in 1962, and now you can learn about this intriguing religion direct from this spiritual authority. Learn about Buddhism from the first American to be ordained (in 1962) as a Tibetan Buddhist monk. This video covers the three jewels of this religion: the Buddha, teaching of enlightenment; the Dharma, teaching the enlightenment itself; and the Sangha, a community of beings trying to implement the Dharma who are trying to become buddhas. Unravel the mystery of the fastest growing religion in our country! 180 minutes on 3 tapes **PBS**

CHRISTIANITY: The First Thousand Years (Series) (1998)
DIRECTOR: ROOS, BRAM 200 min., color **AE**

CHRISTIANITY: The Second Thousand Years (Series) 200 min. **AE**

CHRISTIANITY IN WORLD HISTORY—TO 1000 A.D. 14 min., color **CORONET**

THE CHRISTIANS: Faith and Fear 39 min., color **MGHF**

THE CHRISTIANS: A Peculiar People 27 B.C.—A.D. 330 39 min., color **MGHF**

FRONTLINE: FROM JESUS TO CHRIST: THE FIRST CHRISTIANS

Explore the life of Jesus and the movement he started, challenging familiar assumptions and conventional notions about the origins of Christianity. Drawing upon new and sometimes controversial historical evidence and interviews with the nation's leading New Testament scholars, the series transports the viewer back 2,000 years to the time and place where Jesus once lived and preached. The film traces Jesus' life, focusing on the events that occurred after he died and on his first followers, the men and women whose belief, conviction, and martyrdom created a major movement that transformed the Roman Empire in the space of only 300 years. 240 minutes on 4 tapes **PBS**

LIVES OF JESUS

A riveting, three-part series examines the role of Jesus as a Jewish priest, a political agitator and a spiritual teacher. Traveling to key locations through Europe and the Middle East, former BBC correspondent Mark Tully asks the question: Was Jesus everything the Christian Church claims, or were the facts manipulated to suit those in power? "Jesus the Jew" focuses on his role as a gifted rabbi during a crisis point in Jewish history, when traditions were in danger of being overwhelmed by the Roman Empire. "Jesus the Rebel" shows how he led a peasant revolution by exposing the spiritual and moral decay of the Roman Empire. "The Hidden Jesus" visits the oldest Christian temple in the world and unearths new gospels so dangerous that they were suppressed. 180 minutes on 3 tapes **PBS**

LONG SEARCH (Series) Buddhism: Footprints of the Buddha (1997) TLF

Web Sources

Information about the Buddha—http://www.vri.dhamma.org/publications/buddha.html

Information related to Buddhism—http://www.fundamentalbuddhism.com/

Information related to Buddhism—http://easternreligions.com/bframe.html

Information related to Buddhism—http://internets.com/buddha.htm

History of Christianity—http://www.pbs.org/wgbh/pages/frontline/shows/religion/

McGraw-Hill Resources

Culture 2.0: Biblical History
Transparencies: MA.4 Early Christianity and Byzantine 1900 B.C.E.–0 C.E.

Sample Test Questions for Chapter 8

Select the letter of the choice that BEST answers the question:

1. The mystery cult devoted to the Egyptian goddess Isis was
   a. one of the most popular of the female-dominated, or matriarchal, cults.
   b. the most popular religious practice among Roman soldiers.
   c. a rival of the cult of the person of the emperor.
   d. a cult with Greek origins.
   Ans: a

2. Which of the following was true of Roman religion?
   a. It encouraged democratization of the society.
   b. It included human sacrifice on a routine basis.
   c. It borrowed the pantheon of gods from the Greeks.
   d. It focused on individual salvation.
   Ans: c

3. Which of the following is NOT true of Mithraism?
   a. Its god slaughtered a bull.
   b. It was the chief rival of Christianity.
   c. It involved baptism.
   d. Its god was born of a virgin.
   Ans: d

4. Paul helped transform Christianity into a major religion by
   a. becoming Jesus' first disciple.
   b. preaching to the Gentiles.
   c. negotiating with Rome.
   d. recording the Sermon on the Mount.
   Ans: b

5. Buddhism differs from Hinduism in that Buddha rejected
   a. meditation.
   b. ethics.
   c. the holy writings.
   d. the caste system.
   Ans: d

6. Siddhartha Gautama, the Buddha, lived in India
   a. at the time of Jesus.
   b. 200 years after Jesus.
   c. 250 years before Jesus.
   d. 450 years before Jesus.
   Ans: d

7. With respect to the prevailing Hindu religion of his time, the Buddha
   a. was a reformer of Hinduism.
   b. was a conservative Hindu.
   c. rejected Hinduism completely.
   d. combined Hinduism with Christianity.
   Ans: a

8. The *goal* of Buddhist practice is
   a. to reinforce the caste system in India.
   b. to achieve personal immortality.
   c. to join religion and Indian political thought.
   d. to extinguish the self and its desires.
   Ans: d

9. The Benares sermon advises the Buddha's followers
   a. to pay no heed to the necessities of life.
   b. to seek happiness through sensual pleasure.
   c. to seek only the higher pleasures of heaven.
   d. to avoid the extremes of self-denial and self-indulgence.
   Ans: d

10. The moral of the story in the Buddha's *Sermon on Abuse* is best described by which·one of the following statements.
    a. An eye for an eye, a tooth for a tooth.
    b. A good person cannot be hurt by an evil one but doing evil harms the evil doer.
    c. Abuse must sometimes be accepted without responding in any way.
    d. God punishes the abuser of a good person.
    Ans: b

11. The actions of the Buddha in the *Sermon on Abuse* are an example of extinguishing the desire for
    a. food.
    b. sex.
    c. revenge.
    d. wealth.
    Ans: c

12. The two main branches of Buddhism in historic times are
    a. Sunni and Shiite.
    b. Mahayana and Hinayana.
    c. Dervishes and Mantras.
    d. Zen and Bodhisattvas.
    Ans: b

13. It is quite likely that Siddhartha would NOT have approved of one of these practices of later Buddhism.
    a. following the Middle Way
    b. following the Eight-fold Path
    c. making monumental statues of the Buddha
    d. seeking nirvana
    Ans: c

14. One common feature of the later development of Christianity in the West and Buddhism in India and China is
    a. that each rejected the cult of saints.
    b. that each became associated with imperial political systems.
    c. that each resisted association with political systems.
    Ans: b

15. The teaching of the Buddha in the Benares sermon can be connected with the later teachings of Jesus, in that both promised personal immortality to their followers.
    Ans: F

Answer the following with a word or phrase.

16. The religious leaders of the Jewish community who debated matters of biblical interpretation were known as teachers or _____.
    Ans: rabbis

17. The renunciation of material comforts is called _____.
    Ans: asceticism

18. The Dead Sea Scrolls are associated with a Jewish sect known as the _____.
    Ans: Essenes

19. The word *Buddha* means _____.
    Ans: Enlightened One

Summary

The first 300 years of the Christian church are almost undocumented and barely visible to historians; then, with the Edict of Milan in 313 C.E., the church flourished, borrowing and adapting organizational and artistic forms that prevailed in Roman imperial culture. Under the leadership of the early Latin church fathers, a uniform Christian doctrine and liturgy were disseminated throughout the Mediterranean area, and Christianity grew from a minor sect into an institutionalized religion. A new symbolic art replaced Roman realistic rendering and Greek humanistic models. The basilica was adopted as the temple form. Well suited to a congregational faith, its floor plan in the West was eventually made to figure a Latin cross.

Buddhism never became a church unified under a single authority with a uniform doctrine and established rituals. Like Christianity, it had a monastic component from the start but not a ministering clergy or a congregational form of worship. The focus in Buddhism was on individual meditation and the achievement of enlightenment, and its art, literature, and music all served those ends.

Outline	Pronunciation Guide

A. The Christian identity
    1. legalization: Edict of Milan
    2. influence of Roman tradition, language, law
    3. role of councils
    4. monasticism
    5. Latin church fathers
B. The early Christian language of faith
    1. symbolism and the arts
    2. art and architecture in the west
        a. the catacombs
        b. early Christian sculpture
        c. the early Christian basilica
    3. Byzantine art and architecture
        a. leadership of Justinian
        b. Hagia Sophia
        c. churches of Ravenna
    4. early Christian music: Gregorian chant
C. The Buddhist identity
    1. monasticism
    2. art and architecture in India
    3. art and architecture in China
    4. Buddhist music in India and China
	Diocletian [deye ow KLEE shun]
	ecumenical [ek yoo ME ni kul]
	Nicene [neye SEEN]
	sarcophagus [sahr KAH fah gus]
	diptych [DIP tik]
	clerestory [KLIR stow ree]
	ambulatory [AMB yoo lah tor ee]
	Hagia Sophia [HEYE yah sow FEE ah]
	San Vitale [SAN vee TAH lay]
	San Apollinare Nuovo
	    [SAN upahl li NAH ray noo OW vow]
	a cappella [ah kah PEL lah]
	chaitya [CHEYET yah]
	Ajanta [ah JAHN tah]
	mudra [MOO drah]
	stupa [STOO pah]
	torana [tor AH nah]
	chatra [SHAT rah]

Key Terms: the Mass, paganism, Edict of Milan, Nicene Creed, the *Vulgate,* Church Fathers, monasticism, liturgy, Latin cross/Greek cross plans, Byzantine style, icon, Ravenna, Gregorian chant, *a cappella,* monophonic, antiphonal, melismatic, *stupa, torana, mudra,* pagoda.

Key Images:	
Book Cover, Murano	Hagia Sophia, Constantinople
Sarcophagus of Archbishop Theodorus	Great Stupa, Sanchi
San Vitale, Ravenna	Pagoda of the Song Yue Temple, Mount Song
Emperor Justinian and His Courtiers, San Vitale	Ajanta frescoes, India
Empress Theodora and Retinue, San Vitale	Gilt Bronze Buddhist Altarpiece

Study Questions

Factual

1. What specific aspects of Roman culture did early Christianity borrow?
2. Give three examples of Early Christian symbolism.
3. Discuss the function of each of the parts of the Early Christian basilica.
4. What was the purpose and value of monasticism?
5. Who was Augustine? What role does allegory play in his view of history (see Reading 2.8)?
6. What is the principal theme of Ambrose's "Ancient Morning Hymn" (Reading 2.6)?
7. Fiero, Figure 9.1. List the figures on the sarcophagus and the symbolic meaning of each.
8. What features unique to the Byzantine style are represented in Hagia Sophia and San Vitale (Figures 9.13 to .20)?
9. What role does the icon play in Byzantine worship and belief?
10. What is the symbolic significance of the Buddhist *stupa?* What do the figures on the gates signify?
11. What features in the Buddhist art and architecture of China are different from those of India?

Challenge

1. Put into your own words the phrase *Christian identity.* How did symbolism work to fix that identity?
2. Fiero, Figure 9.7. What does each panel of the Murano book cover describe? Which figures are more or less important depending on their position?
3. Outline the specific contributions of each of the Latin Church Fathers.
4. What, if anything, strikes you most personally about Augustine's *Confessions* (Reading 2.7)? What kind of personality do you envision him to be?
5. Discuss the use of allegory in the writings of Augustine. Does allegory function in a manner similar to symbolism in the visual arts? If so, how so? How do *symbolism* and *allegory* work to convey abstract ideas?
6. What are the main differences between the Latin and Greek cross church? Were the decorative media similar?
7. Describe in your own words the effects of the Buddhist chant (Morning prayers) from the Music Listening Selection I–3. How does it compare with Gregorian Chant (I–2)?
8. Write a comparison of Reading 1.3, "Hymn to the Aten," and Reading 2.6, "Ancient Morning Hymn". What observations can you make about the continuity of the humanistic tradition?

9. Compare the Early Christian church with the Buddhist *stupa*. What differences and similarities do you detect in function and in form? Can you offer any similar comparison of Figures 9.20 (*Empress Theodora and Retinue*) and Figure 9.34 (*The Empress as Donor with Attendants*)?

Strategies for Discussion/Lecture

1. The chapter focuses on symbolic art and lends itself to a slide lecture/discussion. As preparation for the images, assign a short written project from among Factual questions #2 and 7 and Challenge question # 5. The concept of *symbolism* can be illustrated by (a) first recalling and comparing realistic Roman pagan representative art (slides or text illustrations) or (b) using Augustine's symbolic interpretation of Noah's Ark (Reading 2.8). From among the following, include at least one that brings Buddhist symbolic art into the discussion for comparison.
2. Christian iconography: Survey the pictures in this chapter representing Jesus. How do representations of the founder of Christianity change over time? Do specific details in these images suggest a change in status of the founder and his disciples? A survey similar to that for Jesus in art can be made for Siddhartha Gautama. Why are there no pictures of the Buddhist founder at Sanchi? What details suggest absorption of Christ and Buddha into their respective imperial cultures?
3. How does the shape/form of the Early Christian church suit what goes on (ritual) in the building? Looking at examples of the interiors of early Christian and Byzantine churches, students might say how each aspect of the structure relates to a *congregational* religion. The video "A White Garment of Churches" is a good choice for introducing the Christian church. The first half, on the Romanesque, can be shown now and the part on Gothic later in the course.
4. *Confessions* (Reading 2.7). Why is Augustine interested in sleep and dreams? Augustine is tormented by "hidden sins which are visible to your eyes, though not to mine" (lines 102–103) as was Paul before him (Romans 7: 15). Why is this inner doubt seemingly absent from Buddhism?
5. Music. One instructor begins the presentation of Chapter 9 by playing the selections of Gregorian chant and Buddhist morning prayer on the cassette provided with the text. No introduction is given. After hearing each once or twice, the class participants are asked, "What do you hear?" and their responses are written on the board. Such answers as "Gregorian chant" and "monody" are set aside until the reports come down to actually perceived details: "I hear all men singing one tune"; "I don't hear any regular beat"; "I can't tell if it's happy or sad." The technical terms might be introduced afterwards.

Chapter 9 Audiovisuals

Video/CD-ROM Sources

THE BYZANTINE EMPIRE 14 min., color **CORONET**

BYSANTIUM: From Splendor to Ruin 52 min., color **FFH**

THE CHRISTIANS: The Birth of Europe 410–1084 39 min., color **MGHF**

THE CITY OF GOD 52 min., color **FFH**

THE GLORY OF BYZANTINE ART

In this program, noted journalist Paul Solman discusses a magnificent display of Byzantine art garnered from 117 collections with Harvard professor and art expert Ioli Kalavrezou. 12 min., color
FFH

Music Resources

Chants de l'Eglise Milanaise (Ambrosian plainsong), Harmonia Mundi, 901295 CD.
Gregorian Chant, Deller Consort, Harmonia Mundi 234.

Web Resources

Christian catacombs of Rome—http://www.catacombe.roma.it/welcome.html

Guide to Early Church documents—http://www.icinet.org/pub/resources/christian-history.html

Byzantine Studies on the Internet—http://www.fordham.edu/halsall/byzantium/

Information about Byzantine art—http://www.artcyclopedia.com/history/byzantine.html

Virtual tour of the churches and monuments of Ravenna—
    http://www.akros.it/comuneravenna/artefruk.htm

Order of St. Benedict—http://www.osb.org/gen/rule.html

Hear Gregorian Chant, visit the Solesmes Abbey—http://www.solesmes.com/anglais/ang_solesmes.html

Information about the Buddha—http://www.vri.dhamma.org/publications/buddha.html

Information related to Buddhism—http://www.fundamentalbuddhism.com/

Information related to Buddhism—http://www.easternreligions.com/bframe.html

Information related to Buddhism—http://www.internets.com/buddha.htm

McGraw-Hill Resources

Music Listening Selection: CD I
    I–2 "Alleluya"
    I–3 "Morning Prayers"
Transparencies: MA.4 Early Christianity and Byzantine 1900 B.C.E.–0 C.E.

Sample Test Questions for Chapter 9

Select the letter of the choice that BEST answers the question:

1. In his *Confessions,* Augustine views intellectual curiosity as
   a. the primary source of our knowledge of God.
   b. together with faith, a major source of our knowledge of God.
   c. a form of temptation, like sensual impulses.
   d. unrelated to matters of faith but valid on its own grounds.
   Ans: c

2. The interior conflict between soul and body in the *Confessions* is probably based on which of the following philosophical positions?
   a. Aristotelianism
   b. dualism
   c. Cynicism
   d. Stoicism
   Ans: b

3. Drawing parallels between the Hebrew Bible and the Christian New Testament, the author of the *City of God* argued that Noah's ark symbolized all the following EXCEPT the
   a. body of Christ on the cross.
   b. Church.
   c. sins of humankind.
   d. Heavenly City.
   Ans: c

4. Jesus and Siddhartha Gautama share all the following characteristics EXCEPT one:
   a. Neither wrote anything.
   b. Both were reformers of the religion they were brought up in.
   c. Both believed in a personal god interested in our inner life.
   d. Both considered outward display of religious observance as contrary to authentic spiritual progress.
   Ans: c

5. In Christian symbolism, the sign of the eagle signifies the evangelist
   a. Mark
   b. Matthew
   c. Luke
   d. John
   Ans: d

6. One common feature of the later development of Christianity in the West and Buddhism in India and China is each
   a. rejected the cult of saints.
   b. became associated with imperial political systems.
   c. resisted association with political systems.
   d. experienced repeated persecution.
   Ans: b

7. The *City of God* explained the decline of the Roman Empire as predestined by the Christian God and leading towards the end of time.
    Ans: T

8. According to Augustine, the obligation of every Christian was to use reason and the intellect to interpret the literal message of God.
    Ans: F

Open Book

9. Fiero, Figure 9.22. The Great Stupa at Sanchi is
    a. the tomb of Siddhartha.
    b. a Hindu temple.
    c. the site of Siddhartha's enlightenment
    d. a mound housing the relics of Siddhartha.
    Ans: d

10. In the *City of God,* it is clear that Augustine's views are heavily based on which sources?
    a. Paul and the Bible
    b. Roman legal theory and the Bible
    c. the writings of Aristotle
    d. the early Popes and the Bible
    Ans: a

11. Fiero, Figure 9.1. A visitor from China might misinterpret the use of the grapevine to be purely decorative, while in fact, it signifies
    a. the church of Rome.
    b. the agricultural profession of the deceased.
    c. the blood of Christ.
    d. the cult of Dionysus.
    Ans: c

12. Unlike the depictions of the founder of Christianity in this chapter, the Buddha is usually shown
    a. more as an ordinary man and less as a god.
    b. meditating or preaching.
    c. more as an emperor than as a poor reformer.
    d. performing miracles among his followers.
    Ans: b

13. Fiero, Figure 9.7. The Murano book cover reveals all but one of the following.
    a. the split between the Roman church and Greek Orthodox church
    b. the miracles performed by Jesus
    c. the borrowing of Roman symbols
    d. symbolic references to the Hebrew Bible
    Ans: a

14. Fiero, Figure 9.10. The presence of female figures is a sign of
    a. the growing importance of women in the church administration.
    b. the use of symbolic figures representing Christian themes.
    c. the cult of the Virgin Mary.
    d. the mercy of Jesus towards fallen women.
    Ans: b

15. Both the chaitya cave in Karli and the Great Stupa at Sanchi evoke the symbolism of
    a. the bo tree.
    b. the virgin birth.
    c. the moment of enlightenment.
    d. the World Mountain.
    Ans: d

16. Figures 8.5, 9.28, 9.30, and 9.35. Looking at these statues of the Buddha in chronological order, we find that, as time goes on, the Buddha is represented less and less as an ordinary man.
    Ans: T

17. Fiero, Figure 9.27. The *torana* or gate illustrates the early stage of Buddhist statuary in that symbols stand for the presence of the Buddha, instead of pictures of him.
    Ans: T

18. While instruments were forbidden in early Christian music, they appear in Buddhist chant.
    Ans. T

19. The early Christian fathers took a specific attitude toward music, holding that it
    a. was essential to ritual.
    b. was a dangerous pleasure.
    c. might only be employed by priests.
    d. had no place in the Mass.
    Ans: b

20. All but the following is true of early Christian liturgical music: it was usually
    a. monophonic.
    b. performed *a capella*.
    c. antiphonal.
    d. written down.
    Ans: d

Summary

As the teachings of Muhammad came to be recorded in the Quran, Muslims throughout Arabia followed the religious, social, and ethical mandates of an energetic new faith known as Islam. Beginning in the seventh century, Islam rapidly expanded beyond the Arabian homeland to establish the most culturally productive civilization since Roman times. Muslims made unique contributions in the disciplines of medicine, astronomy, and mathematics, as well as in poetry and prose, architecture, the visual arts, and music. The high degree of technical craftsmanship in the arts is matched by a sophisticated taste for complex, abstract design. Compositions marked by lyrical repetition and infinite extension are evident in both the literature and the visual arts of Islam. Muslim scholars translated into Arabic the valuable corpus of Greek writings, which they transmitted to the West along with the technological and scientific inventions of their own and East Asian civilizations. As the geographic intermediaries between Asia and Europe, Muslims created the first truly global culture.

Outline	**Pronunciation Guide**

A. The religion of Islam
   1. Muhammad and his time
   2. the Quran
   3. the spread of Islam
B. Islamic culture
   1. scholarship
   2. poetry and prose
     a. secular poetry
     b. Sufi poetry
     c. prose tales
   3. art and architecture
   4. music
	Allah [AH LAH]
	Muhammad [moo HAHM ed]
	kaaba [KAH bu]
	hijra [HIJ rah]
	jihad [jee HAHD]
	muezzin [myoo E zin]
	mihrab [mi RAHB]
	Avicenna [ah vee SAY nah]
	Sunni [SOON ee]
	Shi'ite [SHEE eyet]
	Sufi [SOO fee]
	Baghdad [BAG dad]
	Rumi [ROO mee]
	Cordoba [kore DOW bah]
	Harun al-Rashid [ha ROON ahl rha SHEED]
	Al-Isfahani [ahl iss fah HA nee]

Key Terms: Quran, bedouin, Kaaba, *hajj*, Five Pillars of Faith, Muslim, *hijra, jihad*, illuminated manuscripts, mosque, *caliph, imam, mullah*, lute.

Key Images	
The Kaaba Dome of the Rock, Jerusalem Court of the Lions, the Alhambra Great Mosque, Cordoba	Leaf from a Koran, Kufic script Niche (*mihrab)* from Iran Illustrations from Islamic manuscripts

Study Questions

Factual
1. What are the Five Pillars of the Muslim faith?
2. What did the teachings of Muhammad borrow from the two faiths that preceded: Judaism and Christianity? In what aspects is it unique?
3. Cite three contributions of Islamic culture to world scholarship.
4. What does *Islam* mean? Does this meaning connect this faith with any other you have studied in this class?
5. In Reading 2.9, from the *Quran*, what do "unbelievers" and "devotees" refer to?
6. In the same reading, what are the social obligations of the practicing Muslim?
7. Briefly describe Baghdad during the golden age of the ninth to eleventh century.
8. What are the major themes of the poems included in Reading 2.10? How does Sufi poetry differ from these?
9. In Reading 2.12, from *The Thousand and One Nights*, the princess tricks the Persian prince with her beauty. What does he trick <u>her</u> with?
10. What features in Islamic art and architecture make this art distinctively different from that which appears in the two preceding chapters?
11. Define briefly: *muezzin, kaaba, Kufic, mirhab, sharia, jihad, hajj.*

Challenge
1. What, according to the Quran, did Muhammad think of the Hebrew prophets and Jesus? How does the Muslim perception of Jesus differ from the Christian? Is the Jewish view closer to the Muslim or the Christian?
2. Describe Muslim equivalents of heaven and hell. Are they the same as in the Judeo-Christian tradition? Do any features of Muslim paradise strike you as characteristic of the wishes of a desert people?
3. Research Muslim attitudes toward women as based on the Koran and as actually practiced in Muslim countries today. Research women of achievement in Islam. Have women become heads of state in any Islamic countries?
4. Describe in your own words your responses to Islamic music (Music Listening Selection I–5). Can you identify the instruments in the piece?
5. Would you have rather lived in Rome or in Baghdad in the year 900? Why?
6. Describe the character of Princess Al-Datma. Find out if females in contemporary Islamic societies would consider her a role model.
7. What is the moral of the tale from *The Thousand and One Nights?*
8. How did Islam come to create a global culture? Consider religious expansion, technology, economic factors, etc.
9. What are the principal features of Islamic poetry as represented in Chapter 10?
10. What are the principal features of Islamic art as represented in Chapter 10? Why is so much Islamic art abstract?
11. Research and discuss the spectrum of belief between moderate and radical interpretations of Islam. Might you find the same spectrum of belief within Christianity and Judaism?

Strategies for Discussion/Lecture

1. A fresh start in introducing Islam to what may be in many instances an uninformed and unappreciative audience is to emphasize the context, and specifically its links (geographic and theological), with Judaism and Christianity. Assigning Factual question #2 is helpful in preparation for lecture/discussion. A close reading of the selection from the *Quran* can focus on key ideas, such as *jihad,* heaven and hell, social norms, and the Muslim view of Jesus and Judaism.
2. Survey the various contributions of Islam to world culture. Which might students consider the most important? Which were transmitted from the Far East? Which were unique to Muslim culture? Which have had the longest lasting effects?
3. Islamic poetry. The lecturer will have no problem introducing the short lyrics: Ibn Zaydun's "Two Fragments" and Ibn Abra's "The Beauty Spot" (Reading 2.10) are of immediate, compelling interest, and can be used as examples of how poetry *suggests* without necessarily saying. Ask the audience, for example, what is it about beauty marks that so fascinates (e.g., Madonna?). Re: Tarafa, "Praise for His Camel," identify aspects that show Muslim origins in a nomadic, male-dominated desert people, whose land is open to trade routes through the Middle East. Unlike the short, suggestive lyrics, Tarafa's method is heavy—perhaps overloaded—with comparison. Rumi's poems (Reading 2.11), with their mind-bending paradoxes, can be compared with other traditions, such as the Buddhist, where "seeing beyond" is the goal.
4. Challenge question #7, on the tale from *The Thousand and One Nights*, would make a good initial discussion question for a class based on student participation. Another would be: "Why didn't the Princess keep her word?" (that is, to marry whoever defeated her in a joust). Either one should produce some interesting conflict, perhaps across gender lines. Is beauty stronger than steel swords? Does the paradise of the *Quran* emphasize the beautiful?
5. If slides are available, a lecture illustrating the range and decorative reach of Islamic art provide a rich contrast with the styles and intention of early Christian, Byzantine, and Buddhist art surveyed in the previous two chapters. Why does Islam prohibit the representation of human beings in public art? What role does human representation play in Islamic manuscripts? How is Islamic calligraphy integrated into the visual arts? What technologies (glass-blowing, ivory-carving, gold-working, mosaic, etc.) did Muslims master in the creation of religious and secular art?

Chapter 10 Audiovisuals

Video/CD-ROM Sources

BELIEFS AND BELIEVERS
    Twenty-four one-hour programs offering a comprehensive look at the nature and function of religions and secular beliefs that comprise today's worldviews; especially see number 16 "Doctrinal Dimensions: Islam, Parts I & II." (two one-hour parts) **CPB**

THE CHRISTIANS: Birth of Europe CRM

THE FIVE PILLARS OF ISLAM 30 min., color **FFH**

ISLAM 19 min., color **MGHF**

ISLAMIC ART
    The religious background of Islamic art forms and their influence on Western art. 30 min. **FFH**

ISLAMIC SCIENCE AND TECHNOLOGY 30 min., color **FFH**

THE MUSLIM WORLD: Beginnings and Growth 11 min., color **CORONET**

ORIENT/OCCIDENT 30 min., color **FFH**

Web Resources

Internet Islamic Historic Sourcebook—http://www.fordham.edu/halsall/islam/islamsbook.html

Information about Islam—http://www.sim.org/islam

The Qur'an—http://www.quarn.ork.uk

Audio readings from the Qur'an—http://www.islaam.com/audio/quran/

Collection of Islamic ceramics at Oxford University's Ashmolean Museum—
    http://www.ashmol.ox.ac.uk/ash/departments/

McGraw-Hill Resources

Music Listening Selection: CD I
    I–4 Traditional Islamic Call to Prayer
    I–5 Arabic-Andalousian *Nouba* (instrumental suite)
Transparencies: MA.5 The Middle Ages 500–1453

Sample Test Questions for Chapter 10

Select the letter of the choice that BEST answers the question:

1. Which of the following was NOT one of Islam's Five Pillars?
    a.   the need to pray five times daily
    b.   the need to give money to the poor
    c.   the need to undertake a pilgrimage to Mecca
    d.   the need to refrain from pork and alcohol
    Ans: d

2. Which of the following does not explain the expansion of Islam?
    a.   It offered uncomplicated rules of conduct.
    b.   It was defended by determined Muslim warriors.
    c.   It tolerated all pagan religions.
    d.   It offered freedom from an uncertain nomadic life.
    Ans: c

3. Arabic poetry
   a. focuses on themes of injustice and retribution.
   b. influenced the troubadour tradition in the West.
   c. only addresses religious topics.
   d. is frequently written in iambic pentameter.
   Ans: b

4. Muhammad claimed he was the last in a series of prophets that included Jesus and Moses.
   Ans: T

5. Like the early Christian church, the decoration of the Islamic mosque grew out of the dictates of the liturgy.
   Ans: F

6. Like the law of the Hebrews, Muslim law bans the worship of idols, because Allah is too remote from our nature and too transcendent a power to be captured in pictures.
   Ans: T

7 Muslim traders introduced to the West the Hindu zero, Chinese paper, and an alternative to the Roman system of numbers.
   Ans: T

8. Although scholars of the Islamic world were excellent copyists, they made almost no original contributions to learning.
   Ans: F

Answer the following with a word or phrase:

9. The holy city of _____ is the destination for the annual pilgrimage and the site of the sacred stone known as the Kaaba.
   Ans: Mecca

10. Muhammad's journey to Medina in 622 is known as _____.
    Ans: *hajj*

11. The holy scripture of Islam is entitled _____.
    Ans: the *Quran*

12. The woman in *The Thousand and One Nights* who tells the story is named _____.
    Ans: Scheherazade

13. From earliest time, Islam has been spread by people whose occupation was
    a. banking.
    b. the priesthood.
    c. trade and business.
    d. midwives.
    Ans: c

14. As regards the Judeo-Christian tradition, Islam represents
    a. a complete break with the Judeo-Christian tradition.
    b. total ignorance of the Judeo-Christian tradition.
    c. acceptance of Jesus but rejection of the Hebrew prophets.
    d. a continuation of the Judeo-Christian tradition.
    Ans: d

15. A crucial element in the advancement of learning in the West was the Muslim transmission of this Hindu creation:
    a. paper
    b. numerals
    c. polytheism
    d. alcohol
    Ans: b

16. In the tale of Prince Behram and Princess Al-Datma, in *The Thousand and One Nights*, Al-Datma is portrayed as
    a. highly religious.
    b. passive and sensual.
    c. pretty but mentally not impressive.
    d. clever and crafty.
    Ans: d

17. The mosque, the Islamic place of worship, is structurally akin to
    a. a courthouse.
    b. a king's palace.
    c. an urban house.
    d. a Bedouin tent.
    Ans: c

18. The concept of religious struggle, both spiritual and militant, is expressed in the word
    a. *jihad.*
    b. *hajj.*
    c. *sharia.*
    d. *mirhab.*
    Ans: a

19. A basic element of the Islamic conception of beauty is variety and unity in nature. This is exemplified in the use of
    a. images of fish and birds.
    b. images of Allah.
    c. landscapes.
    d. repeated decorative motifs.
    Ans: d

Chapter **11** **Patterns of Medieval Life**

Summary

Charlemagne attempted to restore the Roman Empire, and he revived crucial elements of its cultural legacy. Much of community life in the Middle Ages, however, was governed by feudalism—a military and political "contract" between members of the nobility—and manorialism, which offered protection to the laboring classes in return for the food they produced. The *Song of Roland,* the Bayeux Tapestry, and the Norman castle all reflect a heroic age focused on warfare, the conquest of land, and the aggrandizement of personal glory. One of the major events of the period was the Crusades, which resulted in a fierce struggle between Christians and Muslims, the revival of East/West trade, and the rise of medieval towns. Works like *Lancelot* reflect the climate of shifting values that affected feudal ideals and the code of courtly love.

Outline	Pronunciation Guide

A. The Germanic tribes
   1. origins and impact on Rome
   2. basic characteristics of Germanic society
   3. Germanic law and literature: *Beowulf*
   4. Germanic art and its influence
B. Charlemagne and the Charlemagne Renaissance
   1. establishment of the Holy Roman Empire
   2. rebirth of classical learning
   3. illuminated manuscripts
C. Feudal Society
   1. disintegration of the Charlemagne Empire
   2. development of feudalism
   3. culture of the feudal nobility
      a. the *Song of Roland*
      b. the Norman castle
      c. the Bayeux Tapestry
   4. manorialism and the medieval self
   5. the Christian Crusades
   6. The medieval romance and courtly love
      a. *Lancelot*
      b. troubadour poetry
   7. the rise of medieval towns
	fealty [FEE ul tee]
	Aachen [AH kun]
	fief [FEEF]
	bourgeois [bur ZHWAH]
	chanson de geste [shan SOWN du ZHEST]
	jongleur [zhan GLUR]
	fabliau [fab lee OW]
	dit [DEE]
	Guinevere [GWEN ah veer]
	Bernard de Ventadour
	    [ber NARD de vent ah DOOR]
	Chrétien de Troyes
	    [kray tee en de TRAHW]
	troubadour [TROO bah door]
	trouvère [troo VER]
	niello [nee EL low]
	cloisonné [klahw zu NAY]

Key Terms: Huns, Franks, Visigoths, Vandals, Carolingian Renaissance, feudalism, code of courtly love, romance, manuscript illumination, *jongleur,* manorialism, *bushido, samurai,* troubadours.

Key Images	
Sutton Hoo Treasure	Lancelot Crossing the Swordbridge
Lindisfarne Gospels	Back cover of the Lindau Gospels
Equestrian Statuette of Charlemagne	Dover Castle
Palatine Chapel, Aachen	Bayeux Tapestry
Vassal Paying Homage to his Lord	Walled City of Carcassonne

Study Questions

Factual

1. Name some of the Germanic tribes and describe their lifestyle.
2. What role did Charlemagne play in early medieval history? What is meant by the Carolingian Renaissance?
3. How did the Viking invasions affect early medieval life in Western Europe?
4. Describe feudalism as a political and military contract. What social classes did it engage?
5. Describe the Bayeux Tapestry. What does it record?
6. Define the following terms: kenning, *cloisonné*, paten, fief, *chanson de geste.*
7. What were the Christian Crusades? What were the effects of the Crusades on the West?
8. What are the principle themes of the troubadour poets?
9. For what audience did Chrétien de Troyes write?
10. Describe briefly the relationship between the serf and the lord of the medieval manor.

Challenge

1. How "barbaric" were the barbarians? Evaluate them on the basis of their technology, traditions, and art. Is *Beowulf* more "barbaric" than the *Song of Roland*?
2. What feudal ideals are reflected in the *Song of Roland* (Reading 2.14)?
3. Compare Roland and Lancelot as heroes. What "brave deeds" do they undertake? What do they value?
4. Compare the life of a serf with that of a lord in the Early Middle Ages.
5. How does music complement the words of the troubadour lyric (Music Listening Selection I–6)?
6. What roles did women play in medieval life? What various attitudes *towards* women do you detect in the readings from this chapter?
7. What were the most important technological developments in the early Middle Ages?
8. What similarities exist between the style and spirit of the Bayeux Tapestry and the *Song of Roland?* How does the romance work, *Lancelot,* differ from both of these?
9. Discuss *Lancelot* as romance literature. How is a romance different from an epic? Are the themes similar? Are the characters different?
10. What changes in society and culture resulted from the rise of medieval towns?

Strategies for Discussion/Lecture

1. As preparation for class, students can be asked to write a short theme in which the values of *Roland* and *Lancelot* are compared, as in Factual questions #3 and 9. The lecturer might organize discussion around the image of the Bayeux Tapestry (for *Roland*) and Figures 11.12 and 11.19 (for *Lancelot*). The following exercises are aimed at highlighting the differences between the heroic phase of the Christian epic and its courtly, romantic phase.

   a. *Song of Roland.* Can there be a Christian tragedy? Having seen Gilgamesh on his journey of discovery, and Achilles made aware of the effects of his anger and regretting it, we can ask, "What does Roland learn in his confrontation with the enemy?" Who are all the people named in stanza 162? Would the audience have known these names? What do they tell you about the probable audience of the Christian epic?

   b. Study the scene in which Roland prepares to die. Why is there in *Roland* no equivalent of the "recognition" scene in the classic epics? Instead, Roland takes pains to orient his corpse in the direction of Spain so that his sovereign lord, Charles, will see that he died facing the enemy (lines 205–208). What does this say about the Christian hero's need to have earthly powers as witnesses to his deeds? Why, in a Christian epic, would it not suffice that God see that Roland was brave?

   c. Compare Lancelot's trials with those of Roland, to bring out the feminization of Lancelot's battle strategy, aimed at winning not the fortress of Saragossa but the heart of Guinevere. The mixture of combat/assault and Christian martyrdom in the imagery of the passage echoes the heroic field at Roncevaux in miniature and sentimentally in line with twelfth-century taste.

   d. Underline the transition from the rough days of Charlemagne to the courtly period of *Lancelot* by comparing the death of Roland with the point at which Lancelot's strength is about to give out in the joust with Meleagant. An unnamed "wise maiden" finds the key to Christian knightly valor: "If he knew that she (Guinevere) was at the window seeing and watching him, his strength and courage would increase." Compare the joust scene pictured in Figure 11, especially the role of women in this scene, and underscore these references to "feminized" feudalism.

2. One instructor approaches *Lancelot* and Christian medieval love lyrics by comparing the final seduction scene with contemporary Indian erotic lyrics from the *Treasury of Well-Turned Verse* (Fiero, Reading 2.24). Students read each aloud and comment on the style and approach to erotic love. Later, Indian temple sculpture can be compared to Christian cathedral sculpture to corroborate the study of the poems.

3. Instructors who prefer close readings of short texts—specifically on a gender issue—will find Bernard de Ventadour's "When I Behold the Lark" a welcome gift of the anthologizer. Seeing what power the poet's mistress exercises over the male speaker's inner self, one wonders if she is not a stand-in of the sovereign lord, himself the stand-in of the sovereign god. In lines 21–24, the poet puts it on the plate in front of us: the man is in love with his own ideals, mirrored in her eyes. Compare the tone and sentiments of the Countess of Dia in this same reading (2.16).

Chapter 11 Audiovisuals

Video/CD-ROM Sources

THE BATTLE OF HASTINGS 30 min., color **FFH**

BRUGES—THE STORY OF A MEDIEVAL CITY (1977) **IFB**

CASTLE
Host David Macaulay leads you on a tour of a thirteenth century Welsh castle, explaining its cultural significance and unique architectural features (including a "murder hole" used to repel intruders). Colorful, detailed animation shows how the castle was built and portrays the lifestyle of its early inhabitants. This program was a Red Ribbon-winner at the American Film and Video Festival and received a Cine Golden Eagle Award. 60 min. **PBS**

CIVILIZATION: The Frozen World 52 min., color **TLF**

EARLY ENGLISH ALOUD AND ALIVE: THE LANGUAGE OF BEOWULF, CHAUCER, AND SHAKESPEARE
In this program, Dr. Joseph Gallagher brings language to life by reciting examples of Old, Middle, and Early Modern English in their original dialects. Includes subtitles in Modern English, where necessary. 28 min., color **FFH**

THE FEUDAL SYSTEM 36 min., color **FFH**

THE LINDISFARNE GOSPELS: A MASTERPIECE OF ANGLO-SAXON BOOK PAINTING
This look at the creation of the Lindisfarne Gospels combines location footage with images from other manuscripts of the period, and reveals the major pages of the Gospels in fascinating close-up. 35 min. **FFH**

MEDIEVAL MANUSCRIPTS
How illuminations were accomplished and how scriptoria functioned. 30 min. **FFH**

MIDDLE AGES: Rise of Feudalism 20 min., color **EBEC**

A WORLD INSCRIBED: THE ILLUMINATED MANUSCRIPT
This program is a concise history of the illuminated manuscript and monastery libraries, and depicts the workings of a scriptorium and the arduous art of copying and illustrating/gilding medieval and Renaissance literature. 23 min. **FFH**

Music Resources

Songs of Chivalry, Martin Best Medieval ensemble, Nimbus NI–5006 CD.
Troubadours (secular vocal music of the twelfth century), Harmonia Mundi, 396/98 LP.
Troubadour songs and Medieval Lyrics, Paul Hillier, Hyperion, A–66094 LP.
Troubadours, Trouvères and Minnesingers (Songs and Dances of the Middle Ages), Augsburg Ensemble for Early Music, Christophorus CD–74519 CD.

Web Resources

Women writers of the Middle Ages—
http://www.millersv.edu/~english/homepage/duncan/medfem/medfem/html

Resources related to Germanic tribes—
http://campus.northpark.edu/history/webchron/westeurope/germanictribes.html

Exhaustive history of the life and rule of Charlemagne—
   http://www.fordham.edu/halsall/basis/einhard.html

History and images of the Bayeux Tapestry—http://www.hastings1066.com/

Resources related to the feudal system—http://members.tripod.com/themiddleages/feudal_system.htm

McGraw-Hill Resources

Music Listening Selection: CD I
   I–6 *"Can vei la lauzeta mover"*
Transparencies: MA.5 The Middle Ages 500–1453

Sample Test Questions for Chapter 11

Select the letter of the choice that BEST answers the question:

1. The Germanic tribes laid the basis for medieval culture by
    a.   preserving Roman and Christian traditions.
    b.   introducing Central Asian elements.
    c.   establishing an elaborate urban structure.
    d.   presenting a less hierarchical society.
    Ans: a

2. Which of the following does NOT characterize the Germanic tribes?
    a.   They were nomadic.
    b.   They were racially and culturally distinct.
    c.   They produced monumental sculpture.
    d.   They did not live in permanent communities.
    Ans: c

3. The term *Middle Ages* is given to the historical period between
    a.   the era of the Germanic tribes and the rise of the Muslim Empire.
    b.   the invasion by the Germanic tribes and the development of the medieval Church.
    c.   the development of the medieval Church and the height of the Muslim Empire.
    d.   the fall of Rome and the Renaissance Era.
    Ans: d

4. Which of the following does not characterize the Middle Ages?
    a.   The peak of the Roman Catholic Church occurred.
    b.   The outlines of modern European states emerged.
    c.   A capitalist economy flourished.
    d.   The first European universities developed.
    Ans: c

5. Charlemagne
   a. borrowed extensively from Chinese culture.
   b. encouraged a rebirth of education and architecture.
   c. instigated a rebellion against classicism in the arts.
   d. established a representative government destined to become a full-fledged democracy.
   Ans: b

6. After his death, Charlemagne's empire disintegrated in part because
   a. there was no single code of law or central government.
   b. Frankish tribes infiltrated his government and assumed power.
   c. Muslims attacked his empire and overturned his son's rule.
   d. he refused assistance to the beleaguered Church of Rome.
   Ans: a

7. With the dethronement of the last Roman emperor in 476 C.E., the Germanic tribes assumed political power over the empire and destroyed its cultural legacy.
   Ans: F

8. A single, all-powerful chieftain dictated the decisions of Germanic assemblies.
   Ans: F

9. Like early Christian art, Anglo-Irish art was abstract and symbolic in character.
   Ans: T

10. Which of the following is not true of feudalism?
    a. It was based on a contract exchanging land for military protection.
    b. It established a vast network with the Far East.
    c. It provided elemental forms of local government.
    d. It carried out a rough and ready justice.
    Ans: b

11. In the *Song of Roland,* Archbishop Turpin promised
    a. elevation in rank for all heroic deeds
    b. forgiveness of sins to all who fought in battle.
    c. material rewards for those who were heroic.
    d. punishment of any who used excessive cruelty.
    Ans: b

12. The celebrated Roman historian who left a detailed account of the Germanic peoples was
    _____.
    Ans: Tacitus

13. The Iron Age tribes that settled the British Isles before the time of Christ were the _____.
    Ans: Celts

14. The Normans were noblemen of France who
    a. struggled with the warriors of Roland.
    b. conquered Anglo-Saxon England in 1066.
    c. contributed little to medieval architecture.
    d. extended their empire to include Eastern Europe.
    Ans: b

15. Medieval society
    a. was comprised primarily of serfs or unfree peasants.
    b. had a large percentage of urban laborers.
    c. was ruled by a series of all-powerful churchmen.
    d. was characterized by an equal division between city and rural populations.
    Ans: a

16. Which of the following was NOT an objective of medieval crusaders?
    a. acquisition of land
    b. recapture of Jerusalem
    c. expansion of commercial networks
    d. unification of Western Europe
    Ans: d

17. The theme of the medieval poem "When I Behold the Lark" is
    a. unrequited love.
    b. the glories of nature.
    c. the life of a wandering minstrel.
    d. the equality of women.
    Ans: a

18. One of the dominant themes in the *Song of Roland* focused on the virtue of the Muslims and the faith of the Christians.
    Ans: F

19. One of the most significant achievements of the Crusaders was the accomplishment of their military goals.
    Ans: F

Answer the following with a word or phrase.

20. The political system of the Middle Ages that put power in the hands of local lords was called
    _____.
    Ans: feudalism

21. The effort to free the Holy Land from the Muslim Turks was known as the _____.
    Ans: Crusades

22. The literary form known as the medieval _____ described tales of adventure and stories of love between men and women of the aristocracy.
    Ans: romance

23. One of the most important developments in medieval society was the emergence of the urban class separating the serfs and the nobles, namely the _____.
Ans: middle class

24. One of the dominant preoccupations of the Germanic tribes was
   a. accumulating wealth.
   b. establishing an empire.
   c. making war.
   d. developing a trade network.
   Ans: c

25. The art of the Germanic tribes was generally
   a. easily transported from place to place.
   b. to be found on the walls of their cathedrals.
   c. in the form of life-size sculptures.
   d. very realistic, reflecting classical influence.
   Ans: a

Summary

During the European Middle Ages, the Roman church was the dominant political and cultural institution. Its doctrine of the afterlife viewed life on earth as painful and transient and consigned it to the lowest level of an elaborate and fixed hierarchy reaching up to the deity. A fundamental shift in salvation theory placed new emphasis on what the individual Christian *does* on earth, rather than on what Jesus accomplished by his sacrificial death (Paul, Augustine). The reckoning or accounting of these good deeds was the function of the clergy who administered the sacraments. This emphasis is apparent in medieval sermons, as well as in major works like *Everyman* and the *Divine Comedy,* while an alternate, more mystical aspect of the medieval mind is represented in the writings of the poet and composer Hildegard of Bingen.

Intellectual life was heightened by the rise of universities and by the effort to synthesize the doctrinal literature of Christianity with the rediscovered writings of Aristotle. For the most part, the dictates of faith and authority governed intellectual inquiry, though the tension between belief and understanding is evident in the *Summa* of Aquinas.

Outline	Pronunciation Guide

A. The medieval church and the promise of salvation
   1. church sacraments
   2. immortality ideology
B. Medieval literature
   1. the literature of mysticism: Hildegard of Bingen
   2. Innocent III on the human condition
   3. *Everyman*
   4. the *Divine Comedy*
C. The power and prestige of the medieval church
   1. the church as a political institution
   2. the rise of mendicant orders
   3. conflicts between church and state
D. Intellectual movements
   1. the medieval universities
   2. scholasticism
	Eucharist [YOO kah rist]
	memento mori
	   [may MEN tow MOW ree]
	Alighieri [ah lee gee E ree]
	Commedia [kow MAY dee ah]
	Cocytus [kow SEYE tus]
	Cassius [KA see us]
	Assisi [ah SEE zee]
	Giotto [JAH tow]
	Bologna [bow LOW nyah]
	Abelard [A be lahrd]
	Aquinas [ah KWEYE nus]
	Summa Theologica
	   [SOO mah thee ow LAH ji kah]

Key Terms: sacraments, morality play, immortality ideology, mysticism, salvation through good works, *terza rima,* immortality, ideology, allegory, heresy, Inquisition, Franciscans, scholasticism.

Key Images	
Mouth of Hell Plan of Dante's Universe Plan of Dante's Inferno	Satan tormenting the souls of the damned in Hell Giotto, Sermon to the Birds

Study Questions

Factual

1. What are the "sacraments," and what role do they play in medieval Christian concepts of salvation?
2. Who was Hildegard and why did she write?
3. Summarize the role and influence of the Roman Catholic Church in medieval life.
4. What attitudes toward humanity are reflected in Pope Innocent's sermon *On the Misery of the Human Condition*?
5. How does God view humans at the beginning of *Everyman*?
6. What classical motifs and personalities figure in the excerpt from Dante's *Inferno* (Reading 2.19)?
7. What are the principal allegorical figures in *Everyman*; what does each stand for?
8. According to Aquinas, should women have been created in the first place? If so, why?
9. Who were each of the following figures: Innocent III, Francis of Assisi, Abelard?
10. Where were the two earliest universities established? Who ran each?
11. Briefly define the following: *memento mori, dies irae, terza rima*.

Challenge

1. What are the main effects created by Hildegard's visions? How does she achieve these? How would you depict them in paintings or film?
2. In the Nicene Creed (Fiero, Reading 2.5) only one sacrament is established as an article of faith, whereas the Lateran council of 1215 set the number at seven (Fiero , Chapter 12). What does this development say about the relationship of church members to the church hierarchy?
3. Review the description of the clergy given by Five-Wits in *Everyman*, lines 527–564. Has any period or society you have studied thus far elevated some humans that high?
4. Study the plan of Dante's *Inferno* (Figure 12.6). How does Dante rank the hierarchy of sin and crime?
5. Try writing a canto in the style of Dante (in *Terza rima*, if you can!), in which you relegate your favorite contemporaries to their deserved places in Hell.
6. Compare the tone and style of Saint Francis' *Canticle of Brother Sun* (Reading 2.21) and Hildegard's *Scivias* (Reading. 2.17). What is the aim of each work?
7. Make a list of appeals to authority in Aquinas' *Summa Theologica* (Reading 2.20), signaled by expressions like "as (name of authority) says."
8. Briefly describe the medieval university at Bologna and compare it with your own.

Strategies for Discussion/Lecture

1. *Everyman* will constitute one focus for presentation of this chapter, and preparatory written work can be assigned from Factual questions #5 and 7, or from material taken from the suggestions following: A slide of Gislebertus' *Last Judgment* (Figure 13.9) or the grisly text illustrations of Hell in Chapter 12 make good accompaniments to a reading of *Everyman,* which may well have been performed in

front of a cathedral portal with the actors pointing to representations of what sinners could expect in the next life.

2. Understanding the shift in salvation theory will help students savor some details of language and image in this play (and in Chaucer later on), such as the Messenger's language that has crept into the theology of salvation (". . . our heaven King/Calleth Everyman to a general reckoning," lines 19–20); this language—perhaps a mirror of urban middle-class preoccupations—can later be contrasted with Luther's return to the more legalistic language of Paul, when God will be restored to his post as supreme judge before whom the believer is a plaintiff. Similarly, God's statement, "There to I had them all elect" (line 54) is new theology, according to which all humans are destined to "make their mansion" in God's glory, with those failing to measure up subject to a reckoning of their deeds in life.

3. Have the students read *Everyman,* lines 527–564, slowly and out loud, and make a board diagram of the secular and sacred lines of authority. The feudal system of allegiances should be to the left and, to the right, the ecclesiastical hierarchy and its "chain of command" reaching up to the angels and God. This will illustrate the unusually powerful role assigned to ordinary priests as administrators of the sacraments and their full import as regards the "monopolization of salvation."

4. *Divine Comedy.* Reading aloud and reflecting on Dante's images provide a beginning at least to a work that is inherently difficult for students to grasp. The schematic, Figures 12.5 and 6, will help to understand the elaborate structure of guilt and punishment and will generally provide surprises to students who imagine their own hierarchy of evil. That public servants who betray their trust are placed so low in Hell should be a classroom issue. Ask students, "If you were to make a Hell would you arrange the crimes and punishments in the same order as Dante?" Dante's *Commedia* has been described as a medieval epic; a comparison of this poem with the other epics students have studied in these chapters makes for interesting discussion.

5. "The Vision of God" from *Paradise,* Canto 33, challenges the student, just as it must have seemed the supreme challenge to the poet, this evocation of the face of God. One instructor invites to class a colleague from the mathematics department able to convey what geometers mean by the incommensurability of square and circle, Dante's image for his attempt to understand how God can be joined to the form of humanity in Jesus. This has also led to interesting speculation as to what the roles of reason and belief are in mathematics.

Chapter 12 Audiovisuals

Video/CD-ROM Sources

ART AND LIFE IN THE MIDDLE AGES: THE LUTTRELL PSALTER   FFH

EVERYMAN IM

THE MEDIEVAL MIND 26 min., color **EBEC**

MEDIEVAL TIMES: The Role of the Church 14 min., color **CORONET**

Music Resources

The Memory of Thomas à Becket (twelfth-century Mass), Schola Hungarica, Hungaroton SLPD–12458 D; MK–12458 CD.
Requiem Mass and Office of the Dead, Paraclete C623 cassette.

The Play of St. Nicholas (twelfth-century liturgical drama), New York Ensemble for Early Music, Musicmasters 20001 X; 20001 W cassette.

Web Resources

Women writers of the Middle Age—
http://www.millersv.edu/~english/homepage/duncan/medfem/medfem.html

St. Francis of Assisi—http://www.americancatholic.org/features/francis/

The Franciscan Order—http://www.pressroom.com/~franciscan/

The Digital Dante—http://www.ilt.columbia.edu/projects/dante/

The complete text of *Everyman*—http://www.fordham.edu/halsall/basis/everyman.html

McGraw-Hill Resources

Transparencies: MA.5 The Middle Ages 500–1453

Sample Test Questions for Chapter 12

Select the letter of the choice that BEST answers the question.

1. The visions that Hildegard records in the *Scivias* come, according to her, from
   a. Church fathers.
   b. a voice from heaven.
   c. Holy Scripture.
   d. her monastic sisters.
   Ans: b

2. Pope Innocent's view of life and death can be summed up as
   a. death is far away, so begin repenting now.
   b. eat, drink and be merry, since God gave us life for our enjoyment.
   c. death is very close: act as if in the moment of death.
   d. half of life should be spent preparing for death.
   Ans: c

3. In the sermon of Pope Innocent III the sinfulness of humankind is said to start
   a. with a child's coming of age.
   b. with a child's conception, before it is born.
   c. at the moment of birth.
   d. at the first contact with the opposite sex.
   Ans: b

4. The construction of the *Divine Comedy* reflects the theme of a
   a. perfectly constructed universe ordained by God.
   b. heroic figure felled by a character flaw.
   c. hopeless love affair doomed by class prejudice.
   d. mythological quest for priceless treasure.
   Ans: a

5. Dante features prominently the number _____ and its multiples because of its religious significance.
   a. four
   b. five
   c. three
   d. ten
   Ans: c

6. Which of the following is NOT true of the medieval Church?
   a. It became the largest landholder in Europe.
   b. It ruled through a vast bureaucracy.
   c. It established a vast network of courts.
   d. Its officials could only be named by the king.
   Ans: d

7. The Inquisition was a
   a. traveling church court.
   b. list of forbidden books.
   c. church council that determined financial policy.
   d. monastic retreat.
   Ans: a

8. The interlocking rhyme scheme of the *Divine Comedy* is known as
   a. blank verse.
   b. *Terza rima.*
   c. dactylic hexameter.
   d. the heroic couplet.
   Ans: b

9. The three human souls who suffer most in Dante's Hell are
   a. three contemporaries of Dante, including one Pope.
   b. companions of Satan from before the creation of humankind.
   c. three persons taken from the Bible.
   d. persons taken from the Bible and from Roman history.
   Ans: d

10. The author of the *Summa Theologica,* who, inspired by Aristotelian logic, systematically examined most of the theological issues of the Middle Ages was
    a.   Thomas Aquinas.
    b.   Francis of Assisi.
    c.   Saint Augustine.
    d.   Dante Alighieri.
    Ans: a

11. In *Everyman,* the role of sacraments shows continuity with the doctrine of the Nicene Creed of the early Christian Church.
    Ans: F

12. Only church officials could give out the sacraments, thereby ensuring a virtual "monopoly" on salvation.
    Ans: T

13. The emphasis placed on good deeds performed in this life was a feature of Christian salvation theory throughout its history.
    Ans: F

14. In his "Ninth Circle of Hell," Dante sketched an imposing figure of Satan burning in flames.
    Ans: F

Open Book

15. In *Everyman* (Reading 2.19), God says that what turns humankind away from spirituality is
    a.   sex.
    b.   work.
    c.   worldly riches.
    d.   the Devil.
    Ans: c

16. In *Everyman,* the words used by Death suggest that God looks at human failings with the eyes of
    a.   a mother.
    b.   a bookkeeper.
    c.   a doctor.
    d.   a gardener.
    Ans: b

17. *Everyman:* In the speeches of Five-Wits we learn that priests occupy the following rank in God's eyes:
    a.   higher than the angels in heaven
    b.   below the Pope, but higher than rulers
    c.   the most powerful of men, especially over women
    d.   more powerful than the Devil
    Ans: a

18. The Mouth of Hell pictured in Figure 12.3 shows _____ locking the gates of Hell.
    Ans: Saint Peter

19. Fiero, Reading 2.20, "The Vision of God," lines 133–138. In this passage, Dante compares the difficulty of knowing God-made-man to the intellectual difficulty that arises out of the incommensurability of a straight line and a curved line.
    Ans: T

20. Fiero, Figure 12.5. The plan of Dante's universe reflects the astronomical theory of
    a. Copernicus.
    b. Ptolemy.
    c. the Arabs.
    d. The Germans.
    Ans: b

21. Fiero, Figure 12.6. The way Dante imagines Hell to be organized shows that he considered the worst sins of humankind to be sins of
    a. the flesh.
    b. murder.
    c. heresy against Christian doctrine.
    d. treachery.
    Ans: d

22. Fiero, Reading 2.20, from the *Divine Comedy*. In line 82, Dante says, "For you are my true master," by which he means
    a. God.
    b. the Roman poet, Virgil.
    c. Beatrice.
    d. The Virgin Mary.
    Ans: b

23. Fiero, Figure 12.7 and Reading 2.20. The picture of Satan eating the souls in Hell is generally faithful to Dante's description, with the exception of which one of the following details.
    a. Dante does not give Satan three mouths.
    b. Dante places Satan in ice not in fire.
    c. Dante does not give Satan a body.
    d. Dante makes Satan the same size as the souls of the damned.
    Ans: b

24. Fiero , Reading 2.20, "The Vision of God," line 127. When Dante refers to "that second aureole," he means
    a. humankind.
    b. Jesus.
    c. the Roman poet, Virgil.
    d. Dante.
    Ans: b

25. Fiero, Figure 12.9, University Lecture. Considered in the light of the text treatment of medieval universities and our own reading of the *Summa Theologica,* we could say that the picture most likely shows
    a.   a professor giving students the results of his original research.
    b.   a professor giving a commentary on some ancient authority.
    c.   a priest translating the Holy Scriptures into a modern language.
    d.   a professor leading his class in a discussion.
    Ans: b

Summary

Medieval churches were the most monumental expressions of the Age of Faith. In the time of Charlemagne, important monastic centers featured a complex of buildings, including wooden-roofed churches whose relics drew frequent pilgrimages. After 1000 C.E., pilgrimage churches were constructed out of stone along the major pilgrimage routes to special shrines. Designed in the Romanesque style using round arches and groined vaults, these churches reflected the themes of redemption and salvation. The Gothic cathedral featured ribbed vaults, pointed arches, flying buttresses, and stained glass. Its sculpture, windows, and other decorative elements comprised a vast compendium of medieval knowledge and reflected the synthesis of all medieval modes of expression. From the Romanesque to the Gothic, there is a clearly emerging trend away from schematic symbolism to a more natural rendering of the human body. Also, a more optimistic view of human destiny can be seen in the themes represented. The Romanesque preoccupation with death and judgment, and with the authoritative figure of God as judge, gives way to more hopeful themes with the mother of Jesus as the preeminent symbol. Medieval music saw the rise of polyphony and full-fledged music drama. The motet and instrumental music took their place alongside the liturgical music of the Church.

Outline	Pronunciation Guide

A. Medieval architecture
    1. the Carolingian abbey church
    2. the Romanesque pilgrimage church
        a. the role of relics
        b. Roman-style construction
        c. architectural sculpture
    3. the Gothic cathedral
        a. functions and origins
        b. architectural features
        c. stained glass
        d. sculpture and sculptural symbolism
B. Medieval painting
    1. illuminated manuscripts
    2. panel painting
C. Medieval music
    1. early medieval embellishments
    2. liturgical drama
    3. development of notation
    4. polyphony
    5. the *dies irae*
    6. the motet
    7. instrumental music
	Saint Sernin [san ser NAN]
	Vézelay [vay ze LAY]
	Autun [ow TUN]
	voussoir [voo SWAHR]
	Suger [soo ZHAY]
	Saint Denis [san de NEE]
	Chartres [SHAHRT]
	Belle Verrière [bel ver ee ER]
	Sainte Chapelle [sant shah PEL]
	Cimabue [chee mah BOO ay]
	Perotin [per ow TAN]
	dies irae [DEE ez IR ay]

Key Terms: abbey church/cathedral, relics, pilgrimage, Romanesque, Gothic, cult of the virgin, stained glass, sequence, polyphony, motet, timbre, *Dies irae,* synthesis, *cathedra,* altarpiece, requiem.

Key Images:	
Plan for an ideal monastery, St. Gall Saint Sernin, Toulouse, Exterior and Interior views Reliquary Statue of Saint Foy Last Judgment, Autun Cathedral Chartres, Exterior and Interior views	Notre Dame de la Belle Verrière Sainte Chapelle, Paris Virgin and Child, Notre Dame, Paris Madonna Enthroned, Cimabue

Study Questions

Factual

1. Study the plan for an ideal monastery (Fiero, Figure 13.1). Look up and identify any label you do not understand (*e.g.*, servitors).
2. What was the function of the reliquary?
3. Why and where did European pilgrims travel in the twelfth century?
4. What was the traditional subject matter of the Romanesque West portal?
5. What is a cathedral? How does it differ from other churches?
6. What are the main structural features of the Gothic cathedral?
7. To whom were most Gothic churches dedicated? Why?
8. What were the results of using a pointed arch instead of a round one?
9. What kinds of paintings were made in the thirteenth century? What purposes did they serve?
10. What was the symbolic value/meaning of the stained glass window?

Challenge

1. Compare text illustrations of Romanesque and Gothic church sculpture. Is the subject matter the same? Does the artist want to produce the same effect on you?
2. Using the text illustrations in Chapter 10 (Islamic Art and Architecture) to refresh your memory, imagine that you are a Muslim pilgrim to Notre Dame of Paris. What strikes you as different in what you see?
3. Locate some examples of Neo-Gothic architecture on your campus or in your town or city. When were they built? What features of medieval Gothic have been retained or rejected?
4. Using Music Listening Selections I–2 and I–7 through 9, compare early church music with church music after the year 1000.
5. Research the technique of producing a painted and gilded altarpiece. In what ways was the medieval artist also a craftsperson?
6. How was stained glass crafted? What legends are associated with the colors in these windows?
7. To what extent are the visions of Hildegard reflected in medieval art? Answer the same question with regard to the writings of Innocent III and Dante.
8. The Gothic era has been called an "Age of Faith"; how is this epithet reflected in the arts?
9. Give some examples of the medieval synthesis in specific works discussed in this chapter, explaining how each constitutes a "synthesis."

Strategies for Discussion/Lecture

1. Part 2 of the film, *A White Garment of Churches*, gives an excellent survey of the Gothic, with many images found in the textbook, including an introduction to the making of stained glass. Students will be prepared for this viewing by writing a preliminary theme drawn from Factual question #6 and Challenge question #1. Part 1 of the film *Romanesque* might be repeated in full or in highlights, to mark the contrast between the two styles. A visit to a local church or cathedral in the neoromanesque or neogothic styles is highly recommended.

2. If neither slides nor *A White Garment of Churches* or similar video are not available, the text illustrations in this chapter are still sufficiently rich and well-selected to bring out developments in structure and style. Students can be asked to look at the series of Gothic facades (Figures 13.15–29) and list features of the Gothic as it passes from the Norman tower of Chartres through Paris and Amiens, and ending in the flamboyant south tower of Chartres.

3. It is hard for American students to see the Gothic as a *functional* style because such exoskeletal features as flying buttresses are in fact beautiful in themselves. If a slide is available, it may help to show the interior of Notre-Dame-du-Travail in Paris (Jules Astruc, 1892). Its steel-girder Gothic can produce a shock of recognition that shows the purpose of rib vaults and buttresses.

4. Music. Half of one class period could easily be devoted to medieval music. The difficulty of talking about music while avoiding highly technical terms can be overcome by playing the samples on the CD in chronological order one or more times and asking students to compare what they hear in each case—just as they surveyed the facades of Gothic cathedrals, listing similarities and differences. It seems a good idea to always repeat one time the selections from the previous listening session, in this case Gregorian chant. The most useful student responses from a humanities perspective are not repetitions of the glossary items, such as "polyphony," but descriptions that point to the whole social context of musical experience, such as "I felt I could dance to it, whereas the Gregorian has no regular beat," "I could sing the tune after hearing it twice, but I doubt I could memorize the Gregorian," "I couldn't tell if it was happy or sad." Favoring nontechnical responses gives confidence to an audience of nonmusicians and respects the immediate and universal appeal of older music. After the general discussion, such terms as *polyphony, melismatic,* and *organum* can be introduced.

Chapter 13 Audiovisuals

Video/CD-ROM Sources

ART OF THE MIDDLE AGES 30 min., color **EBEC**

CATHEDRAL

Combining spectacular location sequences and cinema-quality animation, this program takes you to France's most famous and awe-inspiring cathedrals. You'll travel in time back to 1214 to explore the design of Notre Dame de Beaulieu, a magnificent Gothic cathedral shaped by cultural and religious forces. Take a close look at the vaulted arches, shimmering stained-glass windows, and dizzying vaulted ceilings. This award-winning program also tells compelling stories of life and death, faith and despair, prosperity and intrigue. Narrated by David Macaulay. 60 minutes on 1 tape **PSB**

CHARTRES CATHEDRAL 30 min., color **EBEC**

THE CHRISTIANS: Faith and Fear 39 min., color **MGHF**

CIVILISATION—Vol. #02: The Great Thaw (1970)
DIRECTOR: CLARK, SIR KENNETH 53 min., color **PBS**

THE FIRST SECULAR MUSIC 60 min., color **FFH**

GOTHIC CATHEDRALS OF EUROPE—ON CD-ROM
This interactive scholarly resource provides an illuminating architectural and historical perspective on 35 of Europe's most treasured Gothic cathedrals. Through moving footage and photographs, users can study architectural details close-up. The CD-ROM can be used with either Windows or Macintosh. **FFH**

THE GREAT CATHEDRAL AT AMIENS FFH

THE JEWELED CITY: THE CATHEDRAL OF CHARTRES
This program offers a narrated tour of the cathedral, along with a historical portrait of the political and religious fervor of the medieval architects who saw it through to completion. **FFH**

LIGHT ON THE STONES: The Medieval Church of Vézelay 24 min. **VM**

MEDIEVAL MANUSCRIPTS
How illuminations were accomplished and how scriptoria functioned. 30 min. **FFH**

ROAD TO SANTIAGO: Parts 1 & 2 CRM

A WHITE GARMENT OF CHURCHES: Romanesque and Gothic 60 min., color **CPB**

Music Resources

Medieval and Renaissance Sounds, 6 volumes, Desto, 47183, 47184, 47190, 47192, 47200, 47201 cassettes.
Music of the Gothic Era, Early Music Consort of London, Deutsche Grammaphone, Arc– 415292 AH CD.
Voices of the Middle Ages, Capella Antiqua Munich, Elektra/Nonesuch, 71171–4 cassette.

Web Resources

Gothic architecture—http://www.geocities.com/Athens/Parthenon/8063/gothic.html

Information about Gothic art—http://www.artcyclopedia.com/history/gothic.html

Medieval art and architecture—http://info.pitt.edu/~medart/

Virtual tour of Chartres Cathedral—http://info.pitt.edu/~medart/menufrance/chartres/charmain.html

Medieval music links—http://classicalmus.hispeed.com/medieval.html

The pilgrimage to El Camino de Santiago—http://www.humnet.ucla.edu/santiago/iagohome.html

Romanesque style of architecture—http://www.geocities.com/Athens/parthenon/8063/romanesque.html

Music Listening Selection: CD I

    I–7 Medieval Liturgical Drama—*The Play of Herod*, Scene Two

    I–8 Hildegard of Bingen: O Successores

    I–9 Three examples of medieval polyphony: Organum: "Rex caeli, Domine."

    Free Organum: Trope, "Agnus Dei."

    Melismatic Organum: "Benedicamo Domino."

    I–10 Three-part Organum, Perotin, "Alleluya."

    I–11 Thirteeth-century Motet "En non Diu!"

    I–12 Estampie.

Transparencies: M.25 Illuminated Manuscript and a Musical Heart

M.24 Structure of the Mass

M.10 Medieval Church Modes

MA.5 The Middle Ages 500–1453

Sample Test Questions for Chapter 13

Select the letter of the choice that BEST answers the question:

1. Carolingian churches were located primarily in
    a. monastic complexes.
    b. towns.
    c. universities.
    d. Italy.
    Ans: a

2. The dominant theme of Romanesque church sculpture at the entrance portal was
    a. redemption and salvation.
    b. the seven deadly sins.
    c. scenes from Jesus' life.
    d. the garden of Eden.
    Ans: a

3. Surveying the musical selections from the period 600–1300 C.E., we discover all the following developments EXCEPT ONE.
    a. purely vocal music to voice plus instruments
    b. monophonic music to polyphonic
    c. strictly Latin lyrics to use of modern languages
    d. strictly male choirs to participation of female singers
    Ans: d

4. In medieval music, the second independent melody that moves in contrast to the given melody is called the
   a. harmony.
   b. counterpoint.
   c. sonority.
   d. polyphony.
   Ans: b

5. All of the following were new kinds of music that emerged in the High Middle Ages EXCEPT for
   a. Gregorian chant.
   b. motet.
   c. *Dies irae.*
   d. estampie.
   Ans: a

6. The most important element of the new musical notation of the eleventh century was that it enabled
   a. amateurs to perform sacred music.
   b. music to be more accurately transmitted from generation to generation.
   c. secular music to flourish in medieval society.
   d. more instruments to be added to the ensembles.
   Ans: b

7. Like its Roman models, the sculpture of Romanesque church is highly humanistic and serene.
   Ans: F

8. Music that includes two or more lines of melody is called _____.
   Ans: polyphony

Open Book

9. Fiero, Figure 13.2, "God as Architect of the Universe." This illustration accurately reflects the notion
   a. that the creator built the universe on the basis of perfect circles.
   b. that the creator built the universe in six days and rested on the seventh.
   c. that the creator built the universe starting with atoms.
   d. that God made the universe in his own image.
   Ans: a

10. Taking Chartres as a summation of twelfth-century imagery, we would conclude that the emphasis in Christian theology in the high Gothic period was on
    a. the judgmental God of the Hebrew Bible.
    b. the redeeming figure of the son of God.
    c. the role of the Virgin Mary as intermediary between humans and God.
    d. the disembodied Holy Spirit.
    Ans: c

11. Fiero, Figure 13.25. West facade, Notre Dame, at Amiens. From the point of view of medieval styles, the look of this facade is
    a. pure High Gothic.
    b. a mixture of Romanesque and Gothic.
    c. pure Romanesque.
    d. a mixture of Greek and Roman elements.
    Ans: a

12. Fiero, Figure 13.3. This image was created for the purpose of
    a   adorning the apse.
    b. warning Christians of sinfulness.
    c. holding sacred relics.
    d. representing the Virgin Mary.
    Ans: c

13. Fiero, Figure 13.15, Chartres Cathedral, aerial view. If we flew over this edifice we could identify it as Gothic by which one of the following features.
    a. the plan of the cathedral
    b. the existence of transepts
    c. the fact that it has towers at the west end
    d. the flying buttresses
    Ans: d

14. Fiero, Figure 13.7. The arches in this church identify its style as Gothic.
    Ans: F

15. The altarpieces prepared for most medieval cathedrals were executed in
    a. oil paints.
    b. stained glass.
    c. tempera.
    d. fresco.
    Ans: c

16. The hymn prepared for the Roman Catholic requiem mass (Mass for the Dead) was known as the
    a. *Dies irae.*
    b. *Scivias.*
    c. *Memento mori.*
    d. organum.
    Ans: a

Chapter **14** Asian Civilizations: The Artistic Record

Summary

Geographically remote from the medieval West, the civilizations of India, China, and Japan flourished between 500 and 1300 C.E. India, where Hinduism inspired the production of sophisticated architecture and sculpture, also generated a large body of Sanskrit poetry, music, and dance. Medieval India honored the Hindu gods in art forms that celebrated the union of flesh and spirit. In China, the Tang and Song dynasties sponsored a Golden Age in poetry and painting. The Chinese surpassed the rest of the world in technological invention and led world production in fine pottery and textiles. Both civilizations pursued philosophies that emphasized holism and the unity of nature. The basic elements of Chinese culture were carried east to Japan in the early sixth century, contributing to the remarkable artistic achievements of the Heian court. Japanese innovations included the world's first psychological novel and new forms of performance art.

Outline	**Pronunciation Guide**
A. India	*rajput* [RAHJ poot]
1. historical context	*sati* [SAH tee]
2. Hinduism in medieval India	**avatar** [AV ah tahr]
3. religious literature	**sitar** [si TAHR]
4. poetry	**Shiva** [SHEE vah]
5. architecture and sculpture	*Puranas* [poo RAH nahz]
6. music and dance	**Khajuraho** [kah joo RAH ow]
B. China	**Kandariya Mahadeo** [ken dar REE ya ma ha DAY oh]
1. Tang and Song dynasties	**Vidyakara** [vi dy ah KAH rah]
2. technological achievements	*mithuna* [mi THOO nah]
3. literature and music	**mudra** [MOO drah]
4. landscape painting	**Li Bo** [LEE POW]
5. crafts	**Du Fu** [doo foo]
6. architecture	**Changan** [SHAHN gahn]
C. Japan	**Hangzhou** [HAHNG jow]
1. prose literature	**Bo Zhu-yi** [BOW choo ee]
2. Buddhism and the arts	**samurai** [SAM or eye]
3. *samurai* culture	**bushido** [BOO shee dow]
4. Nô drama	**Murasaki Shikibu** [moo rah SAH kee SHEE kee boo]

Key Terms: medieval Hinduism, *Puranas,* Chinese examination system, neoconfucianism, nature lyrics and landscape painting, pagoda, raga, tala, sitar, mudra, Chinese opera, pagoda, Silk Road, samurai, bushido, *yugen.*

Key Images:	
Shiva Nataraja, Lord of the Dance Kandariya Mahadeo temple, Khajuraho Mithuna Couple Mi Yu-jen, *Cloudy Mountains*	[Other examples of Tang and Song painting] Tomb Figurines, Tang Dynasty Examples of Chinese ceramics and porcelain Jokei, *Kongorikishi* East Pagoda of Yakushiji, Nara, Japan

Study Questions

Factual

1. Who are the three principal gods of Hindu mythology, and what does each represent?
2. What are the unique characteristics of Chinese poetry? With what themes were Chinese poets most concerned?
3. What are the three basic formats of Chinese painting?
4. Name five technological inventions that may be credited to the Chinese.
5. Describe everyday life in China based on the scenes depicted in Figures 14.10, 11, and 12.
6. What unique contributions did the Chinese make in the area of stoneware crafts and architecture?
7. How did the prose novel serve the culture of medieval Japan?
8. What are the main features of Japanese Nô drama?

Challenge

1. What concepts concerning the nature of the universe are represented in the statue of Shiva (Fiero, Figure 14.2)? Is there anything in Western medieval art to which such a figure might be compared?
2. Discuss the differences between Gothic sculpture in western Europe and Hindu sculpture in India.
3. Describe the Chinese examination system. Are any offices in the United States filled by competitive exams?
4. What attitudes towards time and nature are reflected in Chinese poetry and painting?
5. The arts of India combine the sensual and the meditative. Test this claim against specific works of Indian literature and art.
6. What features can you detect in the Music Listening Selections from India and China (Music Listening Selections I–13, I–14) that make these musical examples distinctive?
7. What attitudes towards time and nature are reflected in Chinese poetry and painting?
8. In your view, how does the Western student benefit from learning about the cultural life of India, China and Japan?
9. Compare the art of medieval Japan with that of medieval India and China. Consider both content and style.
10. It is said that Japanese culture is both delicate and fierce; defend this viewpoint with examples from this chapter.
11. What role does gesture and form play in the art of Japanese drama (see Reading 2.27). Can similar approaches to studied form be found in the visual arts of Japan?

Strategies for Discussion/Lecture

1. Assigning a minitheme from either Factual question #2 or Challenge question #4 is helpful in preparing for class discussion. A preparatory essay or theme could also be based on a comparison of the Hindu temple and the Gothic Cathedral, or a comparison of just the statuary pictured in Chapters 13 and 14..

2. Chinese poems can be matched to paintings in the same section. The love poetry of India can be contrasted to both the Chinese lyrics and to Christian poems like those of the troubadours. If there are any students in the class who speak Chinese, ask them to read some Chinese poems aloud. This will quickly make the point concerning the links between the Chinese language and Chinese music.

3. Many examples in the chapter invite discussion of the role of the female in East Asian societies. What evidence is there concerning the nature of the life styles of upper class women? How are women pictured in Hindu art? In Chinese art? Why were Japanese women able to play music, but not perform in staged drama?

4. Chinese landscape. One way to bring home the Chinese view of humans in the natural world is to ask students to turn to Figure 14.15, for example, and cover the caption of the photo without reading it. Ask them to give a title to the picture. All responses will feature water, mountains, trees, and some may even refer to the human structures in the scene. Only after uncovering the caption will they begin to assess the place of human artifacts in these pictures. How does this put into relief our own view and the Chinese view of the place of humans in the natural environment?

5. The arts of India combine the sensual and the meditative. Test this claim against specific works of literature, art, and music presented in this chapter. Ask students if they can find any comparable examples in Western art.

6. Ask students to write a diary entry on the order of Lady Murasaki's. The entry should record vivid impressions based on the student's immediate environment and its occupants. Challenge question #10 also works well in prompting class discussion.

Chapter 14 Audiovisuals

Video/CD-ROM Sources

ANCIENT SPIRITS: THE GARDENS OF JAPAN & CHINA
China has the oldest garden tradition in the world. For centuries, the country's dramatic topography has inspired poets, painters, and gardeners. In a tour of exquisite gardens, we learn the role of water and rocks in the Chinese sanctuary, and how Chinese methods were splendidly adapted to the Japanese landscape. (1995) 30 min. **HTG**

ART OF INDONESIA: TALES FROM THE SHADOW WORLD
Girding the equator like a string of emeralds, the 13,000 Islands of Indonesia are dotted with steaming volcanoes, cascading waterfalls, and temple ruins such as Borobudur, the largest Buddhist monument in the world. This documentary explores Indonesia's ancient treasures and its "shadow world"—the rituals, myths, and performances by which the harmony of the universe is maintained. Weaving together old Javanese poetry, sculpture, stunning landscapes, and music, this visually splendid film shot in Java and Bali introduces viewers to the symbols that have permeated Indonesian culture for more than a thousand years. (1990) 28 min. **HTG**

CHINA: The Golden Age (Sui and Tang dynasties) 23 min., color **IU**

CHINA'S COSMOPOLITAN AGE: The Tang (1980) 60 min., color **CPB**

CHINESE ART: Of Heaven, Earth and Man 23 min., color **IU**

CHINESE ART: Treasures of the National Palace Museum
This program spotlights 20 works of Chinese art seldom ever seen outside of the National Palace Museum. 26 min., color **FFH**

CHINESE BRUSH PAINTING 30 min., color **RMI**

EARLY ENGLISH ALOUD AND ALIVE: THE LANGUAGE OF BEOWULF, CHAUCER, AND SHAKESPEARE
In this program, Dr. Joseph Gallagher brings language to life by reciting examples of Old, Middle, and Early Modern English in their original dialects. Includes subtitles in Modern English, where necessary. 28 min., color **FFH**

ESSENCE OF BEING JAPANESE, THE (Japan Past & Present) (1989)
DIRECTOR: ANTOINE, JEAN 53 min., color **FFH**

FIVE MILLENNIA OF CHINESE ART: A SPIRITUAL JOURNEY—ON CD-ROM
This elegant CD-ROM replicates the experience of touring the Chi-Shan Garden and the museum's four floors of galleries. Windows only. **FFH**

THE GANGES 45 min., color **FFH**

THE GENIUS THAT WAS CHINA John Merson and David Roberts NOVA (1990)—**PBS**

JAPAN PAST AND PRESENT
An introduction to the complexities, disparities, dichotomies, and beauties of Japan and the Japanese, then and now. Approximately 50 minutes each **FFH**

THE ORIENTAL COLLECTION (British Museum, London) 26 min., color **FFH**

THE TALE OF GENJI
This extraordinarily beautiful program traces the plot of *The Tale of Genji* through the panels of a series of illustrated handscrolls dating from the early twelfth century. (English, 60 min.) *Journal of Japanese Studies*, Winter 1996. Recommended: Video Rating Guide for Libraries **FFH**

Music Resources

The Best of Chinese Orchestral Music, Harmonia Mundi, 8.240389 CD.
Chinese Classical Instrumental Music, Folkways, 6812 cassette.
Music of India: Traditional and Classic, Folkways, 4422 cassette.
Phases of the Moon (traditional Chinese music), CBS MK–36705 CD; MT–36705 cassette.
Religious Music of India, Folkways, 4431 cassette.

Web Resources

Chronology and timeline of medieval India—http://www.itihaas.com/medieval/

History and resources about medieval India—http://www.goindiago.com/history/medieval.htm

Resources relating to medieval India—http://historymedren.about.com/msubind.htm?once=true&

The Tang dynasty—http://campus.northpark.edu/history/webchron/china/tang.html

The Song dynasty—http://www.china-contact.com/www/history/song.html

Resources related to Nô—http://www.bridgewater.edu/~dhuffman/soc306/199grp2/noh.htm

McGraw-Hill Resources

Music Listening Selection: CD I
I–13 Indian Music, *Thumri*
I–14 Chinese Music, *"Ngoh Wai Heng Kong"*

Sample Test Questions on Chapter 14

Select the letter of the choice that BEST answers the question:

1. In the 700s C.E., the _____ invaded northern India.
   a. Chinese
   b. Afghans
   c. Slavs
   d. Muslims
   Ans: d

2. Indian architecture and art was influenced primarily by _____ tradition.
   a. Buddhist
   b. Muslim
   c. Japanese
   d. Korean
   Ans: a

3. Taking the Kandariya Mahadeo temple sculptures as representative works of developed Hinduism, we can reasonably guess that the Muslim invaders of the eighth century found them objectionable because
   a. the gods are represented with unreal human bodies.
   b. the statues are cast in metal.
   c. Islam forbids the representation of God.
   d. the statues reveal too much of the human body.
   Ans: c

4. In medieval Hinduism, the gods of Indian mythology came to be known as "incarnations" of Brahman, that is,
   a. sati.
   b. avatars.
   c. *rajputs.*
   d. mudra.
   Ans: c

5. In Japan, Paradise and "salvation" were anticipated by followers of
   a. the emperors.
   b. the *samurai.*
   c. Nô theater.
   d. Hinayana Buddhism.
   Ans: d

6. The scriptural language of medieval India equivalent to Latin in the West was
   a. Pali.
   b. Hindi.
   c. Sanskrit.
   d. Bengali.
   Ans: c

7. Before modern times, literacy in China was restricted because of
   a. the predominance of the chief noble families.
   b. the unavailability of printed books.
   c. the lack of a system of public education.
   d. the nature of written Chinese script.
   Ans: d

8. The members of the Chinese ruling class chosen by competitive examinations are sometimes known as
   a. mandarins.
   b. scribes.
   c. dukes.
   d. shoguns.
   Ans: a

9. The Chinese method of vaulting that allows overhang of the multiple roofs of the pagoda is known as
   a. Gothic arch.
   b. barrel vaulting.
   c. cantilever.
   d. seven-tiered bracket.
   Ans: d

10. The sensuality of temple sculpture in medieval India is matched by Indian lyric poetry.
    Ans: T

11. In China, in contrast to the medieval West, women were permitted to take the examinations for civil service.
    Ans: F

12. As in the West, the invention of movable type in China in the middle of the eleventh century led to a revolution in the communication of ideas.
Ans: F

13. One feature of medieval Chinese literature that sets it in contrast to contemporary Western writing is that it is largely lacking in religious sentiment.
Ans: T

14. One aspect of Chinese poetry that distinguishes it from Western verse is the presence in earliest times of nature and natural imagery.
Ans: T

Open Book

15. Fiero, Figure 14.12 (Song Dynasty painting) and Figure 11.15 (Bayeux Tapestry). A comparison of these roughly contemporaneous art works shows that medieval China
    a. was, as in the West, a period of territorial struggle.
    b. was stable and peaceful, as reported by Marco Polo.
    c. was at about the same level as the West in rendering perspective.
    d. had a tradition of painting scenes of violent action similar to the West.
    Ans: b

16. Fiero, Reading 2.25 (Tang and Song poetry). One selection shows the influence of Chan (Zen) Buddhist riddles.
    a. Watching the Mt. Lushan Waterfall
    b. Chuang Chou and the Butterfly
    c. Spring Rain
    d. Farewell Once More
    Ans: b

17. Fiero, Figure 14.15. This landscape is typical of the Chinese view of the place of human works as they fit into nature, namely,
    a. that the works of humankind dominate those of nature.
    b. that the works of humans have no place in nature.
    c. that the works of humans properly fit the scene of mountain, tree, stream.
    d. that the works of humans always occupy the foreground.
    Ans: c

18. Fiero, Figure 14.9. The statue of this *Luhan* is evidence of
    a. the importance of Buddhism in China.
    b. the use of the figure as a reliquary.
    c. the avoidance of realism in Chinese art.
    d. the technique of bronze-crafting .
    Ans: a

19. Page 165, Figure 14.211, East pagoda of Yakushiji, Nara, Japan. The timber style of this wood pagoda originated in
    a. China
    b. Japan
    c. Mongolia
    d. Korea
    Ans: a

20. Fiero, Figure 14.22, *Kichijoten,* painted wood, Kyoto, Japan. This statue belongs to Buddhist practice in Japan, that is
    a. the purest form of Hinayana Buddhism.
    b. modified Hinayana Buddhism imported from China.
    c. a Japanese adaptation of Mahayana Buddhism.
    d. Buddhism tainted with Christianity.
    Ans: c

21. In medieval Japan, the *samurai* were
    a. a guild of priestly swordsmen.
    b. a class of warriors who held land in return for military service, like European vassals.
    c. rural judges specializing in land disputes.
    d. a class of freelance warriors without ties to the land.
    Ans: b

22. Fiero, Figure 14.26, *Ko-omote* Nô mask. This fifteenth-century mask marks the beginning of female actors in the Japanese Nô theater.
    Ans: F

BOOK 3

The European Renaissance, the Reformation, and Global Encounter

---

PART I   The Age of the Renaissance *1300 – 1600*

Chapter **15** Adversity and Challenge: The Fourteenth-Century Transition

Summary

The fourteenth century witnessed the collapse of the medieval synthesis; it marked the beginning of an age of transition during which the West rose to a position of global dominance. The Black Death and the Hundred Years' War contributed to the decline of feudalism and manorialism. By the end of the century, the population of western Europe had decreased by at least one-third; death became a principal motif in literature and art. The loss of church prestige (through the Avignon Papacy and the Great Schism) inspired movements of devotional piety, mysticism, and religious reform. Social realism and rising secularism are reflected in the works of Boccaccio and Chaucer, where credible, individualized characters replace the older allegorical and stereotypical heroes of medieval literature. Realistic detail and a new expressiveness also characterize the art (Giotto) and music (Machaut) of the period. In religious expression, devotional piety was a major theme. An age of turmoil, the fourteenth century effected the transition between the medieval and the modern world.

Outline	Pronunciation Guide
A. Historical context 　1. Black death 　　a. Boccaccio's narrative 　　b. political and economic effects: 　　　France and England 　2. Hundred Years' War 　3. Decline of the church 　　a. Avignon Papacy and the Great 　　　Schism 　　b. anticlericalism and devotional piety B. Literature in transition 　1. Boccaccio 　2. Christine de Pisan 　3. Chaucer C. Art and music in transition 　1. Giotto 　2. devotional realism and portraiture 　3. *ars nova* in music	**Avignon** [AH veen YOWN] **Boccaccio** [bow KAH chow] *Decameron* [de KA me rahn] **Giotto** [JAH tow] **Prato** [PRAH tow] **Jean Pucelle** [ZHAHN poo SEL] **Ambrogio Lorenzetti** 　[am BROW jow low ren ZET ti] **Jean Le Bon** [ZHAHN Le BOWN] *chiaroscuro* [kyah row SKOO row] *grisaille* [gree ZEYE] **Sluter** [SLOO tur] **Machaut** [mah SHOW]

Key Terms: plague, Dance of Death, constitutional monarchy, Hundred Years' War, Great Schism, anticlericalism, devotional piety, social realism, *ars nova*

Key Images:	
Limbourg Brothers, *February* Dance of Death Giotto, *Madonna Enthroned*	Giotto, *Lamentation* (Arena Chapel) Sluter, *Well of Moses* A. Lorenzetti, *Madonna del Latte*

Study Questions

Factual

1. What was the Black Death? Where and how did it begin? What were its results for western Europe?
2. What events affected the position of the Catholic church in the fourteenth century?
3. In what ways did warfare change in the West between 1300 and 1500?
4. What were the main results of the Hundred Years' War?
5. Using the figures in your text, describe three examples of "devotional realism" in the visual arts of the late fourteenth century.
6. What is the basis for the structure of Chaucer's *Canterbury Tales*?
7. What are the main features of Giotto's painting style?
8. What were the principal features of the *ars nova* in music?

Challenge

1. Why is the fourteenth century known as the century of adversity and change?
2. In what ways does the threat of AIDS resemble that of the Black Death? How might a plague like the Black Death affect your own community?
3. How does Boccaccio's "Tale of Filippa" illustrate a new attitude toward women in society? What aspects of this tale are representative of social realism?
4. Give examples from the literature and art in this chapter in which vivid pictorial and psychological details replace generalizations and abstractions.
5. The fourteenth century was a great age of mystics. Who were some of these figures and what did they contribute?
6. What were the landmark developments in the rise of England's constitutional monarchy?
7. The name *ars nova* is associated with fourteenth-century music. In what ways might it also be applied to other forms of expression in this century?

Strategies for Discussion/Lecture

1. Offer a brief lecture on the main forces contributing to trauma and transition: the Black Death, the Hundred Years' War, and the Avignon Papacy and Schism. These three events were crucial to changes in all aspects of European life and culture.
2.. Boccaccio's "Tale of Filippa" is short enough to read in class; discussion could take the form of a debate for and against the judge's decision: should the law enter the bedroom of citizens? Does Filippa's objection to the "double standard" applied here anticipate modern feminism?
3. Chaucer's realism is a major departure from prior narrative style. Ask students if they remember the physical features of the Wife of Bath, the Miller, and Alison. The lecturer can then apply the sense of physical detail to the art of devotional realism and to Giotto and Lorenzetti where the bodily presence of Jesus and the living maternity of Mary are so apparent.
4. *Ars Nova* is best appreciated in direct listening: first to the three examples of Early Medieval Polyphony (I–9) and Perotin's "Alleluya" (I–10), followed by Machaut (I–15).

Chapter 15 Audiovisuals

Video/CD-ROM Sources

CHAUCER'S ENGLAND 30 min., color **EBEC**

CIVILISATION - Vol. #03: Romance and Reality (1970)
    DIRECTOR: CLARK, SIR KENNETH 53 min., color **PBS**

THE EARLY RENAISSANCE and THE HIGH RENAISSANCE 60 min. ea., color **CPB**

ENGLISH POETRY PLUS—ON CD-ROM FFH

FAITH AND FEAR: Reaction to the Black Death 40 min., color **CRM**

GIOTTO AND THE PRE-RENAISSANCE 50 min., color **KV**

JOAN OF ARC 26 min., color **CA**

LEONARDO DA VINCI: The Visionary Intellect 24 min., color **AE**

MEDIEVAL ENGLAND: The Peasants' Revolt 31 min., color **LCA**

PRINCES AND PRELATES CRM

Web Resources

History of the Black Death—http://www.byu.edu/ipt/projects/middleages/lifetimes/plague.html

Women writers of the Middle Ages—
http://www.millersv.edu/~english/homepage/duncan/medfem/medfem.html

Biographical information about Boccaccio—http://www.newadvent.org/cathen/02607a.htm

Resources related to Chaucer—http://geoffreychaucer.org/

Giotto biography and links—http://www.christusrex.org/wwwl/francis/

Giotto's frescoes—http://www.kfki.hu/~arthp/html/g/giotto/padova/index.html

Giotto's frescoes—http://www.kfki.hu/~arthp/html/g/giotto/s_croce/bardi/index.html

Information related to Limbourg Brothers and *Les Tres Riches Heures du Duc de Berry*—
http://christusrex.org/www2/berry/index.html

McGraw-Hill Resources

Music Listening Selection: CD I
    I–15 Machaut: *"Ite Missa Est Deo Gratias"* from *Mass of Notre Dame*
    I-16 Anonymous, *Summer Is Icumen In*

Sample Test Questions for Chapter 15

Select the letter of the choice that BEST answers the question:

1. The Great Schism was
    a. a break between the pope and the kings of western Europe.
    b. a definitive break with the nobility by the peasants.
    c. a rivalry between two competing popes.
    d. the dissolution of the Holy Roman Empire.
    Ans: c

2. All of the following are associated with a definition of "modernity" EXCEPT
    a. entrepreneurial capitalism.
    b. advancing technology.
    c. unity of Christendom.
    d. increasing literacy.
    Ans: c

3. In his preface to his collection of tales entitled the *Decameron,* Boccaccio
    a. described how the Black Death destroyed Byzantium.
    b. related the effects of the Black Death on the people of Florence.
    c. discussed the elaborate rituals associated with death.
    d. focused on the spiritual rebirth of the church.
    Ans: b

4. According to Boccaccio, the strategies used by the population to deal with the plague included all of the following except
   a. moderate eating and drinking.
   b. excessive eating and drinking.
   c. fleeing from the sick.
   d. relying upon Muslim doctors and medical theories.
   Ans: d

5. The political fallout of the Black Death included
   a. the outbreak of working class rebellions.
   b. growing political democratization.
   c. consolidation of the aristocracy's power.
   d. allowing the middle class the right to vote.
   Ans: a

6. All except which of the following contributed to the rise of constitutional monarchy in England:
   a. the Jacquerie
   b. the signing of the Magna Carta
   c. the expansion of the Great Council
   d. Parliament's frequent meetings
   Ans: a

7. Fiero, Reading 3.3, from Christine de Pisan's *Book of the City of Ladies*. We learn from the dialogue with Reason that one reason Christine succeeded in the face of society's opposition to women's intellectual advancement is that she had the support of both her parents.
   Ans: F

8. Fiero, Reading 3.4, Chaucer. The most accurate summary of Chaucer's ability to describe people is:
   a. He concentrates on moral character and leaves the physical to the imagination.
   b. He describes men physically, but not women.
   c. He describes peoples' surroundings rather than the people themselves.
   d. He gives a rich mix of both the physical and moral of both genders.
   Ans: d

9. In Boccaccio's "Tale of Filippa," the defendant in the trial argues that the law on adultery
   a. lacks a provision that the act must be witnessed.
   b. is unfair to the party outside the marriage contract.
   c. was passed without the consent of those it affects.
   d. provides a penalty that is cruel and unusual.
   Ans: c

10. European warfare became more "modernized" with the introduction of all of the following EXCEPT
    a. the foot soldier.
    b. the longbow.
    c. gunpowder.
    d. the cavalry.
    Ans: d

11. Reformers like John Wyclif demanded
    a. the end of Church bureaucracy.
    b. the end of Church taxation.
    c. widespread use of Latin.
    d. greater numbers of parish priests.
    Ans: a

12. The technique of *chiaroscuro* used by Giotto involved
    a. an emphasis on Gothic line and flattened figures.
    b. the use of dramatic gestures.
    c. defining figures through the use of light and shadow.
    d. the use of realistic background.
    Ans: c

13. In the second half of the fourteenth century, the Black Death, which was carried by fleas, destroyed between one-third to one-half of the population.
    Ans: T

14. In his short story featuring Madame Filippa, Boccaccio argued against current law that punished women more severely than men for committing adultery.
    Ans: T

15. In devotional literature and painting of the fourteenth century, artists emphasized the righteous wrath of Christ as he punished sinners.
    Ans: F

16. In his introduction to the *Decameron,* Boccaccio offers two possible causes of the Black Death, namely, the just anger of God and the influence of celestial bodies.
    Ans: T

Answer the following with a word or phrase.

17. The celebrated document of English constitutional history, the _____, proclaimed that the king could not levy new taxes without the consent of the nobility.
    Ans: Magna Carta

18. The first European struggle between the emerging nation states was called _____.
    Ans: The Hundred Years' War

19. _____ were essentially pardons that freed sinners from temporal penalties for their sins.
    Ans: Indulgences

20. In his _____, Chaucer depicted a variety of characters making a pilgrimage to the shrine of Thomas à Becket.
    Ans: *Canterbury Tales*

21. NOT among the major characteristics of ars nova music:
    a. aural expressiveness
    b. rhythmic complexity
    c. a return to monophony
    d. the use of isorhythm
    Ans: c

Summary

The earliest efforts at recovering and studying classical literature, a phenomenon known as "classical humanism," occurred in Italy in the fourteenth century. Petrarch, the "father of humanism," glorified the classical Latin past and encouraged the spirit of revival that marked the Age of the Renaissance. Subsequent humanists (such as Ficino and Pico) expanded Petrarch's mission to include Greek manuscripts; at the same time, they advanced the quest for individualism and the unity of all knowledge. Alberti, Castiglione, and Machiavelli applied the ideals of the classical heritage in the civic and social domains. Female humanists wrote letters and treatises of a proto-feminist character. The value of a classical education, the virtue of self-confident individualism, and the viability of the autonomous state were among the uniquely modern concerns of the Renaissance humanists.

Outline	Pronunciation Guide

A. Classical humanism
 B. Italy and the Renaissance
   1. the Italian city-states
   2. Petrarch
     a. father of humanism
     b. development of the sonnet
   3. Ficino and Pico
   4. Alberti
   5. Castiglione
   6. female humanists: Cereta and Marinella
   7. Machiavelli
	Verrocchio [ver OWK yow]
	 Medici [ME di chee]
	 Lapo da Castiglionchio
	     [LAH pow dah kas ti LYOWN kee ow]
	 Canzoniere [kan zow NYAY ray]
	 Ficino [fee CHEE now]
	 Pico della Mirandola
	     [PEE kow de lah mi RAHN dow lah]
	 Alberti [al BER tee]
	 Sforza [SVOR tza]
	 Castiglione [kas ti LYOW nay]
	 sprezzatura [spret sah TOO rah]
	 Marinella [mah ree NEL a]
	 Machiavelli [ma kee ah VEL lee]
	 virtù [vir TOO]
	 studiolo [stoo dee OH loh]
	 l'uomo universale
	     [loo OW mow oo nee ver SAH lay]

Key Terms: classical humanism, Platonic Academy, Urbino, individualism, sonnet, Fall of Constantinople (1453), *virtù, l'uomo universale*, Neoplatonism.

Study Questions

Factual

1. Define the term *renaissance*. Why did the Renaissance take place in Italy?
2. Why is Petrarch called the "father of humanism"?
3. What are the main features of the Petrarchan sonnet?

4. How does Alberti describe the "idle man"? What is Alberti's opinion of the business of money-making? What, according to him, is the value of wealth?
5. Which of Pico's assertions concerning the place of the individual in the world reflects Neoplatonism?
6. What are the basic characteristics of Castiglione's courtier? The court lady?
7. What were the basic concerns of the female humanists, Cereta and Marinella?
8. What, according to Machiavelli (Reading 3.11), are the duties of a prince? Is it better, according to Machiavelli, for the ruler to be loved or feared? What does the prince learn from the lion? From the fox?

Challenge
1. Describe in your own words what is meant by the phrase *classical humanism* and why it was particularly important to the cultural and intellectual movement known as the Renaissance.
2. "I am like a man standing between two worlds: I look forward and backward." So wrote Francesco Petrarch as the pivotal figure between the medieval and modern worlds. Comment.
3. Do you detect the influence of Aristotle's *Ethics* in the Alberti reading? If so, explain.
4. Compare Castiglione's view of the well-rounded person with your own. Are there any qualities you think desirable that Castiglione overlooks? Does he cite qualities that you find unimportant today?
5. How does Joan of Arc (Chapter 15) compare with the qualities called for in the court lady in Reading 3.9? How does Christine de Pisan compare?
6. What defects does Marinella list in her complaint against the male sex? How do these compare with the defects men traditionally ascribe to women?
7. Alberti, Castiglione, and Marinella meet in heaven. What might each have to say about the ideal role of womankind in Renaissance society?
8. How does Machiavelli's image of the Prince reflect or contradict the Renaissance concept of individualism? Humanism?
9. Why is Machiavelli often called "the first political realist"? Do nations and their rulers today operate in the manner described by Machiavelli?
10. Medieval people thought of truth as preexisting, that is, as handed down from antiquity in the form of biblical or classical writing. As far as you can tell from this chapter, did Renaissance thinkers actually break with this point of view? Defend your answer with specific references to the material in the chapter.

Strategies for Discussion/Lecture

1. A written assignment from Factual question #1 or Challenge questions #1, 2, and 9 work well for the lecturer and for discussion. Suggestion #2 below can also be assigned before or during class as a way of bringing home the orientation of the first humanists towards past texts. The lecturer will want to underscore the political context of the small Italian city-state that underlies the various descriptions of the "well-rounded person."
2. Reading 3.5 (Petrarch copying Cicero by hand) can be used as an experiment in reading comprehension that will also introduce students to a technology—and a job description—that the photocopying machine has eliminated. Have the class go back to Chapter 15, page 12, and copy out Christine de Pisan's ten-line poem. See if they have anything like Petrarch's experience: "For just in proportion as the writing is slower than the reading does the passage make a deep impression and cling to the mind." This technique of slowing down the reading can be applied later to lyric poetry.
3. Challenge questions #4, 5, or 6 may be assigned as mini-themes in preparation for class discussion. Distinctions between upper-class males and females (according to Castiglione) are a starting place

for further comparisons: between lower, middle, and upper class women; between literary figures (such as Christine) and housewives; between all men and women as perceived by Marinella, etc. How do Renaissance perceptions differ from modern-day norms and ideals?

4. In the three selections on education (Pico, Alberti, Castiglione) it will be mostly up to the instructor's prompting to help students appreciate what the text author calls their departure "from exclusively feudal and Christian educational ideals." Pico's statement that human nature is *situated* but not determined is quite radical (see Sartre, *Existentialism,* Chapter 35), and Alberti's conclusion on money-making breaks with Aquinas and the Greeks, a sure sign that the ancient ideal of the citizen-soldier has been replaced by more practical, citified ideals.

Chapter 16 Audiovisuals

Video/CD-ROM Sources

ART OF THE WESTERN WORLD
Program 3: The Early Renaissance in Florence & The Early Renaissance in Northern Europe **HTG**

THE BEGINNING: THE EMERGENCE OF THE RENAISSANCE FFH

CIVILISATION—Vol. #04: Man—The Measure of All Things (1970)
DIRECTOR: CLARK, SIR KENNETH 53 min., color, sound **PBS**

AN INTRODUCTION TO THE ITALIAN RENAISSANCE
Giorgio Vasari's *Lives of the Artists* has been the basis of art criticism since the sixteenth century. This dramatized program cleverly illustrates how each great master developed techniques by building upon the work of his predecessors. The lively discussion between Master Vasari and his apprentice reveals the innovations of Giotto, Ghiberti, Donatello, Uccello, Masaccio, della Francesca, Botticelli, Leonardo, Raffaello, and Michelangelo. Images of selected masterpieces illustrate the Roman influence on Renaissance art and reinforce the concepts of perspective, balance, *chiaroscuro,* composition, and realism. This charming guide to the Italian masters provides an excellent foundation for high school students. 29 min., color **FFH**

POWER OF THE PAST WITH BILL MOYERS: FLORENCE
Guided by art historians and Florentine citizens, Bill Moyers tours the city's rich Renaissance legacy, seeking the sources of our common artistic, architectural, and cultural heritage. Through interviews with novelist Umberto Eco and filmmaker Franco Zeffirelli, Moyers explores the centuries-old roots of key contemporary ideas, such as the preeminence of the individual. Join Bill Moyers as he views masterpieces by Michelangelo and frescoes in the Brancacci Chapel—the first look on film at these magnificent frescoes since they were restored. 90 minutes on 1 tape **PBS**

THE PURE RADIANCE OF THE PAST: THE REVIVAL OF ANCIENT ARCHITECTURE FFH

RENAISSANCE: Its Beginnings in Italy 26 min., B&W EBEC

RENAISSANCE AND RESURRECTION 55 min., color ABC NEWS

RENAISSANCE: A FRESH LOOK AT THE EVOLUTION OF WESTERN ART

In this dynamic six-part series filmed on location all around Europe, acclaimed art critic Andrew Graham-Dixon promotes a deeper understanding of the Renaissance. **FFH**

THE RENAISSANCE OF FLORENCE—on CD-ROM

A virtual journey through Renaissance Florence. **FFH**

THE SPIRIT OF THE RENAISSANCE 31 min., color **EBEC**

Web Resources

Machiavelli—http://www.sas.upenn.edu/~pgrose/mach/

Laura Cereta: A Renaissance Feminist—http://www.sas.upenn.edu/~ebbeler/writs/cereta.html

Artists of the Italian Renaissance—http://www.italian-art.org/

Selected letters of Petrarch—http://www.fordham.edu/halsall/source/petrarch1.html

Biographical information and writings of Petrarch—http://petrarch.petersadlon.com/

McGraw-Hill Resources

Transparencies: MA.6 The Renaissance 1350–1600

Sample Test Questions for Chapter 16

Select the letter of the choice that BEST answers the question:

1. The center of early Renaissance humanism was
   a. Italy.
   b. Spain.
   c. Germany.
   d. England.
   Ans: a

2. All of the following statements are true about the Renaissance EXCEPT
   a. it began as a revival of Greco-Roman culture.
   b. its ideas appealed to members of the nobility.
   c. it occurred in the least feudalized part of Europe.
   d. it flourished in an anticlerical environment.
   Ans: b

3. Petrarch was one of the first poets to write in the _____ form.
   a. epic
   b. sonnet
   c. satiric
   d. lyrical
   Ans: b

4. In his *Oration,* Pico proclaimed
   a. the importance of pursuing the spiritual life.
   b. the centrality of free choice.
   c. the need to sharpen debating skills.
   d. his adherence to Medici politics.
   Ans: b

5. In his *Oration,* the *manner* in which Pico imparts his views on human nature is
   a. as a quotation of God speaking to Adam.
   b. as a commentary on Aristotle's *Ethics.*
   c. in his own voice, like a professor.
   d. in the form of a dialogue between two humanists.
   Ans: a

6. In his knowledge of foreign languages, Pico was unusual for his time in that he could read
   a. Latin.
   b. Italian.
   c. Arabic.
   d. French.
   Ans: c

7. According to Castiglione, the primary obligation of the well-rounded male courtier was to
   a. learn rhetoric.
   b. become an accomplished musician.
   c. ensure that a ruler rules wisely.
   d. acquire knowledge of the classics.
   Ans: c

8. *The Prince* depicts individuals as being generally
   a. complicated.
   b. worthy.
   c. selfless.
   d. fickle.
   Ans: d

9. The author of *The Prince* urged governments to employ all BUT which of the following?
   a. ruthless methods
   b. mercenaries
   c. war
   d. deceit
   Ans: b

10. The fairest summary of Machiavelli's advice to the prince on doing good vs. doing evil is
    a. doing good is always the best course.
    b. doing evil is never justified.
    c. do evil but balance evil with good deeds.
    d. do good if you can, evil if you must.
    Ans: d

11. Like the city-states of ancient Greece, those of the Early Italian Renaissance
    a. were eventually unified in a single empire.
    b. were ruled by a military aristocracy.
    c. engaged in a fierce commercial rivalry.
    d. enhanced the status of women.
    Ans: c

12. Many Renaissance humanists were affiliated with the Roman Catholic church.
    Ans: T

13. One of the major tenets of humanistic thought was that the educated individual should withdraw
    from involvement in political life.
    Ans: F

14. According to Alberti, only a lack of education prevented women from realizing their full intellectual
    potential.
    Ans: F

15. The *Book of the Courtier* reflected the Renaissance preoccupation with the intrinsic moral value of
    individual action rather than outward appearance.
    Ans: F

16. Fiero, Reading 3.6, from Petrarch's *Canzoniere*, Sonnet 132. The overall impression we get of the
    relation between the speaker in the poem and his lady is:
    a. the speaker is in charge of the relationship.
    b. the speaker is a victim of the lady.
    c. the lady's family is the cause of the speaker's problems.
    d. the speaker is looking forward to better days.
    Ans: b

17. Fiero, Reading 3.7, from Pico's *Oration on the Dignity of Man*. In the reading, Pico has God create
    humankind, assigning it the following rank in creation:
    a. higher than the angels in heaven.
    b. half animal, half angel.
    c. in the image of God, male and female.
    d. free to design its own nature.
    Ans: d

18. Fiero, Reading 3.8, from Alberti's *On the Family*. According to Alberti, humans are absolutely free
    to choose their own nature and not to blame for choosing one activity over another, or indeed no
    activity at all.
    Ans: F

19. Fiero, Reading 3.8, from Alberti's *On the Family*. On the whole, Alberti reflects the ancient Greek and Roman value that business is a dishonorable profession.
Ans: F

20. Fiero, Reading 3.9, from Castiglione's *Book of the Courtier*. As regards the purpose of the male and female courtiers' education, the word that Castiglione uses most often is
a. to know.
b. to entertain.
c. to impress.
d. to achieve self-satisfaction.
Ans: b

21. Fiero, Reading 3.11, from Machiavelli's *The Prince*. A good many of the author's recommendations to the prince are qualified by the fact that his actions are judged by the masses of mankind, and for Machiavelli, the masses are
a. always deceived by appearances.
b. seldom wrong all the time.
c. not educated but crafty and hard to fool.
d. sometimes wrong as individuals, but rarely as a group.
Ans: a

22. The Florentine family that provided patronage for Ficino and other Renaissance humanists and artists was the _____.
Ans: Medici

23. The studiolo of Federigo da Montefeltro was located in the city of _____.
Ans: Urbino

24. Lavinia Fontana's subject (Figure 16.9) was clearly a member of which class?
a. Lower
b. Middle
c. Upper
d. Clerical
Ans: c

25. In Marinella's *Nobility of Women* (Reading 3.10) she points to the errors of which thinker as the basis for misogyny:
a. Pico
b. Plato
c. Aquinas
d. Aristotle
Ans: d

26. Marinella claims that men dress up like soldiers and "play the daredevil" (page 42) in order to
    a. impress women.
    b. intimidate everyone.
    c. earn greater respect.
    d. prepare for actual combat.
    Ans: b

Chapter 17 Renaissance Artists: Disciples of Nature, Masters of Invention

Summary

During the Renaissance, a thriving middle class joined church and court to patronize the arts. The dual emphasis on material wealth and classical culture in Florence and elsewhere in Italy led artists to revive classical themes, such as portraiture and the nude. Donatello, Brunelleschi, Alberti, Botticelli, and other Early Renaissance artists copied the remains of classical art and studied the writings of classical theorists. At the same time, Renaissance artists brought to the study of nature a passion for scientific objectivity. They investigated the mechanics and proportion of the human body and the effects of light on matter, and they devised new techniques (such as linear perspective and oil painting) for reproducing three-dimensionality on a two-dimensional surface. Leonardo da Vinci epitomizes the tradition of the Renaissance artist-scientist, yet he also advanced the High Renaissance search for unity of design, an ideal of proportional balance and harmony that marked the art and architecture of the High Renaissance. In Rome, Michelangelo brought heroic vitality to the sculpture, painting, and architecture; while in Venice, Titian's sensuous nudes advanced the bold use of color in the oil medium. As in the visual arts, Renaissance music, no longer church-dominated, moved in the direction of natural expressiveness. Northern Renaissance composers dominated the musical scene with compositions that emphasized expressive unity of design. As the printing press stimulated musical performances, the madrigal became a popular form of secular entertainment, and instrumental music and dance emerged as independent genres.

Outline	Pronunciation Guide
A. Renaissance art and patronage	**Giorgio Vasari** [JOR jow vah SAH ree]
B. The early Renaissance	**Donatello** [dah nah TEL low]
1. the classical nude	**Pollaiuolo** [pahl leye oo OW low]
2. the classical revival in architecture	**Botticelli** [bah ti CHEL lee]
3. portraiture	*Campanile* [kam pah NEE lay]
4. the artist as scientist	*Palazzo Vecchio* [pah LAT sow VE kee ow]
a. Masaccio	**Palazzo Rucellai** [ROO chel leye]
b. Brunelleschi	**Pazzi** [PAT see]
c. Leonardo	**Santa Croce** [SAHN tah KROW chay]
C. The high renaissance	**Brunelleschi** [broo ne LES kee]
1. painting: Leonardo and Raphael	**Alberti** [al BER tee]
2. architecture: Bramante and Palladio	**Jan van Eyck** [YAHN fan EYEK]
3. Michelangelo and heroic idealism	**Arnolfini** [ahr nowl FEE nee]
4. painting in Venice: Titian	**Verrocchio** [veh ROH kyow]
D. Renaissance music and dance	*condottiere* [kahn da TYEHR ee]
1. Dufay	**Masaccio** [mah SAH chow]
2. Josquin des Prez	**Ghiberti** [gee BER tee]
3. the madrigal	
4. instrumental music	
5. choreography and dance	

	Raphael [RAH feye el]
	Bramante [brah MAHN tay]
	Palladio [pah LAH dee ow]
	Titian [TISH en]
	Dufay [doo FEYE]
	Josquin des Prez
	[zhahs kan day PRAY]

Key Terms: Early and High Renaissance, secular patronage, revival of classical antiquity, empirical study of nature, linear perspective, aerial perspective, microcosm/macrocosm, *condottiere*, word painting, harpsichord, madrigal.

Key Images	
Donatello, *David*	Raphael, *The Alba Madonna*; *The School of*
Masaccio, *The Tribute Money*	*Athens*
Ghiberti, *Gates of Paradise* (Baptistry, Florence)	Michelangelo, *David*; *Pieta*; Sistine chapel
Brunelleschi, Pazzi Chapel	ceiling
van Eyck, *Marriage of Giovanni Arnolfini and*	Bellini, *Procession of the Reliquary*
His Bride; Self Portrait	Bramante, *Tempietto*
Botticelli, *Birth of Venus*	Palladio, *Villa Rotonda*
Verrocchio, Equestrian statue of Colleoni	Titian, *Venus of Urbino*
da Vinci, *Mona Lisa; Last Supper*	Alberti, Santa Maria Novella, Florence

Study Questions

Factual
1. Cite specific examples of Renaissance art that drew directly on classical themes and subjects.
2. What devices did Renaissance artists use to make their paintings more lifelike?
3. What classical subjects did Renaissance artists favor in their artworks?
4. Why did Leonardo conclude that painting was superior to poetry (Reading 3.12)?
5. How does Leonardo distinguish Judas from the rest of the apostles in the *Last Supper*?
6. What is the theme of Raphael's *School of Athens*? What figures appear in the painting? Why are they there?
7. How did the printing press affect Renaissance music and musical performance?
8. What were the basic characteristics of Josquin des Prez's music?
9. Name and describe five Renaissance musical instruments.
10. What new developments occurred in the area of dance during the age of the Renaissance?

Challenge
1. How, in his architecture, did Alberti unite the classical and Christian traditions?
2. "Almost all the art *before* the Renaissance was created by people for whom the *notion of art* did not exist." Discuss this assertion, offering examples of the new self-consciousness and individualism of Renaissance artists.
3. Renaissance artists shared the ancient Roman artist's view of art as illusion. In what ways did Renaissance artists outreach their ancient predecessors in creating works of art that gave the illusion

of reality? By what techniques were they assisted?

4. Leonardo da Vinci has been described as the first scientific illustrator. Comment and give specific examples.

5. The clearest dependence on classical tradition occurred in Renaissance architecture. Defend or refute this statement by citing specific examples in the illustrations for this chapter.

6. In what way was the art of Jan van Eyck different from that of the Florentines? In what way did Titian's style differ from that of most Florentines?

7. What changes do you detect in the music of the Renaissance (Music Listening Selections I–15 to I–18)? With what kinds of modern music would you compare the madrigal?

8. Research the symbolism of Botticelli's Venus in *Birth of Venus*. Is there general agreement on the meaning of the painting?

9. Discuss or debate the Renaissance belief that harmoniously proportioned buildings produce ideal citizens.

10. Research the figures depicted in Raphael's *The School of Athens,* then speculate on the painter's treatment of them. For example, Diogenes is sprawled on the stairs at Aristotle's lower left. What might Raphael be suggesting by placing him there and in such a pose?

11. Discuss the changing role of artists and their patrons between the Middle Ages and the High Renaissance.

Strategies for Discussion/Lecture

1. Using slides or the illustrations in the chapter, lead a class discussion that focuses on the claim that is made in the title of this chapter. To what extent were Renaissance artists "disciples of nature," that is, people who tried to understand and recreate the appearance of the real world? To what extent were they "inventors" of a new visual style? What is this style and how does it differ from the images depicted, for instance, in Chapter 15?

2. Thematic unity for a slide lecture might be provided by drawing on the key concepts: humanism, individualism, and empiricism. The popularity of portraiture in this era, for instance, can be shown as another form of self-conscious individualism; Verrocchio's *Colleoni* epitomizes the spirit of *terribilità*; Pollaiuolo, van Eyck, and Leonardo are avid empiricists, etc. As slides are shown, students may be asked to identify key concepts in the artworks. In using these concepts, the lecturer is able to draw on the basic ideas and themes already discussed in Chapter 16.

3. The Early and High Renaissance period tendencies in art might focus on a lecture/discussion of the two Davids (Donatello, Figure 17.1 and Michelangelo, Figure 17.35). It can be particularly effective if students are asked to read the account of David's character and exploits in 1 Samuel, 16–17. What moment does each sculptor choose to depict from the biblical narrative?

4. Those stressing continuity with Roman antiquity can use Alberti's Palazzo Rucellai (Figure 17.11) to recall the principle of superimposition of orders (recalling the Colosseum, Fiero, Chapter 6), which will also carry forward to seventeenth- and eighteenth-century facades. The different requirements of church and secular buildings are contrasted in Alberti's Santa Maria Novella (Figure 17.12).

5. Fiero, Figure 17.19. Single-point perspective typically wins approval from beginners in art appreciation, and in comparison, Giotto and earlier painters may be judged "primitive." Discussion should follow on the subject of the image (or the viewer) in space: Renaissance artists attempted to locate figures accurately in space and to scale, and did so by means of a highly artificial and false representation of the way we actually see. How does the camera accommodate background and foreground imagery? Any success here will ease your students' transition to the cubists (in Fiero Book 6), who reject the artificiality of the perspective technique.

Chapter 17 Audiovisuals

Video/CD-ROM Sources

APOCALYPSE: THE REINVENTION OF CHRISTIAN ART
In the years preceding the Lutheran movement, a sharp evolutionary divergence occurred between the art of northern and southern Europe. In this program, hosted by Andrew Graham-Dixon, Michelangelo's controversial painting on the ceiling of the Sistine Chapel, which pushed the limits of Christian art, and Raphael's deeply humanistic *School of Athens* are contrasted with Matthias Grünewald's disturbing *Crucifixion* and other works of the Northern Renaissance. The works of Donato Bramante, Pieter Brueghel the Elder, Albrecht Dürer, and Luca Signorelli are featured as well. A BBC Production. 60 min., color **FFH**

BOTTICELLI—ON CD-ROM The artistic universe of Sandro Botticelli is explored in this marvelously interactive CD-ROM. Available for Windows only. **FFH**

CIVILIZATION: The Hero as Artist 52 min., color **TLF**

THE HIGH RENAISSANCE: Rome and Florence—The Artist as Genius, Art of The Western World Series 30 min., color **CPB**

I, LEONARDO DA VINCI 52 min., color **MGHF**

JAN VAN EYCK
The Virgin of Chancellor Rolin is analyzed as a complex painting, difficult to decipher. 32 min. **FFH**

JOURNEY OF THE MAGUS: Artists and Patrons in Renaissance Italy   FFH

LEONARDO DA VINCI This program examines ten elements in da Vinci's *The Virgin, the Infant Jesus, and Saint Anne* and refers to the first sketches of this painting to explore its hidden meanings. 30 min. **FFH**

LEONARDO DA VINCI—ON CD-ROM
All of the master's paintings plus a large selection of his drawings and reference works for careful study. Available for Windows only. **FFH**

LIFE AND WORKS OF MICHELANGELO, THE
His timeless genius adorns palaces and museums of his native Italy. Enjoy a detailed view of the life of Michelangelo, from his childhood to his final architectural achievements in Rome. His sculptures and paintings, such as the Pieta, his David statue, the tomb of Pope Julius II, and the Sistine Chapel frescoes, are a feast for the eyes. 60 min. on 2 tapes **PBS**

THE MEDICI—ON CD-ROM
A wealth of information on the art collections, court life, and business and social activities of the most influential family of Renaissance Florence. Recommended: CD-ROM User **FFH**

MICHELANGELO (1964) **EBBC**

MICHELANGELO—ON CD-ROM
This interactive masterpiece takes a close look at the work and life of one of the most significant artists in history **FFH**

MICHELANGELO: THE LAST GIANT 68 min., color **MGHF**

MUSIC AND ART: Italy and Music and the Court: The German Court of Maximillian I, Music and The Renaissance Series 30 min. each, B&W **IU**

MYSTERY OF THE MARRIAGE: JAN VAN EYCK'S *THE ARNOLFINI MARRIAGE* **FFH**

OUT OF DARKNESS, MAN AND MUSIC Series 53 min., color **FFH**

THE PURE RADIANCE OF THE PAST: The Revival of Ancient Architecture **FFH**

RAPHAEL: AN ARTIST FOR THE VATICAN—ON CD-ROM This virtual tour of the Stanze and Loggia, the Sala dei Chiaroscuri, and the Chapel of Nicholas V showcases their magnificent frescoes and reveals the world of the Renaissance as seen through the eyes of Raphael. Available for Windows only. **FFH**

RENAISSANCE AND RESURRECTION (1978) **CRM**

THE RENAISSANCE, Music in Time Series 60 min., color **FFH**

THE RENAISSANCE OF FLORENCE—on CD-ROM
A virtual journey through Renaissance Florence. **FFH**

RIDDLE OF THE DOME: FLORENCE CATHEDRAL AND FILIPPO BRUNELLESCHI **FFH**

Music Resources

The Age of Humanism (1540–1630), New Oxford History of Music, Educational Record Sales, 157 Chambers Street, New York, NY 10007.
Ceremonial Music of the Renaissance, Das alte Werk, SWAT 9524–B.
Fifteenth-Century Netherlands Masters, Decca DL 79413.
Guillaume Dufay, *Hymns (with Introductory Gregorian Chants from the Cambrai antiphonal)*, Schola Hungarica, Hungaroton HCD–12951.
Medieval English Music (from the fourteenth and fifteenth centuries), Hilliard (Vocal Ensemble), Harmonia Mundi HMA–190.1153.
Medieval and Renaissance Sounds, 6 volumes, Desto, 47183, 47184, 47190, 47192, 47200, 47201 cassettes.
Music of Shakespeare's Time, Nonesuch HG–73010.

Web Resources

Botticelli—http://www.ibiblio.org/wm/paint/auth/botticelli/

Botticelli—http://www.artchive.com/artchive/B/botticelli.html

da Vinci's sketches and artwork—http://library.thinkquest.org/3044/

da Vinci's most famous artwork—http://www.mcs.csuhayward.edu/~malek/Vinci.html

The *Mona Lisa*—http://www.pbs.org/treasuresoftheworld/a_nav/mona_nav/main_monafrm.html

The *Mona Lisa*—http://artchive.com/artchive/L/leonardo/monalisa_text.jpeg.html

Biographical information about Michelangelo—http://www.michelangelo.com/buon/bio-index2.html

Biographical information about Michelangelo—http://hometown.aol.com/dtrofatter/michel.htm

Biographical information about Michelangelo—http://www.ibiblio.org/wm/paint/auth/michelangelo/

Biographical information about Michelangelo—http://archive.com/artchive/M/michelangelo.html

Pope Julius II and Michelangelo—http://ourworld.compuserve.com/homepages/OLDNEWS/sistine.htm

The Sistine Chapel—http://www.kfki.hu/~arthp/tours/sistina/indedx.html

The Sistine Chapel—http://www.christusrex.org/wwwl/sistine/40-Judge.html

The Sistine Chapel—http://www.science.wayne.edu/~mcogan/Humanities/Sistine/index.html

Michelangelo's works at Oxford University's Ashmolean Museum—
    http://www.ashmol.ox.ac.uk/ash/departments/

Jan van Eyck's *Giovanni Arnolfini and his Bride*—
    http://artchive.com/artchive/V/van_eyck/arnlfini_text.jpg.html

Renaissance music links—http://classicalmus.hispeed.com/rena.html

Art of the High Renaissance—http://www.artcyclopedia.com/history/high-renaissance.html

Biography of Raphael—http://www.artchive.com/artchive/R/raphael.html

Raphael's more familiar paintings—http://www.mcs.csuhayward.edu/~malek/Raphael.html

Raphael's *School of Athens*—www.ge-dip.etat-ge.ch/athena/raphael/raf_ath4.html

McGraw-Hill Resources

Music Listening Selection: CD I
    I–17 Dufay, "Kyrie I"
    I–18 di Lasso, *"Matona Mia Cara"*
    I–19 Morley, "My Bonnie Lass She Smileth"
    I–20 Des Prez, "Tulerant Dominum Meum"

Sample Test Questions for Chapter 17

Select the letter of the choice that BEST answers the question:

1. Renaissance art included all but which of the following characteristics?
   a. naturalistic depiction of the world
   b. renewed interest in classical themes and styles
   c. quest for an underlying unity of design
   d. glorification of the feudal order
   Ans: d

2. Neoplatonist views held that
   a. objects of physical beauty moved the soul to desire union with God.
   b. artists should possess the same privileges as philosopher-kings.
   c. art should be based on classical myths.
   d. art should be subsidized by the state.
   Ans: a

3. In his construction of the Pazzi Chapel, Brunelleschi was among the first Renaissance architects to employ
   a. flying buttresses.
   b. a hexagonally organized floor plan.
   c. proportional ratios.
   d. the groined vault.
   Ans: c

4. The artistic equivalent of the literary biography and autobiography was the
   a. portrait.
   b. gold coin.
   c. still life.
   d. cartoon.
   Ans: a

5. Brunelleschi defined the laws of _____ as a tool for creating the appearance of two- and three-dimensional space.
   a. color
   b. perspective
   c. line
   d. geometric fusion
   Ans: b

6. Leonardo da Vinci is viewed as a harbinger of the scientific revolution primarily because of his
   a. many mechanical inventions.
   b. effort to find the rules of nature through observation.
   c. reliance on abstract speculation.
   d. accurate illustrations of human anatomy.
   Ans: b

7. Michelangelo's Sistine Chapel paintings depict the
   a. crucifixion of Christ.
   b. creation and fall of humans.
   c. Apocalypse.
   d. Last Supper.
   Ans: b

8. The many-faceted genius who designed the dome of Saint Peter's cathedral was
   a. Brunelleschi.
   b. Alberti.
   c. Michelangelo.
   d. da Vinci.
   Ans: c

9. Renaissance musicians Josquin des Prez and Dufay enhanced musical tradition by developing
   a. polyphonic compositions for the lute.
   b. homophony and five-tone intervals.
   c. complex harmonies and expressive polyphony.
   d. instrumental music for the spinet.
   Ans: c

10. In his *Last Supper,* da Vinci depicted the moment when Jesus promised his disciples eternal life.
    Ans: F

11. In music as well as in the visual arts, Italian artists made more innovations than their Northern European counterparts.
    Ans: F

Answer the following with a word or phrase.

12. _____ is defined as the dependence on direct observation of the natural world.
    Ans: Empiricism

13. The master portraitist of the High Renaissance whose depictions of the Madonna and Child were frequently theatrical and idealized was _____.
    Ans: Raphael

14. The multi-talented artist who created the marble statue of David, the symbol of Florence's defiance and determination, was _____.
    Ans: Michelangelo

15. The Venetian artist known for his painterly use of color is _____.
    Ans: Titian

16. The most popular form of secular music was the _____, an unaccompanied song that focused on a theme of romance or whimsical complaint.
    Ans: madrigal

17. In his sacred music, the Franco-Flemish composer, Guillaume Dufay, sometimes used popular tunes.
    Ans: T

18. The composer Josquin des Prez was one of the most effective practitioners of a technique wherein pieces of melody are repeated quickly in various voices, the one overlapping the next, a procedure known as
    a. counterpoint.
    b. polyphony.
    c. word painting.
    d. imitation.
    Ans: d

19. In the Renaissance, the polyphonic nonsacred vocal genre that was the equivalent of the motet in church music was called the
    a. *cantus firmus.*
    b. madrigal.
    c. spinet.
    d. saltarello.
    Ans: b

20. On the whole, the Renaissance saw the emergence of the first professionals in music and dance and the decline of the amateur.
    Ans: F

Chapter **18** **Africa, the Americas, and Cross-Cultural Encounter**

Summary

Beginning in the fifteenth century, as European nation-states pursued programs of expansion and exploration, the continents of Asia (dominated by Europe), Africa, and the Americas increasingly came into contact. The civilizations of Africa and the Americas share some startling features that set them apart from those of the early modern West. Tribal organization and an animistic view of nature characterized the diverse cultures that flourished in Africa and the pre-Columbian Americas. The literature, music, and art of the kingdoms of West Africa reflect the communal and spiritual nature of African society. The largely oral traditions of music and poetry have powerfully influenced the modern West. Among the pre-contact Native American peoples, only the Maya left a system of writing; however, the genius of the Maya, Aztec, and Inca civilizations is still visible in the ruins of their great cities. The once-flourishing Native American tribes found throughout the Americas left ritual art forms that testify to a holistic and deeply spiritual worldview. The Euro-African/Euro-American encounters of the sixteenth century were marked by troubled patterns of intercourse and exchange that have affected the destinies of modern societies in three continents.

Outline	Pronunciation Guide

A. Cross-cultural encounter
     1.   prior to 1450
     2.   after 1450: expansion; technology; navigational aids
B. Africa's cultural heritage
     1.   general features
     2.   West African kingdoms
     3.   African literature
          a.   epic
          b.   myth
          c.   poetry
     4.   African music and dance
     5.   African sculpture
     6.   Cross-cultural encounter
          a.   Muslims in Africa
          b.   Europeans in Africa
B. The Americas:
     1.   general features
     2.   Native American arts
     3.   Maya civilization
     4.   Aztec and Incan empires
     5.   cross-cultural encounter
	Sudan [soo DAN]
	Ghana [GAH na]
	Mali [MAH lee]
	Benin [be NEEN]
	Bambara [bahm BAH rah]
	Sundiata [sun dee AH tah]
	kachina [kah CHEE nah]
	Quetzalcoatl [ket sahl kow AH tel]
	Tlaloc [TLA lahk]
	Coatlique [koh aht lee KAY]
	Uxmal [ush MAHL]
	Chichén Itzá [CHI chen IT sah]
	Tenochtitlán [te nawch tee TLAN]
	Yaxchilan [yahsh chee LAHN]
	Yucatan [yoo kah TAN]
	conquistadores
	     [kahn kees tah DOW rays]
	Cortés [kor TEHZ]

Key Terms: animism, Sudan, trans-Saharan trade, oral literature, fetish, art of masks, Mesoamerica, Mayan ceremonial centers, Inca, Mali, *griot,* scarification, *kachina,* Navaho Night Chant, *conquistadores.*

Key Images	
Oba of Benin	Zuni Warrior Kachina, Hopi
Gabon-Bakota reliquary	Maya Temples, Chichén-Itza, Yucatan
Congo Nail Fetish	Maya Ceremonial Lintel and ceramics
Edo head of a Queen Mother	Inka tunic
Antelope Headpiece, Bambara Tribe	Aztec manuscripts; sun Disc (Calendar Stone)

Study Questions

Factual

1. What factors—political, economic, and technological—contributed to increased global travel in the age of the Renaissance?
2. Describe the kinship system characteristic of African life. How does your relationship to your kin differ from the African system?
3. What aspects of African life did the Muslim, Ibn Battuta, find most congenial? Most unusual?
4. What qualities in African expression are distinctively tribal and communal?
5. According to the speaker in *Sundiata,* which is more valuable, speaking or writing? Why does the *griot* take pride in his role?
6. Identify specific examples of metaphor and simile in the African poems included in Readings 3.20 and 3.21.
7. In the Cheyenne tale, "How the Sun Came" (Reading 3.19), is the emphasis on the origin of the physical universe or on human relationships?
8. Why was blood such an important fluid among the early peoples of the Americas?
9. What were the unique features of Maya culture? Which of these were preserved by the Aztecs?
10. What similarities can be found between African art and the art of the Americas?

Challenge

1. Apply the concept of *animism* to the arts of Africa.
2. Discuss and give examples of the ways in which the arts of ancient African and Native American peoples reflect a holistic view of nature. Are there analogies here with other civilizations, such as those of Asia?
3. African masks and fetishes and Native American sculpture are now to be seen in museums of fine art. What would you say is missing when we remove these objects from their cultural context? Is their value changed by being placed and looked at in museums?
4. In Reading 3.14, *Sundiata,* the *griot* says, "The world is old, but the future springs from the past." Apply this observation to an overview of the materials you have covered from Chapters 1 to 18. Describe the patterns of continuity. Does the future, indeed, "spring from the past"?
5. In what ways does abstraction give power to African sculpture? Use illustrations in the text to cite specific examples. Can any similarities be found between African art and Native American totems?
6. Research and compare the myths of origin among African and Native American tribes. (Both are readily available in English translation.)

7. What are the main characteristics of African music as reflected in the Music Listening Selections I–21 and 22? Are any of these features apparent in today's popular music, such as Afro-pop, rap, etc.?

8. What similarities can you detect between the Navaho Night Chant (Music Listening Selection I–23), the Gregorian Chant (I–2), and the Buddhist Chant (I–3)?

9. Speculate on why so little of African sculpture is centered on the naturalistic representation of human individuals.

10. The introduction to *The Humanistic Tradition* began with a story from the land of the Pygmies (Fiero, Reading 1, "The Story of Rock Picture Research"). Read *The Forest People* by Colin M. Turnbull (N.Y. Simon and Schuster, 1962) for an update on Pygmy life. Do you find similarities with the earlier account by Leo Frobenius?

11. Fiero, Figure 18.16, Cliff Palace, Mesa Verde, Colorado. Find out the function of the circular structures. What do they tell us about Anasazi social life?

12. What aspects of Aztec life and culture most impressed Cortes? Why so?

13. Research the life and personality of Las Casas; why was he called the "Apostle to the Indians"?

Strategies for Discussion/Lecture

1. Cultural relativity is a natural theme for this chapter, which introduces cultures practically destroyed by the those cultures discussed in Chapters 15–18. The lecturer might focus on the clash between worldviews, social organization, religion, etc. of African and Native American people and their European contemporaries (Factual questions 1, 5). How or in what manner might a Florentine or a native of Madrid or Paris regard the art and culture of the Mali folk, the Maya, the Aztecs? In turn, how might an individual from any of these cultures look upon European paintings and sculptures, such as Michelangelo's *David*? From here, the lecturer might move to a consideration of the Muslim view of African culture (Reading 3.17).

2. For the lecturer wanting preparation on Mexico, Michael D. Coe, *Mexico* (New York, Thames and Hudson, 3rd edition, 1984) is essential. This culture, geographically closest to us, tends to be far less well understood than the civilizations of medieval Europe or ancient Greece. A modest beginning at correcting this imbalance would be to concentrate on some of ancient Mesoamerica's achievements, beginning with its cuisine, and including its pyramid building.

3. The social class of the Portuguese soldier shown in Figure 18.11 is worth stressing, since the vanguard of colonization in both Africa and Mesoamerica consisted of military men accompanied by priests. Would such social classes be likely to take notice of the astronomy, mathematics, horticulture, and medicine developed over millennia by the "savages" of these lands? Is it surprising that Spanish missionaries destroyed the literature of the Maya, when they were fully engaged in burning the books of "enemies of the faith" of their own race and culture?

Chapter 18 Audiovisuals

Video/CD-ROM Sources

ARTIST UNKNOWN: THE SEARCH FOR AFRICAN HISTORY

Lonnie James, a young British man of African descent, journeys to the war-shattered central African kingdom of Benin to discover the origins of a carved mask purchased in London. A BBC Production. 50 min. **FFH**

1492: COLUMBUS AND THE AGE OF DISCOVERY
Eight-part series prepared for Columbian Bicentennial (1992) 50 min. ea., color **CPB**

THE AFRICANS
Nine one-hour series filmed in location in 16 African countries (1985) color **CPB**

AFRICA'S GIFT: Ivory Coast, Senufo (1973) 35 min., color **WEBC**

THE ANCIENT AFRICANS 27 min., color **IM**

ATLANTIC SLAVE TRADE (1974) 17 min., color **UEUWISC**

THE BAMBARA OF MALI (1973) 10 min., color **UMNAV**

BENIN KINGSHIP RITUALS (1962) 40 min., color **IUASP**

CONQUISTADORS: WITH MICHAEL WOOD
The conquest of the New World in less than 50 years is one of history's most profound events—and remains one of its greatest adventures. British historian Michael Wood captures the bravery, endurance, greed, cruelty and suffering involved in these 16th-century explorations. Wood turns his attention to the Americas to follow four amazing tales: Cortes' dramatic conquest of the Aztecs in Mexico; Pizarro's daring overthrow of the Incas in Peru; Orellana's obsessive search for El Dorado and discovery of the Amazon; and Cabeza de Vaca's pivotal crossing of the North American continent. 240 minutes on 2 tapes **PSB**

THE DOGON MMA

THE DOGON OF MALI: Cliff Dwellers of Bandiagara, Mali (Dogon) (1973) 10 min., color **UMNAV**

ODYSSEY: INCAS, THE
From the breathtaking heights of Machu Picchu to jungle valleys and desert floors, this program travels the spectacular world of the ancient Incas. Visit an empire that stretched across some of the globe's highest peaks and covered 350,000 square miles. It is an amazing story, unveiling how the Incas—without the wheel—conquered this vast, unforgiving land and created one of the most impressive civilizations the world has ever known. 60 minutes on 1 tape **PBS**

THE FALL OF THE MAYA
How the story is still being unraveled of the rise and fall of the Maya. (23 min.) Recommended: School Library Journal, Video Rating Guide for Libraries **FFH**

THE MAYA
Visit the city-temple of Palenque in Mexico where the bones of long-dead children and mysterious inscriptions are valuable clues to the secrets of the ancient Mayans. 50 min. **AE**

THE PRIEST AND THE NGNANGA
Cameroon—treats the world of the traditional African healer. 29 min., color **FFH**

WONDERS OF THE AFRICAN WORLD WITH HENRY LOUIS GATES JR.
Set out on an expedition with one of the country's most revered intellectuals, Henry Louis Gates, Jr., as he traces the roots of twentieth-century Africa. Travelling by land and sea, he's on a mission to locate legendary towns and palace ruins unearthing the often disturbing truths in modern cities and suburbs. Into the Sudanese desert he begins at the pyramids of Giza and travels through Aswan, Jebel Barkal and Kerma to dig up the dirt on 4,000-year-old remains. Through Kenya and Tanzania he goes, stopping to explore the Swahili culture, finding descendants from medieval Persian mariners along the way. Through Ghana and Benin he unravels the truth behind slave trade. While in search of the lost Ark of the Covenant, Gates discovers mummified bodies of Ethiopia's kings. That's not all! On a quest to fulfill his childhood dream to find Timbuktu's books, he finds more surprises. Visit with some of the most fascinating people, tour magnificent ancient cities and gain powerful new perspectives on some of the most colorful cultures rich in history. Nominated for NAACP Image Award: Outstanding News, Talk or Information Special and Outstanding Literary Work, nonfiction. 360 minutes on 3 tapes **PBS**

THE WORLDS: Out of the Past 60 min., color **CPB**

Music Resources

Africa: Ancient Ceremonies, Dance Music, and Songs of Ghana, recorded by Stephen Jay, New York: Nonesuch Records, 1979.
Anthology of Music of Black Africa, Everest 3254/3, recorded with sponsorship of l'Institut Français d'Afrique Noire and the Musée de l'Homme, in conjunction with UNESCO; may be ordered from Everest Records, 10920. Wilshire Blvd, Suite 410, Los Angeles, California 90024.
Indian Music of the Pacific Northwest Coast, Folkways, 4523, two-cassette set.
The Music of Africa, 1971, one LP disc, traditional and modern music, brief descriptions of each selection, AH.
Music of the Sioux and Navajo, Folkways, 4401 cassette.
Fiero, Music Listening Selections CD-I
    I-21 The Music of Africa—Senegal: Greetings from Podor
    I-22 The Music of Africa—Angola: Gangele Song
    I-23 Music of the Navajo—The Night Chant

Web Resources

Information about Christopher Columbus—http://lcweb.loc.gov/exhibits/1492/intro.html

The ancient kingdom of Ghana—http://www.ecfs.org/projects/FLS/5N/Nsghana/home.html

The Guggenheim Museum's online exhibit, *Africa: The Art of a Continent*—
    http://www.artnetweb.com/guggenheim/africa/index.html

East Africa—http://www.yale.edu/swahili/

Resources related to Africa—http://www-sul.stanford.edu/depts/ssrg/africa/history.html

Resources related to African dance—http://www.artslynx.org/dance/afro.html

Resources related to African myths—http://www.artsmia.org/mythology/african.html#top

Information about Mayan history and culture—http://mars.cropsoil.uga.edu/trop-ag/the-maya.htm

The Inca Trail and Machu Picchu—http://www.raingod.com/angus/gallery/photos/south-america/peru/incatrail.html

Resources related to native peoples of the Americas—http://www.mayalords.org/

Sample Test Questions for Chapter 18

Select the letter of the choice that BEST answers the question:

1. Which one of the following did NOT constitute a major part of the trade in commodities across the Sahara in the time of the early state of Ghana.
   a. slaves
   b. gold
   c. wood
   d. salt
   Ans: c

2. The author of *Sundiata: an Epic of Old Mali,* tells us that the functions of the poet typically include all BUT one of the following.
   a. entertainment
   b. keeping historical records
   c. providing examples of good past behavior to the current king
   d. keeping a record of past promises made
   Ans: a

3. Djeli Mamoudou Kouyaté, the author of *Sundiata,* learned the art of the poet, or *griot,* from
   a. his father.
   b. training by the guild of professional *griots.*
   c. books on the art of the *griot.*
   d. village songs and stories.
   Ans: a

4. One of the common elements among the diverse African society was
   a. monotheistic worship of a single god.
   b. a kinship system emphasizing communal well-being.
   c. a rejection of ritual.
   d. a rigid caste system like that of India.
   Ans: b

5. Many African religious beliefs included all BUT which of the following?
   a. Natural objects carried spiritual power.
   b. Ancestral spirits acted as guides to the living.
   c. Ritual was less important than veneration of the priests.
   d. Honoring tribal spirits was essential for security.
   Ans: c

6. Many of the West African kingdoms emerged in the geographical region known as the
   a. Sahara.
   b. Great Rift.
   c. Congo.
   d. Sudan.
   Ans: d

7. The earliest West African kingdom was that of
   a. Ghana.
   b. Songhai.
   c. Timbuktu.
   d. Mali.
   Ans: d

8. African poetry featured themes of
   a. social rank and social conflict.
   b. the importance of the elderly.
   c. the sufferings of hell.
   d. praise for heroes and rulers.
   Ans: d

9. Examples of the African myths about death reflect a belief in
   a. purgatory and the life to come.
   b. a stern and repressive deity.
   c. an intimate relationship between gods and humans.
   d. Original Sin.
   Ans: c

10. The dominant element in African music is
    a. rhythm.
    b. harmony.
    c. melody.
    d. dissonance.
    Ans: a

11. The only known pre-Columbians to produce a written language were the
    a. Cheyenne.
    b. Maya.
    c. Tinglit.
    d. Hottentots.
    Ans: b

12. In the five centuries before contact with Europeans, the most illustrious Native American civilizations arose in
    a. the region near the Bering Strait.
    b. the area known as Meso-Mesoamerica.
    c. Peru.
    d. Florida.
    Ans: b

13. In Cortés' letter to the king (Reading 3.20), the Aztec practice he most disapproved of is
    a. their treatment of women.
    b. human sacrifice.
    c. their restricted diet.
    d. the shabby housing of the poor.
    Ans: b

14. The largest Native American states were theocratic, which means a
    a. fusion of religious and political power.
    b. rigid social structure.
    c. totalitarian government.
    d. highly militaristic monarchy.
    Ans: a

15. The Mayan civilization is known for all of the following EXCEPT
    a. terraced temples.
    b. its calendar.
    c. its legacy of thousands of books.
    d. the belief in the sanctity of blood.
    Ans: c

16. Among the functions of Mayan ceremonial centers was experimental observation in the field of
    a. chemistry.
    b. biology.
    c. astronomy.
    d. weather prediction.
    Ans: c

17. Central to the religious ritual of the largest Native American states was
    a. human sacrifice.
    b. worship of the moon.
    c. the priesthood of all citizens.
    d. large iron masks of the gods.
    Ans: a

18. Native American myths and folktales feature themes similar to those of
    a. the Hebrew Bible.
    b. Africa.
    c. Europe.
    d. Scandinavia.
    Ans: b

19. The phrase that BEST describes Cortés' reaction to the city of Tenochtitlán is:
    a. He finds little to like in the city.
    b. He finds the city poorly designed from a strategic perspective.
    c. He finds their religion attractive, if somewhat "barbarian."
    d. He is impressed by Aztec material achievements but disapproves of their religious practices.
    Ans: d

20. The first European nation to engage in the slave trade was
    a. Holland.
    b. England.
    c. France.
    d. Portugal.
    Ans: d

21. Unlike the works of Greek poets, *Sundiata* was written to exalt individualism and the common person.
    Ans: F

22. One striking characteristic of the selections of African poetry (Reading 3.16) is their lack of any reference to violence and death.
    Ans: F

23. The dominant belief in African culture (prior to the coming of Islam and Christianity), which held that spirits inhabited all things in nature is called _____.
    Ans: animism

24. Fiero, Figure 18.2, Prostrate Muslims. From what you know about Islam, the posture of these worshipers might best be described as
    a. submission to the head priest.
    b. submission to God in fellowship.
    c. the equivalent of facing the Vatican, in prayer.
    d. homage paid to the chieftain.
    Ans: b

25. Body painting and tattooing. The anthropologist, Claude Levi-Strauss (*Tristes tropiques*) discovered that Brazilian aboriginals were puzzled that he had no tattoos: "Without tattoos, how can you distinguish the humans from the animals?" This observation can be applied to some illustrations in Chapter 18, namely _____.
    Ans: Figures 18.3, 18.7, 18.10, 19.21

26. Fiero, Reading 3.14, from *Sundiata, An Epic of Old Mali*. The griot, Djeli Mamoudou Kouyaté, is very explicit about the extent of his knowledge and its accuracy. The reading as a whole indicates that he knows all there is to know for someone in his position, but that he will not tell all.
    Ans: T

27. Fiero, Reading 3.14, from *Sundiata, An Epic of Old Mali*. The griot, Djeli Mamoudou Kouyaté, shares with Socrates (*Phaedrus*) the conviction that the invention of writing ruins people's memory.
    Ans: T

28. During his stay in Mali, the Muslim traveller, Ibn Battuta, appears to approve of the way the residents encourage young people to memorize the Quran.
    Ans: F

29. What most surprises the Muslim traveler, Ibn Battuta, about the men of Mali is their
    a. arrogance in the presence of women.
    b. laxity about daily religious prayers.
    c. drunkenness.
    d. lack of jealousy.
    Ans: d

Summary

In Northern Europe, the years 1500 to 1650 were marred by political, religious, and social upheaval. Northern humanists, whose critical study of early Christian manuscripts awakened them to the original ideals and practices of the faith, clamored for reform. The key figure in the Protestant Reformation, Martin Luther, contended that Scripture was the sole basis for religious belief and that faith (rather than good works) was the key to salvation. The art and music of the Northern Renaissance reflect the influence of Christian humanism as it responded to the spirit of reform, as well as new forms of patronage and the wonders of print technology. In literature, the satires of Erasmus, More, and Cervantes attacked existing institutions and values. Woodcuts and engravings made popular images cheaply and readily available. Human nature and human destiny are central to the prints of Dürer, the paintings of Brueghel and Bosch, and the essays of Montaigne; but in the tragedies of William Shakespeare, these themes take on unsurpassed monumentality and profundity.

Outline	Pronunciation Guide

A. Historical context
  1. the impact of technology
  2. Christian humanism and the Northern Renaissance
    a. *devotio moderna*
    b. Erasmus
B Luther and the Protestant Reformation
  1. Luther's program of reform
  2. impact of Luther's protests
  3. music and the Reformation
C. Northern Renaissance Art
  1. Dürer
  2. Grünewald
  3. Bosch
  4. Brueghel
D. Northern Renaissance literature
  1. Erasmus and More
  2. Cervantes and Rabelais
  3. Montaigne
  4. Shakespeare
    a. sonnets
    b. *Othello* and *Hamlet*
	devotio moderna [dee VOW tee oh mow DER nah]
	ars moriendi [AHRS moh ree EN dee]
	imitatio Christi [im ee TAH tee oh KRIS tee]
	Wittenberg [VIT en berk]
	Cranach [KRAH nahk]
	intaglio [in TAHG lyow]
	Dürer [DU rer]
	Grünewald [GROO ne vahld]
	triptych [TRIP tik]
	Bosch [BAHSH]
	Hans Baldung Grien [HAHNTS BAHL dung GREEN]
	Brueghel [BROY gul]
	Holbein [HOWL beyen]
	Don Quijote [don kee HOW tay]
	Sancho Panza [SAHN chow PAHN zah]
	Rocinante [row see NAHN tay]
	Montaigne [mahn TAYN]
	Iago [YAH gow]
	Desdemona [dez de MOW nah]

Key Terms: Christian humanism, *devotio moderna,* lay piety, indulgences, Reformation, Anabaptists, woodcut/engraving, satiric novel and essay, printing press, Shakespearean sonnet, secular drama.

Key Images	
Dürer, *Erasmus of Rotterdam* Dürer, *Knight, Death, and the Devil* Grünewald, *Isenheim Altarpiece*	Bosch, *The Garden of Delights* Brueghel, *Triumph of Death*; *Wedding Dance* Holbein, *Sir Thomas More*

Study Questions

Factual

1. What were Luther's main complaints against the church? What reforms did he seek? What were the results of Luther's protests?
2. What professions does the speaker (Folly) single out in Erasmus' *The Praise of Folly* (Reading 3.22)? Do you agree with her?
3. What political and social ideals are set forth in More's *Utopia?*
4. How do parents in More's *Utopia* (Reading 3.23) train their children to scorn gold and silver?
5. How did the age of exploration and expansion influence More and Montaigne in their writings?
6. Why does Montaigne use classical quotations in his essay *On Cannibals* (Reading 3.25)?
7. What was the significance of the following: the Guttenberg Bible; the Peasant's Revolt; the Battle of the Armada.
8. Define the following terms: quatrain, couplet, blank verse.
9. How does the technique of woodcut differ from engraving?
10. How does the art of Brueghel differ from that of his northern contemporaries, Grünewald, Bosch, etc.?
11. What are the principal characteristics of Hamlet, as reflected in the excerpt in Reading 3.27?
12. What factors contributed to the popularity of Shakespeare's plays in his own time and place?

Challenge

1. Assess the effects of the printing press on Western society of the early modern era.
2. How does the Lutheran chorale express the spirit and the sentiment of the Protestant Reform?
3. In what ways did Northern artists break with the medieval past? In what ways did they perpetuate earlier subjects and styles? How do they differ from Italian Renaissance artists?
4. What are the unique features of Dürer's style? What did he learn from Italian art?
5. Offer a verbal description of Bosch's *The Garden of Earthly Delights.* Why are there so many different interpretations of this triptych?
6. Why in your view was the sixteenth century a time in which satire was revived as a popular genre? When and by whom was the genre formerly used (see Chapter 6)?
7. Don Quijote (Reading 3.24) seems to be powerfully influenced by what he reads in books. Can too much reading make Jack not only dull, but a buffoon?
8. Try to see two film versions of Shakespeare's *Othello*: Othello played by Laurence Olivier and Othello played by William Marshall. Compare the interpretations of the main characters offered in each production. Alternately, do the same with Shakespeare's *Hamlet*, of which numerous film versions exist (see Audiovisuals).
9. How does *Othello* compare as dramatic experience with the plays *Antigone* (Chapter 4) and *Everyman* (Chapter 12)?
10. Montaigne's essay *On Cannibals* depicts the natives of Brazil in a much more favorable light than their French contemporaries, who were engaged in the horrors of religious civil war. Interestingly

enough, Montaigne concludes that Europeans are incapable of seeing virtue and accomplishment in "people who don't wear pants." Do moderns share this bias? To what extent may Montaigne's essays be regarded as satiric?

Strategies for Discussion/Lecture

1. A central theme for this chapter is the "shattering" of the old order. Ask students to find examples of this phenomenon in the chapter. Luther's *Address to the German Nobility* can easily escape notice. Ask students to imagine a document this controversial and confrontational addressed by a local clergyman to the governors of all the states, urging them to call a council for the purpose of deposing the appointed authorities of the organized faiths. The repeated references to usurped authority take on a new significance in context. One might also raise the question of current movements for religious renewal: what does today's religious revivalism have in common with that of the sixteenth century?

2. Prompt students to consider Northern versus Italian Renaissance culture by emphasizing the importance of Christian humanism in the North, a revival of the "classic" aspects of Christianity, rather than of the Greco-Roman ideals. Follow comparing Northern Renaissance art with Italian Renaissance art. For instance, compare Grünewald's *Isenheim Altarpiece* (Figure 19. 9) with any one of a number of Italian crucifixion scenes, for instance, Pietro Perugino's *The Crucifixion with the Virgin, Saint John, Saint Jerome and Saint Mary Magdalene,* National Gallery of Art, Washington. Nearly contemporary with the Grünewald, the Perugino is all serenity and composure and bathed in daylight showing life going on as usual. The comparison also makes a good term-paper project.

3. It is worthwhile to compare the impact of print technology on early modern culture with that of computers and other forms of digital technology on our own. The writings of Marshall McLuhan, especially *Understanding Media* (1964), remain intriguing to students, who generally understand and appreciate his insights.

4. Some will want to concentrate on Shakespeare's *Hamlet* or *Othello* and lecture/discuss in relation to a performance on video. To what extent does the personality of the unique (and flawed) individual unfold in the dramatic art? What devices does Shakespeare employ to win our sympathy for the main figures? How does a staged performance of either play differ from the cinematic versions?

Chapter 19 Audiovisuals

Video/CD-ROM Sources

APOCALYPSE: THE REINVENTION OF CHRISTIAN ART
In the years preceding the Lutheran movement, a sharp evolutionary divergence occurred between the art of northern and southern Europe. In this program, hosted by Andrew Graham-Dixon, Michelangelo's controversial painting on the ceiling of the Sistine Chapel, which pushed the limits of Christian art, and Raphael's deeply humanistic *School of Athens* are contrasted with Matthias Grünewald's disturbing *Crucifixion* and other works of the Northern Renaissance. The works of Donato Bramante, Pieter Brueghel the Elder, Albrecht Dürer, and Luca Signorelli are featured as well. A BBC Production. 60 min., color **FFH**

HIERONYMUS BOSCH
A look at Bosch's work collected by Philip II and housed in the Prado. 30 min. **FFH**

BRUEGHEL THE ELDER: HIS LIFE AND ART

This program presents Brueghel's life and work, from his early landscapes in Italy to the great allegorical works that made him one of the most original and influential painters of the Flemish school. 25 min., color **FFH**

JOHN CALVIN 29 min., color **University of Utah Educational Media Center**

THE CHRISTIANS: Protest and Reform CRM

CIVILISATION—Vol. #06: Protest and Communication (1970)

DIRECTOR: CLARK, SIR KENNETH 53 min., color, sound **PBS**

ALBRECHT DÜRER: IMAGE OF A MASTER

This timeless program examines the life and work of the peerless painter and printmaker, focusing on some of his most important pieces. 20 min. **FFH**

EARLY ENGLISH ALOUD AND ALIVE: THE LANGUAGE OF BEOWULF, CHAUCER, AND SHAKESPEARE

In this program, Dr. Joseph Gallagher brings language to life by reciting examples of Old, Middle, and Early Modern English in their original dialects. Includes subtitles in Modern English, where necessary. 28 min., color **FFH**

MARTIN LUTHER AND THE PROTESTANT REFORMATION 30 min., B&W **TLF**

THE REFORMATION 52 min., color **MCHF**

THE REFORMATION: Age of Revolt 24 min., color **EBEC**

RENAISSANCE: A FRESH LOOK AT THE EVOLUTION OF WESTERN ART

In this dynamic six-part series filmed on location all around Europe, acclaimed art critic Andrew Graham-Dixon promotes a deeper understanding of the Renaissance. **FFH**

TUDOR AND STUART LONDON (1500-1666): COURT AND COMMONS (1991)

DIRECTOR: GREEN, BENNY 20 min., color, sound **FFH**

SHAKESPEARE

For full Shakespeare filmography visit: http://us.imdb.com/M/person-exact?Shakespeare%2C+William

10 THINGS I HATE ABOUT YOU (1999)

(based on *The Taming of the Shrew*)

DIRECTOR: Gil Junger **AZ**

BEHIND THE SCENES: THE TEMPEST

The great adventure of creating a world on a theatre stage comes to life in this program, where viewers witness production of Shakespeare's *The Tempest*. Julie Taymor's inventive use of shadow puppetry and extraordinary masks combines with human actors to create a uniquely theatrical experience. Viewers learn about the many artistic decisions that lead to a finished production. 30 min. 1992 **HTG**

CRITICAL GUIDE TO SHAKESPEARE
A six-part series, filmed on location in Stratford-upon-Avon, from the Emmy Award-winning Cromwell Production team. 30 min. each **FFH**

THE GREAT HAMLETS
In these programs, Trevor Nunn talks with some of the greatest actors of the twentieth century about their interpretations of Hamlet. 55 min. ea. Recommended: Shakespeare Newsletter **FFH**

HAMLET (1996)
DIRECTOR: KENNETH BRANAGH AZ

HAMLET
The melancholy Dane and a rich cast of characters come alive in this multimedia seminar that investigates the text, history, and themes that fuel Shakespeare's immortal tragedy. **FFH**

THE HOW AND WHY OF POISONING OTHELLO IM

THE INTERACTIVE SHAKESPEARE LIBRARY
This series of CD-ROMs provides students with a wide range of powerful tools with which to analyze and interpret six of Shakespeare's greatest works. All CD-ROMs are fully compatible with either Windows or Macintosh. **FFH**

LOVE'S LABOUR'S LOST (2000)
DIRECTOR: KENNETH BRANAGH **AZ**

O (2001)
(based on *Othello*)
DIRECTOR: TIM BLAKE NELSON **AZ**

OTHELLO (complete play) MCHF

OTHELLO
DIRECTOR: ORSON WELLES 92 min., color **AZ**

OTHELLO on CD-ROM FFH

OTHELLO: A Critical Guide FFH

WILLIAM SHAKESPEARE
Featuring delightful dramatized extracts from some of Shakespeare's best-known plays, memorable depictions of life in Elizabethan times, expert commentary, and critical analysis, this program provides a colorful and informative glimpse into the remarkable world of William Shakespeare. 46 min. **FFH**

SHAKESPEARE: A MIRROR TO MAN LCA

SHAKESPEARE AND HIS THEATRE: THE GLOBE FFH
SHAKESPEARE AND HIS THEATRE: THE GENTLE SHAKESPEARE

Shakespeare's life and work, the landmarks associated with his plays, and his major dramatic motifs. 31 min. **FFH**

SHAKESPEARE IN LOVE (1998)
DIRECTOR: JOHN MADDEN **AZ**

THE SHAKESPEARE MYSTERY
The plays of William Shakespeare often dealt with royal intrigue. In fact, his masterpieces offer an "insider's" view of the politics of European courts of his time. But was Shakespeare a political insider? Some scholars doubt Shakespeare's authorship of these works, suggesting that the real bard was Edward De Vere (1551-1604), a poet, courtier, and high-ranking earl in Elizabethan England. Scholars search for clues in Shakespeare's work for his true identity. This unsolved mystery surrounding the greatest author in the English language will shake the viewer to the literary and historic core. (1989) 60 min. **HTG**

SHAKESPEARE'S SONNETS
Fifteen sonnets read by Ben Kingsley, Roger Rees, Claire Bloom, and Jane Lapotaire, then analyzed by a noted critic or writer. 150 min. **FFH**

THE TRAGEDY OF OTHELLO IM

Music Resources

Shakespeare Songs and Consort Music, Deller consort, Harmonia Mundi HMC–202; HMA–190.202 CD.

Web Resources

Sources related to Martin Luther—http://www.icinet.org/pub/resources/text/wittenberg/wittenberg-home.html

Biographical information about Martin Luther—http://www.luther.de/e/index.html

Sir Thomas More—http://www.luminarium.org/renlit/tmore.html

Shakespeare—http://daphne.palomar.edu/shakespeare/

Shakespeare's Globe Theatre—http://www.rdg.ac.uk/globe/home.html

Art of the Northern Renaissance—http://www.artcyclopedia.com/history/northern-renaissance.html

Albrecht Dürer's *St. Michael's Fight against the Dragon*—
http://artchive.com/artchive/D/durer/stmichael.jpg.html

Biographical information and images of Hieronymus Bosch—http://www.3dresarch.com/bosch/

Biographical information and images of Brueghel—
http://www.kfki.hu/~arthp/html/b/bruegel/pieter_e/index.html

Biographical information about Cervantes'—http://www.csdl.tamu.edu/cervantes/english/index.html

Biographical information about Rabelais—http://www.pantagruelion.com/p/rabelais.html

Biographical information and readings of Montaigne—
   http://www.orst.edu/instruct/phl302/philosophers/montaigne.html

McGraw-Hill Resources

Music Listening Selection: CD II
   II–4 *"Ein Feste Burg ist unser Gott"*
Transparencies: MA.6 The Renaissance 1350–1600

Sample Test Questions for Chapter 19

Select the letter of the choice that BEST answers the question:

1.   Luther's salvation doctrine was based principally on the words of
     a.   Jesus.
     b.   Augustine.
     c.   Erasmus.
     d.   Paul.
     Ans: d

2.   NOT associated with the northern European movement known as the "devotio moderna":
     a.   lay piety
     b.   anti-clericalism
     c.   mysticism
     d.   empiricism
     Ans: d

3.   Don Quijote decides to do battle with the "wild giants" for all the following reasons EXCEPT one.
     a.   to get rich
     b.   to serve God
     c.   because he felt driven by destiny
     d.   to serve his king
     Ans: d

4.   Luther posted his Ninety-five Theses on the door of the Cathedral at
     a.   Rome.
     b.   Augsburg.
     c.   Wittenberg.
     d..   Heidelberg.
     Ans: c

5. Don Quijote forbids Sancho to come to his rescue in battle, unless the attackers are "mere rabble, people of low birth." He explains that this is because Sancho is
    a. a serf.
    b. not Spanish.
    c. not Christian.
    d. not a knight.
    Ans: d

6. The Christian humanist movement in Northern Europe focused primarily on
    a. reviving the ideas and practices of the early Christians.
    b. establishing absolute equality of the sexes.
    c. encouraging more devotion among the clerical orders.
    d. recruiting working-class members for the monasteries.
    Ans: a

7. Germans distrusted the Church of Rome because it
    a. refused to recognize the Holy Roman Emperor.
    b. discouraged the sale of indulgences.
    c. operated much like an Italian princely court.
    d. prevented German unification.
    Ans: c

8. Luther asserted that _____ alone, rather than good works, was necessary for an individual's salvation.
    a. prayer
    b. tithing
    c. baptism
    d. faith
    Ans: d

9. Protestant reformers wished to eliminate from Christian practice all BUT which of the following?
    a. monasticism
    b. indulgences
    c. absolute papal authority
    d. a number of the sacraments
    Ans: a

10. In general, Anabaptists rejected
    a. a secular state.
    b. ceremony and ritual.
    c. equality of the sexes.
    d. limitations of baptism.
    Ans: b

11. Driven by the principles of the Reformation, anti-ceremonial Protestants
    a. destroyed art works.
    b. rejected long sermons.
    c. encouraged more papal taxation.
    d. urged the veneration of holy relics.
    Ans: a

12. Bosch's *The Garden of the Earthly Delights*
    a. exalted the intellectual ability of the individual.
    b. included symbolism derived from astrology and alchemy.
    c. preached the joys of the material world.
    d. insisted on the primacy of the clerical orders.
    Ans: b

13. During the sixteenth century, the system of "balance-of-power" politics enabled Europeans to enjoy a period of unprecedented peace.
    Ans: F

14. Predestination is the belief that one's destiny, either to eternal life or to hell, had been determined from the day of one's birth.
    Ans: T

Answer the following with a word or phrase.

15. The European credited with the invention of the printing press was _____.
    Ans: Gutenberg

16. _____, frequently called the "Prince of Humanists," skillfully made use of the printing press in his attacks on church corruption.
    Ans: Erasmus

17. An Augustinian monk and author of the *Ninety-Five Theses,* _____, sought to reform Catholicism rather than establish a new religion.
    Ans: Martin Luther

18. The creator of extraordinary engravings and woodcuts, _____ displayed a deep piety and a commitment to religious reform.
    Ans: Dürer

19. The Flemish artist, _____, warned of the corruption of the material world and the punishments awaiting sinners in his triptych, *The Garden of the Earthly Delights.*
    Ans: Bosch

20. Inspired by Plato, _____ wrote the *Utopia,* which described an ideal society based on cooperation and communal living rather than materialism and competition.
    Ans: More

21. Fiero, Reading 3.22, from Erasmus' *The Praise of Folly*. The passage is explicit about the mass of mankind: "Thus the worst art pleases the most people." In his attitude about the taste and abilities of most people, Erasmus resembles his predecessor,
    a. Christine de Pisan.
    b. Machiavelli.
    c. Donatello.
    d. Alberti.
    Ans: b

22. Reading the selection from Erasmus' *The Praise of Folly*, a modern reader is most likely to be surprised by the low esteem in which this profession is held:
    a. law
    b. astrologers
    c. theologians
    d. medicine
    Ans: d

23. Fiero, Reading 3.23, from More's *Utopia*. One of the premises of More's political views is that an insufficient amount of life's essentials inevitably leads to moral decay.
    Ans: T

24. In most societies you would expect to find gold and silver in the money, or backing up the money; in More's *Utopia*, however, and for carefully chosen reasons, you find gold and silver in
    a. women's jewelry.
    b. swords.
    c. chamber pots.
    d. religious vessels.
    Ans: c

25. In Shakespeare's Sonnet #130 (Reading 3.26) the author pokes fun at
    a. his literary colleagues.
    b. the Petrarchan love sonnet.
    c. romance among the elderly.
    d. his former mistress.
    Ans: b

BOOK 4

Faith, Reason, and Power in the Early Modern World

PART I   The Age of the Baroque

Chapter **20** The Catholic Reformation and the Baroque Style

Summary

In the wake of the Protestant Reformation, the Roman Catholic Church launched a reform movement in much of Europe. The writings of Ignatius of Loyola and Teresa of Avila set the tone for a new, more mystical Catholicism. The arts of the seventeenth century reflect the religious intensity of the Catholic reform movement, as well as the ambitions of rival Western nation-states. The Baroque style, which came to dominate Western Europe and Latin America between 1600 and 1750, was born in Italy. Mannerist artists anticipated the Baroque style by their figural distortions, irrational space, bizarre colors, and general disregard of Renaissance "rules." Works by Caravaggio and Bernini featured contrasts of light and dark, an expanded sense of space, and the operatic staging of subject matter. Counter-Reformation churches were ornate theaters for the performance of Catholic ritual. The music of Giovanni Gabrieli reflected the taste for emphatic contrasts in baroque art. The most important development in music was the birth of opera, the integration of text and music to create music-drama.

Outline	Pronunciation Guide

A. Historical context of the Catholic reformation
  1. the Catholic Reformation in Europe
  2. Catholicism's reach into Asia and Latin America
B. Development of Catholic mysticism
  1. Ignatius of Loyola's *Spiritual Meditations*
  2. autobiographical writings of Teresa of Avila
  3. poetry of Richard Crashaw
	Gianlorenzo Bernini [jahn low REN zow ber NEE nee]
	Avila [AH vee lah]
	Buonarroti [bwow nah ROW tee]
	Parmigianino [pahr mee jah NEE now]
	Tintoretto [tin tow RET tow]
	Leonardo da Vinci [lee ow NAHR dow dah VIN chi]
	Caravaggio [kar a VAHJ jow]
	Artemesia Gentileschi [ahr te MEE zee ah jen ti LES kee]
	baldacchino [bahl dah KEE now]

C. Development of the Baroque style 　　1. roots in mannerism 　　2. general character 　　3. contributions of Caravaggio and 　　　Bernini 　　4. Counter-Reformation architecture D. Early Baroque music 　　1. sacred music of Palestrina 　　2. polychoral compositions of Gabrieli 　　3. birth of opera—Monteverdi	**Giacomo da Vignola** [jah kow mow dah VEE nyow lah] **Francesco Borromini** [fran CHES kow bow row MEE nee] **San Carlo alle Quattro Fontane** [san KAHR low ahl lay KWAHT trow fown TAH nay] **Andrea Pozzo** [ahn DRAY ah POT tsow] **Giovanni Gabrieli** [jow VAHN nee ga bree AY lee] **Claudio Monteverdi** [KLAHW dee ow mahn te VER dee] **Pronunciation Key: apple, play, ah** (altar), **egg, keep, inch, eye, glow, booze, outfit, bulk, u** in book, **single, shin, chapter, just, zebra, zhivago, canyon**

Key Terms: Council of Trent, mannerism, *trompe l'oeil,* Baroque, opera, libretto, overture, aria, recitative, polychoral, dynamics, concertato.

Key Images	
Bernini, *The Ecstasy of Saint Teresa* Saint Peter's Cathedral, Rome Tintoretto, *The Last Supper* Gentileschi, *Judith Slaying Holofernes* El Greco, *The Agony in the Garden*	Caravaggio, *The Crucifixion of Saint Peter* Borromini, San Carlo alle Quattro Fontane, 　　Rome Pozzo, *Apotheosis of Saint Ignatius*

Study Questions

Factual

1. How do each of the following illustrate the Catholic Reformation emphasis on the immediacy of religious experience: Loyola's *Spiritual Exercise,* Teresa of Avila's vision, Caravaggio's *The Crucifixion of Saint Peter?*
2. How does the stylistic term *mannerism* apply to El Greco's *The Agony in the Garden?* Pamigianino's *Madonna of the Long Neck?*
3. How did Bernini achieve "theatrical effect" in his sculpture and architecture?
4. What is *trompe l'oeil?* Show how it works in an illustration of the interior of an Italian baroque church.
5. When, where, and why did opera emerge as a form of artistic expression?

Challenge

1. Describe the distortions that Parmigianino and El Greco introduced into their paintings (Figures 20.4 and 20.7). What effect do you think the painters wanted to achieve?
2. What features of form and content do you consider most sensuous in Bernini's *The Ecstasy of Saint Teresa* (Figure 20.2)? Which specific aspects of the piece are sensuous and which are mystical? Do the two overlap?
3. In what way are the fountains of Rome typical of Baroque expression?

4. Discuss opera as the ultimate example of the baroque taste for theatricality. Does extravagant display of emotion come across to the listener in Monteverdi's *Orfeo* (Music Listening Selection II–2)?
5. Discuss the excerpt of Gabrieli's music in Music Listening Selection II–1 using these terms: polychoral, dynamics, concertato.
6. Research the influence of the Catholic Baroque style on the art and architecture of Latin America.

Strategies for Discussion/Lecture

1. Student written preparation for the chapter might take the form of a comparison of the two Last Suppers (page 12) to bridge the Renaissance and the Baroque. The instructor will do well to prepare the students for the intriguing mixture of authoritarianism and theatrical promotion of sensualism that characterizes such Catholic art works as Bernini's *The Ecstasy of Saint Teresa,* then move on to a closer study of precepts in Reading 4.1. Here students may be on familiar ground as they recall medieval Christian practices and doctrine: hierarchy, sacraments, celibacy, relics, pilgrimages. What has changed? The doctrinaire tone of Rule 13 says it sufficiently and clearly.
2. Two Last Suppers. An effective comparison, suggested by the text author, is between the last suppers of Tintoretto and Leonardo (Figures 20.5 and 20.6). Try projecting them side by side onto the blackboard, and ask a member of the class to draw the main lines of the composition with a board marker. This will produce two contrasting schematics side by side.
3. St. Peter's in Rome. Does the *baldacchino* of Bernini (Figure 20.14) within the seat of Roman Catholic authority make a sensual appeal? Compare its columns to Bernini's exterior colonnade. Is the mixture of authoritarianism with sensualism analogous to that which one might observe in the excerpt from Ignatius of Loyola?
4. Il Gesù and San Carlo alle Quattro Fontane. Mindful of the dates of construction, compare exteriors and interiors of these two churches, perhaps tracing the facades to call attention to architectural elements.
5. Monteverdi. Relate the dynamics of the music (contrast, tone color, etc.) to the principal features of Baroque art.

Chapter 20 Audiovisuals

Video/CD-ROM Sources

BERNINI'S ROME 30 min., B&W **IU**

CIVILISATION—Vol. #07: Grandeur and Obedience (1970)
 DIRECTOR: CLARK, SIR KENNETH 53 min., color **PBS**

EL GRECO: REDISCOVERING A MASTER 29 min., color **FFH**

REALMS OF LIGHT: The Baroque 60 min., color **CPB**

REALMS OF LIGHT: The Baroque in Italy and Austria 30 min., color **CPB**

A REPUTATION: THE RAPE OF ARTEMISIA GENTILESCHI
 In 1612, Artemisia Gentileschi accused a fellow artist of rape. This program reconstructs how the male-dominated art community of Rome falsified her promiscuity and destroyed her reputation. **FFH**

Music Resources

Palestrina, Giovanni. *Missa Papae Marcelli*, Phillips, The Tallis Scholars, Gimell CDGIM-339.

Web Resources

History of the Catholic Reformation—
    http://mars.acnet.wnec.edu/~grempel/courses/wc1/lectures/32cathreform.html

Resources about the Catholic Reformation—http://newadvent.org/cathen/12700b.htm#ll

Biographical information about Teresa of Avila—http://www.ccel.org./t/teresa/teresa.html

Resources related to Richard Crashaw—http://www.crashaw.plus.com/

Biographical information about Richard Crashaw—www.luminarium.org/sevenlit/crashaw/

Resources related to Baroque music—http://www.ipl.org/exhibit/mushist/bar/index.htm

Resources related to the Baroque Age—http://history.evansville.net/baroque.html

McGraw-Hill Resources

Music Listening Selection: CD II
    II–1 Gabrieli, *"In Ecclesiis"*
    II–2 Monteverdi, *Orfeo*
Transparencies: MA.7 Early Modern World 1600–1789

Sample Test Questions for Chapter 20

Select the letter of the choice that BEST answers the question:

1. Which one of the following statements best expresses the relationship between the *Spiritual Exercises* by Ignatius of Loyola and Baroque art?
    a. Like Bernini, Ignatius makes an unqualified appeal to the senses as the basis for belief.
    b. Ignatius shows an indifference to the senses and a strong authoritarian stance on church dogma.
    c. Ignatius combines an appeal to the senses and an insistence on obedience to the authority of the church.
    d. Unlike Bernini, Ignatius sees no role in religion for the senses.
    Ans: c

2. The history of the early modern era in Western Europe included the development of all the following EXCEPT
    a. competing religious theologies.
    b. geographic expansion.
    c. the beginnings of the state system.
    d. a new era of peace among nation-states.
    Ans: d

3. The Society of Jesus insisted on intensive prayer and meditation, accompanied by lifelong asceticism as outlined in Loyola's
   a. *Confessions.*
   b. *Praise of Folly.*
   c. *Spiritual Exercises.*
   d. *The Church Militant.*
   Ans: c

4. All of the following characterized the Baroque era in the West EXCEPT the
   a. establishment of colonial empires.
   b. Catholic Reformation.
   c. appearance of constitutional regimes.
   d. Scientific Revolution.
   Ans: c

5. Giovanni Gabrieli became celebrated for his
   a. anticlassical paintings.
   b. design of Saint Mark's Cathedral in Venice.
   c. authorship of a Jesuit handbook.
   d. polychoral religious music.
   Ans: d

6. The devout English Catholic who composed mystical religious poetry like *The Flaming Heart* was
   a. Robert Cramner.
   b. Richard Crashaw.
   c. Thomas More.
   d. Henry Boleyn.
   Ans: b

7. The term "Baroque style" in painting is characterized by all the following EXCEPT
   a. symmetrical composition.
   b. illusionistic effects.
   c. strong contrasts of light and dark.
   d. theatrical flamboyance.
   Ans: a

Answer the following with a word or phrase.

8. The last stage of Renaissance art, which seemingly renounced symmetry, idealism, and naturalism, was called _____.
   Ans: mannerism

9. The sculptor and architect _____ designed the colonnade of Saint Peter's in Rome.
   Ans: Bernini

10. The seventeenth-century Italian composer who wrote *Orfeo,* one of the first full-length operas in history, was _____.
    Ans: Monteverdi

11. The Catholic Reformation leader who founded the Jesuits was _____.
    Ans: Ignatius of Loyola

12. The seventeenth-century Italian painter who preferred to portray violent scenes from the Bible was
    _____.
    Ans: Artemisia Gentileschi

Open Book

13. Chapter 20: Compare Tintoretto's *The Last Supper* (Figure 20.5) with Leonardo da Vinci's fresco
    (Figure 20.6). One compositional element that is typically Baroque is
    a. the horizontal, rectangular format.
    b. the oblique positioning of the table.
    c. the depiction of all twelve disciples.
    d. the placement of Jesus at the center of the canvas.
    Ans: b

14. Compare two facades (Figures 20.16 and 20.18). Even if you didn't know the dates of the two
    structures, you would place San Carlo alle Quattro *later* than Il Gesù on the basis of this feature.
    a. the use of classical columns
    b. the use of statues in niches
    c. the narrow width of the facade
    d. the undulating entablatures on both levels.
    Ans: d

15. The facade of Saint Peter's is a *neoclassical* design, not an exact copy of Greek and Roman models.
    This is clear from which one of the following features.
    a. the dome, which was unknown in antiquity
    b. the use of a pediment
    c. the use of paired columns
    d. the placement of columns on plinths
    Ans: c

16. The paintings by Caravaggio and Gentileschi
    (Figures 20.9 and 20.10)) have in common:
    a. the use of strong obliques.
    b. light/dark contrastspillars.
    c. Biblical subject matter.
    d. all of the above.
    Ans: d

17. Page 14, Figure 20.8, *The Supper at Emmaus*. The manner of rendering the outstretched hands of the
    two figures on the right is known as
    a. foreshortening.
    b. *intaglio.*
    c. mannerism.
    d. linear perspective.
    Ans: a

Summary

In the new nation-states of the West as in the empires of the East, seventeenth-century art reflects the influence of absolutism. In the France of Louis XIV, artists made luxury, size, and technical refinement the symbols of wealth and authority. French art combined classical themes and design principles with Baroque features, as seen in the Palace at Versailles. The king established strict guidelines for the fine arts, all of which reflected the neoclassical idea that the mind should prevail over the passions. Outside of France such artists as Velásquez and van Dyck produced elegant portraits of the ruling classes, while Rubens produced dramatic allegories of royal authority.

In the Near East, Suleiman, ruler of the Ottoman Empire, established a pattern of princely patronage that was imitated by subsequent Muslim rulers in Persia and India. Their architectural monuments represent the wealth, authority, and artistic vision of a privileged minority. In China too, at the Forbidden City of the Ming and Qing emperors, the arts flourished as an expression of royal majesty. The aristocratic style legitimized and glorified the power of the ruling elite throughout Europe and Asia.

Outline	**Pronunciation Guide**
A. Introduction 1. the age of absolutism 2. the classical Baroque style B. Louis XIV and the establishment of French absolutism 1. Versailles a. lifestyle by protocol 2. patronage of the arts a. creation of academies b. Poussin and the academic style c. portraiture 3. aristocratic painting outside France a. Velásquez b. Rubens c. van Dyck 4. music and dance at the court of Louis XIV—Lully	**Suleiman** [SOO lay mahn] **Tokugawa** [tow koo GAH wah] **Versailles** [ver SAHY] **Mansard** [man SAHR] **Perrault** [pe ROW] **Louis Le Vau** [LOO ee le VOW] **Girardon** [zhi rahr DOWN] **Poussin** [poo SAN] **Velásquez** [ve LAHS kez] **La Rochefoucauld** [lah rowsh foo KOW] **Molière** [mowl YER] **Jourdain** [joor DAN] **Cléonte** [klay AHNT] **Dorimene** [dow ree MEN] **Covielle** [kow VYEL] **Jahangir** [ye HAHN geer] **Shah Jahan** [SHAH je HAHN]

<table>
<tr><td>

    5. neoclassicism and French literature
        a. La Rochefoucauld
        b. Racine
        c. Molière—*Le Bourgeois Gentilhomme*
C. Absolute power and the aristocratic style beyond Europe
    1. Suleiman and the Ottoman Empire
    2. the Moguls of India
    3. China under Ming and Manchu (Qing) rule
    4. Tokugawa Japan

</td><td>

Mogul [MOW gul]
haiku [HEYE koo]

</td></tr>
</table>

Key Terms: absolutism, classical Baroque, academies, Ottoman Empire, Moguls, Ming and Manchu (Ching), neoclassicism, maxim, aristocratic portrait, porcelain, Forbidden City, *haiku,* Zen, "floating world."

<table>
<tr><td colspan="2">

Key Images:

</td></tr>
<tr><td>

Rigaud, *Portrait of Louis XIV*
Versailles, Palace and gardens
Versailles, Hall of Mirrors
Poussin, *Arcadian Shepherds*
Lorrain, *The Marriage of Isaac and Rebekkah*
Velásquez, *The Maids of Honor*
Rubens, *Rape of the Daughters of Leucippus*

</td><td>

Imperial Mosque, Isfahan
Red Fort, Delhi
Taj Mahal, Agra
Forbidden City, Beijing
Ming Dynasty: Tapestries and porcelains
Japanese woodblock prints and ink brush scrolls

</td></tr>
</table>

Study Questions

Factual
1. What luxury items were used to embellish the palace at Versailles?
2. Which Royal academies did Louis XIV create? Why were they founded?
3. Who were the major artistic figures in the creation of the Baroque aristocratic style?
4. What are the main features of the aristocratic portrait? Which figures in your text best illustrate this genre?
5. Who were the Moguls? What kind of art patronage did they provide?
6. What kinds of literature were available in China to those who could read?
7. Where, when, and how did formal ballet and choreography originate?
8. Summarize the action of Molière's *Le Bourgeois Gentilhomme* (Reading 4.13).
9. What were the main features of the aristocratic style in Tokugawa Japan?

Challenge
1. Why is the seventeenth century often called the Age of Absolutism?
2. How does the complex at Versailles—gardens and chateau—illustrate classical baroque style and the grandeur and absolute power of Louis XIV?
3. Compare the palace complex at Versailles to the Mogul and Chinese complexes illustrated in this chapter. What differences do you see, if any, in the Eastern complexes?

4. What is the message of Poussin's *Arcadian Shepherds?*
5. Apply some of the *Maxims* of La Rochefoucauld to the characters in the *Le Bourgeois Gentilhomme.*
6. Does Molière's *Bourgeois Gentilhomme* support or undermine the concept of nobility?
7. Do the female characters in the *Bourgeois Gentilhomme* represent a distinct point of view on what is happening in the play?
8. Why do you think the Taj Mahal has captured the imagination of so many artists and poets over the centuries? Find out what the inside of this mausoleum looks like. Is it as extraordinary as the exterior?
9. It is suggested in the text that Eastern art lacks the heroic urgency and strong sense of individualism that may be found in the paintings of Western artists, such as Poussin and Rubens. Does the art of the Moguls and the Manchu generally confirm this point of view? What features do you find in the visual arts of India and China that are lacking in Western painting?
10. Madame de Pompadour is said to have owned two telescopes and to have influenced the commercial popularity of fine porcelain. What other kinds of influence did she wield? Do a short research project that offers a thumbnail sketch of this remarkable seventeenth-century woman.
11. What are the basic characteristics of the aristocratic portrait? Which figures in your textbook illustrate this genre?
12. Research and report on either of the following: the Japanese tea ceremony; kabuki theater.

Strategies for Discussion/Lecture

1. If two classes are devoted to this chapter, one can be spent on "global" absolutism as seen in the arts of elites in France, the Ottoman Empire, and China, and the second on Molière's play. A slide lecture or lecture with text illustrations will serve the first best, and if possible, a video used in conjunction with the reading of the *Le Bourgeois Gentilhomme.*
2. If no filmed performance of Molière's play is available, work through the play in selected sections, distributing parts to be read aloud by students, asking the nonreaders to summarize and comment on the passages read.
3. Find other examples of "the aristocratic style" in this or other eras. How was this style manifested in the young American continent? Was there an aristocratic style in Africa? In Maya culture?
4. Ask students to identify (in their own town or university campus) public buildings that reflect the aristocratic style, or which combine authority, stability, impressive scale, and the use of neoclassical detail.
5. Ask students to identify geometric shapes in Figures 21.2 and 21.4. Imagine the view from the apartments over the topiary in the north flower bed. What would move a culture to change a natural form into a geometric one? A picture of a Japanese bonsai would make a stimulating contrast.

Chapter 21 Audiovisuals

Video/CD-ROM Sources

THE AGE OF ABSOLUTE MONARCHS IN EUROPE 14 min., B&W **CORONET**

LE BOURGEOIS GENTILHOMME MGHF

CHINA: The Manchu Ruler (1977) 19 min., color **IU**

COMEDY OF MANNERS: Molière: The Misanthrope 52 min., color **FFH**

DAILY LIFE AT THE COURT OF VERSAILLES (1986)
DIRECTOR: DELOUCHE, DOMINIQUE
This is the story of France as reflected in Versailles, from its construction by Louis XIV to its abandonment by Louis XVI during the French Revolution. French w/English narration 60 min., color **FFH**

THE LAST EMPEROR
DIRECTOR: BERNARDO BERTOLUCCI (1987) **AZ**

PETER PAUL RUBENS
This program examines two portraits of Hélène Fourment in which she appears in suggestive apparel, and projects from them what the others, the nudes which she destroyed, might have looked like. 32 min. **FFH**

THE SUN KING 30 min., B&W **IU**

THE TAJ MAHAL: A LOVE STORY **FFH**

VERSAILLES 34 min., color **EVN**

Music Resources

Chinese Opera: Songs and Music, Folkways 8880, cassette.
François Couperin, Concerts Royaux (4), Claire, See, Moroney, Ter Linder, Harmonia Mundi 901151, CD.

Web Resources

The Taj Mahal—http://www.taj-mahal.net/topEng/index.htm

The Taj Mahal—http://www.liveindia.com/tajmahal/index.html

The Taj Mahal—http://users.erols.com/zenithco/tajmahal.html

The Taj Mahal—http://www.angelfire.com/in/myindia/tajmahal.html

Kabuki sounds and makeup, plus summaries and explanations of major plays—
http://www.fix.co.jp/kabuki/kabuki.html

Virtual tour of China's Forbidden City—http://www.chinavista.com/beijing/gugong/!start.html

Biographical information about Molière—http://www.site-moliere.com/bio/index.html

Virtual tour of the Chateau de Versailles and biographical information about Louis XIV—
http://www.chateauversailles.fr/en/

Rubens, biographical information and images—http://www.mcs.csuhayward.edu/~malek/rubens.html

McGraw-Hill Resources

Transparencies: MA.7 Early Modern World 1600–1789

Sample Test Questions for Chapter 21

Select the letter of the choice that BEST answers the question:

1. Louis XIV strengthened governmental authority by all the following methods EXCEPT
   a. spending large sums of money on the military.
   b. levying heavy taxes on the nobles and the Church.
   c. choosing first-rate advisers.
   d. recognizing the propaganda value of the arts.
   Ans: b

2. The classical Baroque style fuses principles of order and symmetry with Baroque
   a. expansiveness and exuberance.
   b. regularity and rigidity.
   c. geometry and marquetry.
   d. rectilinear organization.
   Ans: a

3. Poussin counseled artists to paint
   a. genre scenes of everyday life.
   b. the bizarre and the grotesque.
   c. only contemporary figures.
   d. heroic and religious scenes.
   Ans: d

4. A brief, concise, and witty saying that sometimes offers practical advice is a
   a. metaphor.
   b. hyperbole.
   c. simile.
   d. maxim.
   Ans: d

5. In *Le Bourgeois Gentilhomme*, Mr. Jourdain
   a. struggled to dress and speak like a nobleman.
   b. challenged the supremacy of the king.
   c. conspired to discredit a fellow merchant.
   d. sought a long-lost twin brother.
   Ans: a

6. In *Le Bourgeois Gentilhomme,* teachers of music, fencing, philosophy, and dancing
   a. establish an academy for noblewomen.
   b. dispute the relative importance of their arts.
   c. are imprisoned for attempted treason.
   d. perform before the assembled court.
   Ans: b

7. During their reestablishment of autocratic power, the Ming rulers in China accomplished all the following EXCEPT the
   a. rebuilding of the Great Wall.
   b. revival of the system of merit examinations.
   c. establishment of a highly regimented and luxurious court life.
   d. establishment of academies of painting and architecture.
   Ans: d

8. Louis XIV established his preeminence by securing the approval of the Estates General, the French legislative assembly.
   Ans: F

9. Absolute rulers, believing that they held their power directly from God, shared authority only with the Church.
   Ans: F

Answer the following with a word or phrase.

10. The symbol of French absolutism constructed during the reign of Louis XIV was the chateau at
    _____.
    Ans: Versailles

11. The author of *Le Bourgeois Gentilhomme,* who exposed the hypocrisy and superficiality of contemporary society, was _____.
    Ans: Molière

12. Known as "the Magnificent," _____ reigned over the Ottoman Empire and encouraged a Golden Age of literature and art.
    Ans: Suleiman

13. Comparable to the palace complex of the French king, the _____, constructed by the Indian Mogul Akbar, inspired admiration for its size, elegant design, and ornate decoration.
    Ans: Red Fort

14. In Japan, court elegance and the aristocratic style were visible in a regime known as the
    _____.
    Ans: Tokugawa

Summary

In seventeenth-century Northern Europe, a number of circumstances shaped the development of the baroque style—the dominance of the Reformed church, the influence of a commercial middle class, and a passionate effort to sustain personal rights and liberties. The study of Holy Scripture was central to the ideals of Pietism and Protestant belief. As a result, artistic expression turned inward to the personal and subjective rather than outward to spectacular forms of display. In the literary domain, the King James Version of the Bible brought the English language to new heights of eloquence. The poetry of Donne and Milton reflected Protestant perspectives of morality, evil, and death. The religious works of Rembrandt present a visual parallel to these literary landmarks by bringing to life the drama of Holy Scripture. His genius was matched in music by Handel and Bach. Handel's oratorios typified the Baroque taste for rich color and dramatic effect. Bach's compositions invested Reformation Christianity with a sublime and deeply personal sense of tragedy.

Outline	Pronunciation Guide
A. Baroque of the protestant north 1. the shaping influence of the Bible 2. the rising middle class 3. Civil War and the English Commonwealth B. Baroque literature 1. King James Version of the Bible 2. poetry of John Donne 3. John Milton C. the expressive arts of the Baroque 1. Christopher Wren 2. Rembrandt 3. Handel and the oratorio 4. Bach: religious music	**van Dyck** [van DEYK] **Douay** [doo AY] **intaglio** [in TAH lyow] **homophony** [how MOF ah nee] **Franz Hals** [FRAHNS HAHLS] **de Hooch** [de HOOK]

Key Terms: Holy Scripture, metaphysical poetry, conceit, etching, homophonic, figured bass, cantata, oratorio.

Key Images	
Wren, Saint Paul's Cathedral	Rembrandt, *The Return of the Prodigal Son* Rembrandt, *Christ Preaching* (etching)

Study Questions

Factual
1. How, where, and why was the King James Version of the Bible produced?
2. What is the theme of Milton's *Paradise Lost?* Who are the central characters?
3. What models did Christopher Wren draw upon when he designed Saint Paul's in London?
4. What is an oratorio? How does it differ from an opera? How is Handel's *Messiah (*Music Listening Selection II–3) typical of "the Baroque sensibility?"
5. What is the difference between etching and engraving (see Chapter 18)?
6. For what instrument(s) did J. S. Bach write most of his religious music?

Challenge
1. Show how the work of Rembrandt and other visual artists in this chapter exhibit the Northern Reformation's emphasis on a return to Holy Scripture.
2. How does the "Protestant devotionalism" of the North Netherlands reveal itself in the paintings of Rembrandt?
3. Why has the stylistic term *metaphysical* been invented to describe the poetry of John Donne? Give details using the examples in this chapter.
4. It is often said that Satan is the most compelling character in Milton's *Paradise Lost.* Do you find this to be so? Read further in the poem and offer your own explanation for this assertion.
5. Compare the original version of Luther's chorale, "A Mighty Fortress is our God" to the setting in Bach's *Cantata No. 80* (Music Listening Selection II–4). How has Bach modified the earlier piece?
6. Do you find the works of art, literature, and music in this chapter more or less "theatrical" than those discussed in Chapter 20? Why so or why not?
7. Compare Handel's *Messiah* (Music Listening Selection II–3) with Milton's *Paradise Lost* (Reading 4.9) for majesty of style and power of expression. Are there any distinct similarities?

Strategies for Discussion/Lecture

1. An introductory lecture might focus on the different sensibilities of the Baroque: the Catholic Baroque in Italy and elsewhere, the aristocratic Baroque in France, and the Protestant Baroque as reflected in Northern Europe.
2. Since this chapter contains a sizeable selection of poetry in English, a good part of the class time might be spent working with students in reading verse correctly and with expression, as outlined in the following suggestions:
   First read aloud the two versions of the Twenty-Third Psalm (Reading 4.6) and invite discussion regarding the effect of each. Then compare the King James Version of the Twenty-Third Psalm with selected lines of Milton. Does poetry have to rhyme? Compare line 1 of the King James Version and the Douay Version up to the semicolon. Is the rhythm the same? What is the secret of the music of the King James Version?
3. Compare the rhythm (by scansion) of the two sonnets by Donne (Reading 4.7). In the second sonnet, what does *viceroy* mean? How does this image relate reason to God and to the individual? Is faith, in this sonnet, a matter of knowing or believing?
4. Reading Milton is generally a challenge for today's students, but taken in small doses and dealing with immediately appealing themes—such as Adam's decision to stick with the fallen Eve (lines 89–98)—he has the power to win over.

For those stressing continuity with the early church fathers, the figure of Augustine can be seen looking over Milton's shoulder in lines 147–151 and in the angel's approving reply, lines 165–168: better to rely on the coming of redemption in Jesus than to inquire into nature's secrets.

5. Rembrandt, Figure 22.4. In the context of Protestantism, the Prodigal Son may be thought of as the image of a "stray sheep." Who has "gone astray"? Is it Rome or Luther? What does *prodigal* mean? To which branch of divided Christianity might the word apply more accurately?

6. Christopher Wren. Compare the facade of St. Paul's Cathedral in London to the Italian Baroque churches from the preceding chapter. How does Wren compare in dynamism and in the use of classical principles?

7. To stimulate class discussion, ask, "What religious scripture was used in your home when you were a child? Did its use have any effects on you in the course of your personal development?"

8. If possible, have the class attend a live performance of *Messiah*, and ask them to describe in writing the most compelling features.

Chapter 22 Audiovisuals

Video/CD-ROM Sources

ART OF THE WESTERN WORLD
    Program 5: The Baroque: Italy and Austria & The Baroque: Spain & the Netherlands **HTG**

JOHANN SEBASTIAN BACH 27 min., color **IFB**

BACH: The Fugue No. 4 in B minor
    Performance and analysis **Pioneer LDCA Catalog No V1013L CAV**

BACH: Brandenburg Concertos No 1–6
    Performance and analysis **Pioneer LDCA Catalog No 071 204-1 LHV CLV**

HANDEL: Messiah
    Performance and analysis **Pioneer LDCA Catalog No PA 86-174 CLV**

REMBRANDT AND HIS PAINTS
    An examination of the work at the Rembrandt Research Project. 27 min. **FFH**

REMBRANDT VAN RIJN This program explores Rembrandt's self-portraits and attempts to determine the secret meanings hidden in the various versions of his face. 30 min. **FFH**

THE RESTORATION OF THE GLORIOUS REVOLUTION 11 min., color **CORONET**

UNQUIET LAND: Civil War in England 25 min., B&W **Universal Studio's Educational and Visual Arts Division**

Web Resources

Georg Frederic Handel—http://www.classical.net/music/comp.lst/handel.html

Directory of J.S. Bach resources—http://www.jsbach.net/bcs/

Resources related to John Milton—http://www.luminarium.org/sevenlit/milton/

Resources related to the life and works of John Donne—http://pages.infinit.net/impulsar/donne.html

Resources related to the English Civil War—http://easyweb.easynet.co.uk/~crossby/ecw/

The Rembrandt Museum in Amsterdam—http://www.rembrandthuis.nl/flash.html

McGraw-Hill Resources

Music Listening Selection: CD II
    II–3 Handel: *Messiah*, "Hallelujah" Chorus
    II–4 Bach: *Cantata No. 80*, final chorus
Transparencies: MA.5 The Middle Ages

Sample Test Questions for Chapter 22

Select the letter of the choice that BEST answers the question:

1. The middle class of the Protestant North
   a. became wealthy from a far-flung trading network.
   b. had little influence on political life.
   c. staunchly supported the absolute monarchs.
   d. joined the nobles in repressing the peasants.
   Ans: a

2. Puritans were
   a. ardent supporters of the papal hierarchy.
   b. Calvinists who demanded stricter religious observances.
   c. allies of King Charles in the Civil War.
   d. soldiers in the royalist army.
   Ans: b

3. *Paradise Lost* has as its theme the
   a. journeys of adventurers to unexplored continents.
   b. suffering in the face of imminent death.
   c. existence of evil in a universe created by God.
   d. ravages of the English Civil War.
   Ans: c

4. The Calvinist Republic, which successfully rebelled against Catholic Spain in 1581, was
   subsequently known as
   a. Belgium.
   b. Luxembourg.
   c. Holland.
   d. Silesia.
   Ans: c

5. As a follower of the Anabaptist sect, Rembrandt movingly depicted
   a. the oppression of women.
   b. the poor.
   c. clerics.
   d. the aristocracy
   Ans: b

6. The Civil War in England led to the execution of a king and the establishment of a commonwealth.
   Ans: T

7. Since Calvinism exalted the human body, large-scale nudes were frequently created by artists in the Protestant North.
   Ans: F

Answer the following with a word or phrase.

8. The architect of the dome of Saint Paul's Cathedral, which combines drama with illusionism, was

   _____.
   Ans: Christopher Wren

9. The creator of the *Messiah* and the developer of the oratorio, _____ became known as "England's greatest composer."
   Ans: Handel

10. The major sources of Bach's religious inspiration were the teachings and hymns of _____.
    Ans: Martin Luther

11. The English poet _____ penned the celebrated metaphor, "No man is an island."
    Ans: Donne

12. _____, a poetic form used in *Paradise Lost*, consists of unrhymed lines of ten syllables each with accents on every second syllable.
    Ans: Blank verse

Open Book

13. *Not* true of Van Dyck's Portrait of Charles I:
    a. The king is shown in full armor.
    b. The tradition of aristocratic portraiture is evident.
    c. Charles bears the symbols of royal monarchy.
    d. It is an equestrian portrait.
    Ans: c

14. Milton's *Paradise Lost,* Reading 4.9, lines 142–169. Choose the expression that best captures the conclusion reached in this dialogue on knowledge between Adam and the angel.
    a. Humans are capable of infinite knowledge.
    b. Happiness has nothing to do with knowledge.
    c. People should be content with their individual capacity for knowledge.
    d. Only God has perfect knowledge: humans will have it in the next life.
    Ans: c

15. Fiero, Figures 21.6 and 21.7. In the clothing of the audience to Jesus' sermon, Rembrandt has suggested that Jesus preached
    a. only to the poor.
    b. to the Roman forces of occupation and the Jews.
    c. to Rabbis and upper-class Jews.
    d. to a broad spectrum of the population.
    Ans: d

16. Milton's *Paradise Lost,* Reading 4.9, lines 27–69. One intriguing aspect of Milton's poem is that in this passage Lucifer upholds the same view on knowledge and happiness as Adam and the angel do.
    Ans: F

Summary

During the seventeenth century, European scientists shattered the medieval view of the cosmos. Kepler determined that the earth followed an elliptical path around the sun, which stood fixed at the center of the solar system, as Copernicus had theorized. Galileo derived the laws of falling bodies from studies of motion on earth. Finally, Newton combined all the findings of his predecessors in a grand synthesis. According to the new view, earth was not a stable center but just another of the "wandering" planets; thus, its inhabitants could no longer be considered central to the universe.

The theory was confirmed by several newly invented scientific instruments, notably the telescope. Concurrently, physics, astronomy, and higher mathematics were established on their modern foundations. While the new science demystified nature, Bacon, Locke, and Descartes developed new theoretical methods for describing and predicting the operations of nature. Some of these revolutionaries were orthodox Catholic believers (Copernicus, Kepler), but most were deists, persuaded that God should be seen as a master "artificer" and the universe a great machine operating according to universal natural laws, independent of divine intervention.

The new learning influenced the arts profoundly. Humans came to be seen as a tiny part of a universe become infinitely large, and advances in optics changed the attitude toward light in Dutch painting. In music, the mechanical improvement of stringed and keyboard instruments led to the emergence of wholly instrumental musical forms with added scope for virtuosity.

Outline	Pronunciation Guide

A. Historical context
   1. roots of the scientific revolution
   2. religious conditions
B. Scientists
   1. Kepler
   2. Galileo
   3. opposition from organized religion
   4. new instruments
C. Scientific method
   1. Bacon and inductive reasoning
   2. Descartes and deductive reasoning
D. Science and religion
   1. deism
   2. Spinoza
   3. Pascal
   4. Locke
   5. Newton
	Giordano Bruno [jor DAH now BROO now]
	Novum Organum [NOW vum or GAN um]
	Cogito, ergo sum [KOW gee tow ER gow SUM]
	Spinoza [spi NOW zah]
	Blaise Pascal [BLAYZ pas KAL]
	Pensées [pahn SAY]
	tabula rasa [TAH boo lah RAH zah]
	Gerard ter Borch [tur BOWRK]
	camera obscura [KA me rah ob SKOO rah]
	Jan Vermeer [YAHN ver MIR]
	Judith Leyster [LEYE sta]
	van Oosterwyck [fon OOST er vik]
	Vivaldi [vi VAHL dee]

E. Influence of the scientific revolution
   1. on prose genres
   2. on Dutch painting
      a. Vermeer
      b. Rembrandt
   3. on music
      a. new instruments and instrumental forms
      b. Vivaldi
      c. Bach

Key Terms: science/*scientia,* heliocentric theory, empirical method, inductive and deductive reasoning, systematic doubt and the *Cogito,* deism, *tabula rasa,* genre painting, *vanitas,* sonata, fugue, concerto.

Key Images:	
de Hooch, *A Dutch Courtyard*; *Family Making Music* Vermeer, *View of Delft*; *Woman Holding a Balance*	Hals, *The Laughing Cavalier* Leyster, *Self-Portrait* Rembrandt, *The Anatomy Lesson of Dr. Nicolaes Tulp*

Study Questions

Factual
1. Briefly explain the contributions of Copernicus, Kepler, and Galileo.
2. Say in your own words how Isaac Newton synthesized the scientific work of his predecessors.
3. Name and identify the "four Idols" from Bacon's *Novum Organum* (Reading 4.8). How does the notion of an "idol" serve Bacon's main purpose in writing this treatise?
4. According to Locke, the human mind at birth is a *tabula rasa.* What did he mean by that?
5. What is genre painting? How did Dutch painting reflect the influence of "the new science"?
6. What is a sonata, a fugue, and a concerto? For what instruments were such pieces written?

Challenge
1. Imagine that Bacon and Descartes have met in the afterlife, and they get into a discussion of Descartes' theory of knowledge. What might Bacon say to Descartes?
2. See Figure 23.10, Jan Vermeer, *View of Delft.* How is the artist's fascination with light reflected in this painting? Do you find Baroque elements in the picture?
3. To illustrate how an *inductive* thinker and a *deductive* thinker would approach the same problem, explain how each would go about answering the following questions: (1) What is heat? (2) Can the future be known or not? (3) Do computers think?
4. With his celebrated statement *"Cogito, ergo sum,"* Descartes hoped to establish at least one thing as absolutely certain. Why do you think it is important for a philosopher to arrive at such a certitude?
5. Descartes concludes that he is "a substance the whole essence or nature of which is to think." How does he arrive at this seemingly unlikely position?
6. Once a visitor to Descartes' home in Holland asked him what he was reading. Descartes took him into his study, where he was dissecting a cow on a table, and said, "This is what I'm reading." Say in your own words what this story says about Descartes as a thinker.

7. Some people consider J. S. Bach the greatest composer of all time. What can be said in support of this view? Do you hear any notable differences between Bach's religious music (Music Listening Selection II–4) and his secular music (Music Listening Selection II–6 and II–7)?

8. Give examples that show that the new learning and the European quest for naturalistic accuracy had a major impact on the visual arts of the seventeenth century.

Strategies for Discussion/Lecture

1. Since the readings on science in the chapter are nontechnical, the lecturer might summarize the shift to heliocentrism and the discovery of general laws of nature, then relate these to the general texts of Bacon, Descartes, and Locke, and lastly, survey the effects of the new learning on painting and music.

    A challenging written theme for class might be to assign the geocentric theory as an example of a Baconian *idol*. Why was the geocentric model so entrenched in people's minds? Are there good reasons for thinking that the earth is the center of the cosmos? The following suggestion elaborates this further.

2. Bacon (Reading 4.10). Using Factual question 3, ask students to identify received notions that they have overcome through better understanding of the facts. If well conducted, the discussion will not produce merely a list of prejudices but examples of the four "idols." Bacon's choice of the word *idol* should also be an issue, since it points to a mechanism that an American thinker called the "fixation of belief," or the investment one has in having the "right" views, even when they are incorrect.

3. A second approach to the chapter would be to organize the material and the lecture around Outline E, 1–3, using slides and illustrations of the key images and the CD recordings as the main focus. In this approach, Bacon and Locke would constitute the intellectual background of the period, with its emphasis on the world of concrete particulars, its fascination with new instruments, etc. Challenge question 7 would make a good written assignment, offering choice and focus on individual works.

4. Descartes is wary of the senses because of their unreliability, while Bacon and Locke are, to different degrees, persuaded that knowledge arises from the senses. A simple test is to ask the class, "Do the senses tell us that the earth rotates at 1,000 mph?" Better (or worse) yet, "What sense experience corresponds to the value of ?" If nobody has gained knowledge of these through the senses, are they then "idols" in Bacon's sense?

5. Classes that are visually oriented might profit from a discussion of the role of realism in painting. How "realistic" are Vermeer's works? What was the function of *camera obscura* in his achieving "photographic" realism? In the still life paintings, what role(s) did symbolism play? Students might be interested to read the fictionalized account of Vermeer's life and time in the novel, *The Girl with the Pearl Earring*, by Tracy Chevalier (Plume, 2001).

Chapter 23 Audiovisuals

Video/CD-ROM Sources

ASCENT OF MAN: The Majestic Clock 52 min., color **TLF**

ASCENT OF MAN: The Starry Messenger 52 min., color **TLF**

CIVILISATION—Vol. #08: The Light of Experience (1970)
   DIRECTOR: CLARK, SIR KENNETH 53 min., color **PBS**

WILLIAM HARVEY AND THE CIRCULATION OF THE BLOOD 33 min., color **IFB**

SCIENCE AND SOCIETY 18 min., color **MGHF**

JAN VERMEER In this program, video graphics are used to focus on the key elements of *The Astronomer* for the purpose of analyzing its structure and composition. 28 min. **FFH**

VESALIUS: Founder of Modern Anatomy 13 min., color **Yale Medical School**

Music Resources

Baroque Music on Authentic Instruments, Collegium Musicum, Budapest, Hungaroton, LPSLPX–12193.

Web Resources

Antonio Vivaldi—http://home.kc.rr.com/vivaldi/

Directory of J.S. Bach resources—http://www.jsbach.net/bcs/

The essays of Francis Bacon—http://ourworld.compuserve.com/homepages/mike_donnelly/bacon_htm

The life and work of Galileo—http://es.rice.edu/ES/humsoc/Galileo

Biographical information and resources related to Johannes Kepler—
http://es.rice.edu/es/humsoc/galileo/people/kepler.html

Biographical information about René Descartes—http://www.utm.edu/research/iep/d/descarte.htm

Defining deductive reasoning—http://ai.eecs.umich.edu/cogarch0/common/capa/reason/html

History of the Scientific Revolution—
http://mars.acnet.wnec.edu/~grempel/courses/wc2/lectures/scientificrev.html

Biographical information about John Locke—http://www.rjgeib.com/thoughts/constitution/locke-bio.html

McGraw-Hill Resources

Music Listening Selection: CD II
    II–5 Vivaldi, *The Four Seasons,* "Spring"
    II–6 Bach, *Brandenburg Concerto* No. 4 in G Major
    II–7 *The Art of the Fugue*
Transparencies: MA.7 Early Modern World 1600–1789

Sample Test Questions for Chapter 23

Select the letter of the choice that BEST answers the question:

1. Among the instruments for measurement invented during the Scientific Revolution was the
   a. compass.
   b. astrolabe.
   c. barometer.
   d. hourglass.
   Ans: c

2. Among the new forms of mathematics developed during the seventeenth century was
   a. calculus.
   b. plane geometry.
   c. algebra.
   d. pythagorean theorems.
   Ans: a

3. The belief in a mechanistic universe fashioned by a Creator (rather than a Redeemer) God is called
   a. atheism.
   b. agnosticism.
   c. deism.
   d. animism.
   Ans: c

4. Dutch painting reflected the influence of the Scientific Revolution in its
   a. preoccupation with light, space, and natural detail.
   b. emphasis on secular scenes.
   c. depiction of the struggle between religion and science.
   d. experimentation with new pigments.
   Ans: a

5. All BUT ONE of the following were musical innovations of the Baroque era.
   a. suite
   b. sonata
   c. concerto
   d. opera
   Ans: d

6. Descartes, *Discourse on Method.* The way Descartes goes about finding something that is absolutely certain is
   a. by trying to doubt everything.
   b. by using geometry as a standard.
   c. by using his certainty that God exists as a standard.
   d. by starting with the proposition "I think, therefore I am."
   Ans: a

7. Opposition to the new science came only from the Roman Catholic Church.
   Ans: F

Answer the following with a word or phrase.

8. The person whom the Inquisition threatened with torture unless he disavowed his scientific theories was _____.
    Ans: Galileo

9. The scientist who discovered the elliptical nature of planetary movement was _____.
    Ans: Johann Kepler

10. The Dutch invention perfected by Galileo that confirmed the truth of Copernicus' ideas was the _____.
    Ans: telescope

11. The process by which scientists draw general conclusions from observation of natural phenomena is known as _____.
    Ans: inductive reasoning

12. The process by which scientists begin with general theories and move toward the definition of particular truths is called _____.
    Ans: deductive reasoning

13. The depiction of everyday scenes, which so appealed to the middle-class Dutch, is called _____ painting.
    Ans: genre

14. Jan Vermeer is thought to have conceived his paintings with the use of an optical device that anticipated the modern pinhole camera, namely,
    Ans: the *camera obscura.*

Open Book

15. Fiero, Reading 4.13. The way Locke refers to innate ideas in lines 8–11 would be called by Bacon an
    a. Idol of the Tribe.
    b. Idol of the Cave.
    c. Idol of the Market Place.
    d. Idol of the Theater.
    Ans: d

16. Fiero, Reading 4.13. Locke's view on the origin of our ideas is best expressed by which of the following statements?
    a. All our ideas come from sensation.
    b. Some of our ideas come from sensation, some cannot arise from sense impressions.
    c. All our ideas either come from sense impressions or are derived from sense impressions.
    d. The senses give unclear ideas, then the mind gives them precision.
    Ans: b

17. Fiero, Figure 23.8, *The Suitor's Visit.* In this picture, the figure at the right is playing the violin, the most technically and mechanically improved instrument of this period.
    Ans: F

18. Fiero, Book 4, pages 45–46. In the following question, match a type of "idol" from Bacon's *Novum Organum* with the numbered errors.
    1. My personal feeling is that the earth is flat.
    2. Marriage is inferior to bachelorhood says Ignatius of Loyola in the *Spiritual Exercises.*
    3. Where I work everyone says that "jealous" means the same thing as "envious."
    4. Heaven awaits all good Christians.
        a. Idol of the Tribe
        b. Idol of the Cave
        c. Idol of the Marketplace
        d. Idol of the Theater
    Ans: 1. a, 2. b, 3. c, 4. d

19. Fiero, Figure 23.10, *View of Delft.* The interest in the new science on the part of Dutch painters may be seen in
    a. The choice of colors.
    b. The size of the canvas.
    c. The choice of the horizon line.
    d. The depiction of scientists in the foreground.
    Ans: c

20. Fiero, Figures 23.4, *Still Life,* and 23.5, *Vanitas.* Based on their views concerning the origin of our knowledge, which of these philosophers would more likely find appeal in the Dutch still life painters' sheer delight in the sensation of seeing?
    a. John Locke
    b. René Descartes
    Ans: a

21. A polyphonic composition in which a single musical theme is restated in sequential phrases is called a _____.
    Ans: fugue

Chapter **24** The Promise of Reason

Summary

The Age of European Enlightenment marks the beginning of the Western notion of social progress and human perfectibility. In political thought, Thomas Hobbes and John Locke advanced the idea of government based on a contract between ruler and ruled. While Hobbes envisioned individuals as surrendering part of their freedom to a supreme central authority, Locke saw government as holding power from the people and as required to exercise the will of the majority. Locke's writings provided the intellectual foundation for the Enlightenment faith in reason. Jefferson, Montesquieu, and Adam Smith were among those who adapted Locke's concept of natural law to matters of political and economic life. The idea that human beings acting according to the principles of reason might achieve the good life on earth produced a zealous optimism among European intellectuals. The *Encyclopédie* symbolized the Enlightenment will to gather and disseminate both theoretical and practical knowledge. The most popular prose genres—satire, journalistic essay, and the novel—addressed all aspects of human behavior in their social context.

Outline	Pronunciation Guide
A. Overview of the European enlightenment 　1. influence of the scientific revolution 　2. rise of literacy 　3. tension between noble and middle classes B. Emphasis on reason 　1. the concept of natural law 　2. development of the social sciences 　3. political theories of Hobbes and Locke 　4. influence of Locke on Montesquieu and Jefferson 　5. economic theories of Adam Smith C. *Philosophes* 　1. nature of the *salon* 　2. the deist view of God 　3. Diderot and the *Encyclopédie* 　4. notion of social progress—Condorcet and Wollstonecraft 　5. new forms of prose: the novel; journalistic essay	*Leviathan* [le VEYE u thun] **Montesquieu** [mahn tes KYOO] *philosophe* [fee low zuf] **Diderot** [dee de ROW] *Encyclopédie* [ahn see klow pay DEE] *salon* [sa LAHN] **Houdon** [hoo DOWN] **Condorcet** [kahn dowr SAY]

Key Terms: natural law, *salon, Philosophes, Encyclopédie, laissez-faire* economics, philosophic optimism, social contract.

Study Questions

Factual
1. How does Hobbes define human nature?
2. Why, according to Locke, are men willing to give up their freedom?
3. Which of Locke's ideas influenced Montesquieu and Jefferson?
4. What did Diderot wish to achieve in his multi-volume *Encyclopédie*?
5. Adam Smith (Reading 4.17) says that the division of labor comes from an inborn human tendency. What is that natural tendency according to Smith?
6. Mary Wollstonecraft's *Vindication of the Rights of Women* has been called "feminism's founding document." Why so? What were the principal aims of this treatise?
7. What, according to Condorcet, were the three main causes of the differences between human beings (Reading 4.19)? Did he believe these could be remedied?
8. What were the most important literary achievements of Joseph Addison, Daniel Defoe, and Alexander Pope?

Challenge
1. You have noticed that the thinkers in this period all tried to base their philosophy on what human beings do by nature. How can we tell what they do by nature, as opposed to what they do by upbringing?
2. Most of the *philosophes* believed in the existence of God. Why then did they also oppose church authority and organized religion?
3. It has been said that Hobbes and Locke might have been influenced by the Chinese concept of the Mandate of Heaven (Chapter 3). Which thinker would have been more attracted to this concept and why?
4. What do you think Condorcet means when he claims that sexual prejudice brings about "an inequality fatal even to the party in whose favor it works?" Can you provide evidence that supports this view—or negates it? How might Mary Wollstonecraft respond to this position?
5. In the time of the first cities (see Fiero, Chapters 1-2) you saw that slavery was widespread in the ancient world, yet in the article on "Negroes" in the *Encyclopédie* the practice is condemned as "contrary to natural law." What does this mean? Can you account for why this new position arose in the period of the Enlightenment?
6. Adam Smith argued that trade restraints imposed by monopolistic mercantile companies, chartered by the English crown, were unreasonable. Does this have any application today? Do you think Smith's views have influenced American foreign trade policies?
7. Enlightenment thinkers were not the first to advance the idea that human nature is bound by moral or "natural" laws. Can you find any similar point of view in Aristotle, Confucius, Cicero, or others?
8. In both Europe and China during the seventeenth and eighteenth centuries, long works of fiction in modern spoken languages became increasingly popular. How might we explain the rise of the modern novel in these regions? Why do you think this genre failed to develop in India and Africa during this era?
9. Do you agree with Hobbes' view of human nature? Is his view of rulership forward or backward-looking?
10. How does Pope's *Essay on Man* reflect the mood of optimism in the Age of Enlightenment?

Strategies for Discussion/Lecture

1. The texts in political philosophy in this chapter (including Rousseau in Chapter 25) can be focused on the notion of natural law, an extension to human nature of the conclusion of the seventeenth century that the entire physical world is governed by universal laws.

   One approach is to offer commentary on the first paragraphs of each of the social-philosophical texts in the chapter. With the exception of Condorcet, all begin with "nature," "necessary natural laws," or "state of nature." Condorcet may be used as an example of the new "faith in reason," since he pretends to predict the human future with the same ease that one might predict a solar eclipse in the year 3000.

2. A lecture or discussion could focus on two of the shortest texts in the chapter, Jefferson's *Declaration* and Abigail Adams' *Letter*. Jefferson's claim that the equality of all people is a "self-evident truth" should not go unchallenged. What standard of self-evidence could he be using in making such a statement? Can it be countered that "people are not created equal"? This instructor's ploy is not intended to encourage skepticism but to underline the fact that the Enlightenment might better be called the Age of Optimistic Faith in Reason, as opposed to the Age of Reason.

   Many students will be surprised by the vigor of Abigail's Adams' statement of purpose. When she asserts that "all men would be tyrants if they could," she may be echoing one general view of human nature characteristic of the times: specifically, wouldn't Hobbes agree with her?

   Adams' letter and the text author's comment on it can also be used to illustrate the insufficiency of reason. In the human community, does it really matter if truth is discovered and freely disseminated—even "self-evident" truth—if nobody has the political will to make the truth prevail?

   Wollstonecraft's *Vindication of the Rights of Women* is an ideal "cap" for these considerations since it deals with matters related to nature versus culture in the social development of women.

3. Divide the class into pro-Hobbes and pro-Locke teams and debate whether ultimate authority should lie in the hands of the ruler or in the hands of the people.

4. Students may be interested to research (and then discuss) Jefferson's views on Blacks based on his own writings, comparing the evidence of his written considerations to the actions he took in his personal and political life. A similar set of contradictions is apparent in the work and person of Mary Wollstonecraft whose *Vindication* is anchored in reason, but who, as a person, was capable of startling irrationality (see Janet Todd's *Mary Wollstonecraft: Revolutionary Life*).

5. Challenge question 1 is effective for discussion of natural law, and it will most likely be answered by students in one of two ways: (1) "You can't discover what is based on nature as opposed to nurture" (facile skepticism), (2) "You do scientific research on babies and the earliest human societies" (the premise of twentieth-century scientism). It may come as a shock to students that *none* of the social thinkers in this chapter ever did a scrap of empirical research on the foundations of natural law. (2) "Since the eighteenth century, has political science confirmed or refuted any of the articles of faith of these founders of the science of human society?"

6. The reading from Adam Smith may be your students' first contact with economics. Is it a science? If so, what are its laws? True to his era, Smith grounds economics in the "propensity in human nature . . . to truck, barter and exchange one thing for another" (lines 5–8). No empirical evidence is given for the existence of this (self-evident?) principle of human nature. If economics derives from "first principles of human nature," why is there not one economics, as there is only one physics? Stimulating insights into Smith's work and its relationship to Condorcet's may be found in a recent publication by Emma Rothchild, *Economic Sentiments: Adam Smith, Condorcet, and the Enlightenment* (Harvard University Press, 2001).

7. Pope's *Essay on Man* (Reading 4.21) shows how the belief in universal laws can lead to conclusions opposite from the progressive views of Jefferson and Adams. Pope's advice on the use of reason is to submit, to inquire no further. For Pope the status quo (WHAT IS) is not to be challenged by any appeal to justice (WHAT IS RIGHT): WHATEVER IS, IS RIGHT.

Students might be asked, "Who in society would benefit from such a view?" or "Imagine Pope's response to Abigail Adams' letter." Alternatively, flip forward to Fiero, Figure 25.5, *Gin Lane,* and apply Pope's maxim. This is basically the strategy used by Voltaire in *Candide* in Chapter 25.

Chapter 24 Audiovisuals

Video/CD-ROM Resources

AN AGE OF REASON, AN AGE OF PASSION 60 min., color **CPB**

ART OF THE WESTERN WORLD
 Program 6: An Age of Reason & An Age of Passion **HTG**

CATHERINE THE GREAT: A Lust for Art
 With dramatic readings from Catherine the Great's diaries, this program investigates a self-professed "glutton for beauty" who feasted daily on Rembrandts, Rubenses, and Brueghels. In less than 40 years, she acquired more masterpieces than the Louvre, often using art as a political weapon. **HTG**

CIVILIZATION : The Smile of Reason 52 min., color **TLF**

THE HERMITAGE: A Russian Odyssey
 This series takes a lingering look at Russia's great bastion of art, the Hermitage Museum of St. Petersburg. Aswirl in Russian art, politics, and history, THE HERMITAGE captures the grandeur and storminess of one of the greatest repositories of art worldwide. 54 min. each 1993 **HTG**

THOMAS JEFFERSON
 DIRECTOR: KEN BURNS
 Revered as the author of the Declaration of Independence yet condemned as a slave owner, Thomas Jefferson has entered a new era of controversy. This penetrating biography first portrays the young Jefferson from the Virginia wilderness, transformed by the philosophic fire of the American Revolution. Torn between his career and family life at Monticello, he suffers heart-rending personal loss even as he pens a new concept in democratic government. Follow Jefferson's rising star as he becomes U.S. Minister to France, enters national politics, fulfills his destiny as President, and begins his busy retirement years. 180 minutes on 2 tapes (1997) **PBS**

JEFFERSON IN PARIS
 DIRECTOR: JAMES IVORY (1995) **AZ**

THE MARKET SOCIETY AND HOW IT GREW 58 min., B&W **NET**

VOLTAIRE PRESENTS CANDIDE: An Introduction to the Age of Enlightenment 34 min., color
 EBEC

The John Locke bibliography—http://www.libraries.psu.edu/iasweb/locke/home.htm

Mary Wollstonecraft—http://www.ucalgary.ca/UofC/Others/CIH/writinglives/wlmslinks.html

Thomas Jefferson—http://www.pbs.org/jefferson/

Biographical information about Denis Diderot—http://www.utm.edu/research/iep/d/diderot.htm

Resources related to Natural Law—http://www.utm.edu/research/iep/n/natlaw.htm

Biographical information and resources related to Adam Smith—http://www.lucidcafe.com/lucidcafe/library/96jun/smith.html

McGraw-Hill Resources

Transparencies: MA.7 Early Modern World

Sample Test Questions for Chapter 24

Select the letter of the choice that BEST answers the question:

1. During most of the eighteenth century, European society was shaken by a struggle between the
   a. landed nobility and the middle class.
   b. middle class and the peasantry.
   c. kings and the middle class.
   d. nobility and the Church.
   Ans: a

2. Hobbes believed that
   a. the final political authority should remain with the people.
   b. social contract should be the source of individual happiness.
   c. human beings are selfish and warlike.
   d. society is best governed by a representative assembly.
   Ans: c

3. Locke affirmed that
   a. human beings are capable of governing themselves.
   b. life is "nasty, brutish, and short."
   c. revolution is never justified.
   d. the preservation of the state was the supreme objective of politics.
   Ans: a

4. Locke asserted the
   a. equality of the sexes.
   b. equality of social classes.
   c. necessity for religious toleration.
   d. overthrow of all monarchs.
   Ans: c

5. Montesquieu generally is credited with pioneering the field of
   a. anthropology.
   b. history.
   c. sociology.
   d. geography.
   Ans: c

6. In writing the Declaration of Independence, Thomas Jefferson was inspired by
   a. Voltaire.
   b. Montesquieu.
   c. Rousseau.
   d. Hobbes.
   Ans: b

7. One of the first champions of equality of the sexes was
   a. Jefferson.
   b. Montesquieu.
   c. Condorcet.
   d. Locke.
   Ans: c

8. The most important form of literary entertainment in the eighteenth century was the
   a. journalistic essay.
   b. novel.
   c. epic poem.
   d. soliloquy.
   Ans: b

9. *Laissez-faire* economics as defined by Adam Smith insisted on
   a. government intervention in business.
   b. state-owned monopolies of major industries.
   c. the law of supply and demand.
   d. restricting foreign imports.
   Ans: c

10. The salons of France, where much debate over Enlightenment thought took place, were organized and directed by
   a. the *Philosophes*.
   b. women.
   c. the king.
   d. the universities.
   Ans: b

11. On the whole, Enlightenment thought assumed that human society, like nature, was governed by natural laws.
    Ans: T

12. The eighteenth century is known for the expansion of the natural, rather than the social, sciences.
    Ans: F

13. Wollstonecraft held that the education of most women was
    a. disorderly and inadequate.
    b. too greatly controlled by the church.
    c. lacking in Latin and Greek.
    d. all of the above.
    Ans: a

Answer the following with a word or phrase.

14. The Enlightenment writer, _____, articulated "philosophic optimism" by arguing that all events, no matter how painful, conformed to a pre-established universal design.
    Ans: Leibnitz

15. The thinker who first advocated the idea of a separation of powers as a defense against totalitarian government was _____.
    Ans: Montesquieu

16. According to _____, governments should protect and increase an individual's rights to life, liberty, and property.
    Ans: Locke

17. The compendium of knowledge that reflected the Enlightenment's bent toward collecting and classifying information was known as the _____.
    Ans: *Encyclopédie*

18. The writer who first suggested that rehabilitation rather than torture would deter crime was _____.
    Ans: Beccaria

Chapter 25 The Limits of Reason

Summary

The Enlightenment faith in the promise of reason was eventually tempered by an equally enlightened examination of the limits of reason, culminating in Kant's *Critique of Pure Reason,* which argued that empirical science was limited by a number of predetermined mental categories. In practical human terms, however, the most glaring failure of the age of reason was the perpetuation of the slave trade. The new intellectual climate was prepared by master satirists Goldsmith, Swift, and Voltaire. Voltaire's *Candide* leveled a comic blow to the prevailing philosophical optimism. Hogarth expressed a similar kind of invective in the visual arts. Questioning the value of reason for the advancement of the human condition, Rousseau argued that society itself corrupted the individual; he championed solitary "man in his primitive state."

Outline	Pronunciation Guide

A. Historical context
   1. reaction against the excesses of rationalism
   2. economic and social conditions: industrialism
   3. the transatlantic slave trade: Equiano; Wheatley
B. Satire
   1. cosmopolitan context
   2. satire in European literature: Swift
   3. satire in Chinese literature
   4. Voltaire
   5. satire in visual art
C. Revolt against pure reason
   1. Rousseau
   2. Kant
	Equiano [ek wee AH now]
	Voltaire [vahl TER]
	Candide [kan DEED]
	Rousseau [roo SOW]
	Kant [KAHNT]
	Li Ruzhen [LEE JOO CHEN]

Key Terms: satire, deism, philosophic idealism, the Third Estate, the Bastille, irony, categorical imperative.

Key Images	
Hogarth, *Marriage à la Mode: The Marriage*	Hogarth, *Gin Lane*

Study Questions

Factual
1. Summarize the conditions and circumstances described by Equiano in his Travels (Reading 4.22).
2. What is the message of Phillis Wheatley's poem, "On Being Brought from Africa to America" (Reading 4.23)?
3. Who is the model for Dr. Pangloss in Voltaire's *Candide?* What features of the character refer to this model?
4. Describe the character of Candide as he is depicted in the early portions of *Candide.*
5. What ills in British society are ridiculed by Hogarth?
6. What did Rousseau mean when he wrote, "God makes all things good; man meddles in them and they become evil"?
7. How would Rousseau reform education? Were aspects of your own education "Rousseauian"?
8. Name the chief causes of the American Revolution and the French Revolution.

Challenge
1. Voltaire mocks the notion that love is ennobling and that warfare is a glorious endeavor. What other traditional attitudes and beliefs does Voltaire satirize in *Candide?*
2. Research projects. Read either Leonard Bernstein's musical comedy *Candide,* or Terry Southern's novel *Candy.* How do these modern adaptations rework the subjects satirized by Voltaire?
3. In criticizing his own society, Voltaire isolated three "great evils": boredom, vice, and poverty. Do you think he was on target for the eighteenth century? Do you think he would single out these evils in today's society, or other ones?
4. Consider the phrases *heroic butchery* and *cool apartments* from Chapters 3 and 6 of *Candide* (Reading 4.25). How do these and other oxymorons enliven Voltaire's prose style?
5. What aspects of eighteenth-century life does Hogarth attack in his art? How does visual satire differ from verbal satire? Can you cite any examples of satire in popular contemporary life? Are there any American political cartoonists of the caliber of Hogarth?
6. Rousseau locates the origins of human cruelty in social interaction. How does he arrive at this? Do you agree with his point of view?

Strategies for Discussion/Lecture

1. A brief lecture summary of the transatlantic slave trade might be followed by class discussion on the conditions and circumstances reflected in the writings of Equiano and Wheatley. Then move to apply the assessments of human nature offered by Swift, Volatire, and Rousseau. What picture of eighteenth-century culture is etched here?
2. The lecturer can bridge the last chapter to the present one by recalling the satirical aspect of Molière's play. Dr. Pangloss in the Baron's chateau is a caricature of the thinker, like Molière's philosopher, yet he, Pangloss—not Voltaire—is "on the inside," lives off the powerful, even promoting a philosophy according to which whatever happens is for the best. Can students recognize the spirit of Pope's "WHATEVER IS, IS RIGHT" in lines 31–39 of *Candide?*
   Li Ruzhen's *Flowers in the Mirror* (Reading 4.26) can be used to emphasize another technique of the social satirist, whereby a never-never land is used as the scene of action (cf. *Gulliver's Travels*).
3. In a recent book by the neurologist, Donald B. Caine (*Within Reason: Rationality and Human Behavior*, Pantheon Books, 2001), it is suggested that the West has placed too much faith in reason as "an all-powerful divine force, with its own supreme mission." Use this observation (or the book

itself) as a starting point for discussion and debate.

4. Kant's major writings are far too difficult to recommend to students at this level, but one of his short, popular essays which shows his kinship with Rousseau can be read with understanding and pleasure: *What is Enlightenment?* (pages 132–139 of the readily available *The Philosophy of Kant,* Modern Library, 1949 and 1977).

5. If slides of Hogarth's engravings are available, these might be used to offer an intriguing, if satiric overview of the ills of the eighteenth century.

Chapter 25 Audiovisuals

Video/CD-ROM Sources

CANDIDE (1972) **TLF**

THE FRENCH REVOLUTION 17 min., color **CORONET**

SEEDS OF THE REVOLUTION: Colonial America 1763–75 24 min., color **Graphic Curriculum**

Web Resources

Kant on the web—http://www.hkbu.edu.hk/~ppp/Kant.html

Biographical information about Jean Jacques Rousseau—
http://www.utm.edu/research/iep/r/rousseau.html

Information about Jonathan Swift—http://www.jaffebros.com/lee/gulliver

Bibliography of major satiric works—http://andromeda.rutgers.edu/~jlynch/biblio/satirebib.html

The Voltaire Society of America—http://humanities.uchicago.edu/homes/vsa/

Biographical information about William Hogarth—http://www.lamp.ac.uk/hogarth/

McGraw-Hill Resources

Transparencies: MA.8 Early Modern World 1789–1914

Sample Test Questions for Chapter 25

Select the letter of the choice that BEST answers the question:

1. In Olaudah Equiano's narrative, one thing contributing to his abduction and enslavement was
    a. the proximity of his village to the sea.
    b. his parents' failure to guard him.
    c. his captor's promise of good food.
    d. his total ignorance of self-defense.
    Ans: b

2. When Candide and his friends were traveling through Portugal, they encountered a natural disaster in the form of
   a. a cyclone.
   b. a drought.
   c. an earthquake.
   d. a plague of locusts.
   Ans: c

3. The British artist who published an extraordinary series of engravings that were biting commentaries on economic and social conditions was
   a. William Hogarth.
   b. Tom Rakewell.
   c. Christopher Wren.
   d. William Pitt.
   Ans: a

4. The peasant grievances that fueled the French Revolution included all of the following EXCEPT
   a. high taxes.
   b. inflation.
   c. royal spending.
   d. redistribution of land.
   Ans: d

5. In his *Discourse on the Origin of Inequality among Men,* Rousseau asserts that civil society began with
   a. speech.
   b. private property.
   c. the family.
   d. the social contract.
   Ans: b

6. In Rousseau's *Discourse,* the result of sexual attraction in humanity's first period is
   a. affection for children.
   b. marriage.
   c. devotion of children to parents.
   d. a purely animal act.
   Ans: d

7. In Kant's view, reason was
   a. falsely based in human habit.
   b. rooted in innate ideas.
   c. useless in making moral judgments.
   d. the keystone for human conduct.
   Ans: d

8. *A Modest Proposal* by Jonathan Swift suggested in jest that the problem of poverty be solved through cannibalism.
   Ans: T

9. Rousseau flatly rejected the Enlightenment belief that progress in the arts and sciences would improve individual conduct.
Ans: T

10. Kant shifted the focus of Western philosophy from questioning the nature of objective reality to examining the mind and its operations.
Ans: T

11. Hume, the ultimate skeptic, doubted that humans could know anything other than the contents of their own minds.
Ans: T

Answer the following with a word or phrase.

12. The author of *Candide,* who aimed much of his invective against organized religion and fanaticism, was _____.
Ans: Voltaire

13. Rousseau began the first chapter of his treatise _____ with the words, "Man is born free, and everywhere he is in chains."
Ans: *The Social Contract*

14. The celebrated slogan of the French Revolution, "Liberty, Equality and Fraternity," was penned by _____.
Ans: Rousseau

Open Book

15. Fiero, Figure 25.4. In Hogarth's engraving, *Marriage à la Mode,* what is placed immediately in the foreground shows that the most important aspect of marriage for these participants is
   a. money.
   b. breeding.
   c. sex.
   d. property.
Ans: b

16. Fiero, Figure 25.5. In Hogarth's *Gin Lane,* the symbols hung outside shops indicate that money is to be made from misery; the trades represented include all BUT ONE of the following.
   a. casket makers
   b. distillers
   c. wig makers
   d. pawn shops
Ans: c

17. In *Gin Lane,* Hogarth has partly concealed in his background, top-center, left, a London building with some connection to the scene before our eyes. This building is most likely
    a. Saint Paul's Cathedral.
    b. a courthouse.
    c. the Houses of Parliament.
    d. the University of London.
    Ans: b

18. The nineteenth-century lithograph *The Hold of a Ship* (Figure 25.1) suggests that
    a. male and female slaves were housed together.
    b. most of the slaves were young.
    c. most of the slaves were female.
    d. all of the above.
    Ans: a

Chapter 26 Eighteenth Century Art, Music, and Society

Summary

Eighteenth-century European art and music reflected the changing character of society and the tastes of its various social classes. The fashionable rococo style expressed the aristocratic affection for an art of delicacy, intimacy, and grace. The materials of this art are luxurious and durable and require a high caliber of craft labor. By mid-century, a reaction against the rococo style occurred among members of a growing middle class, who identified their interests with the rational ideals of the European Enlightenment. Encouraged by the *philosophes'* demand for an art of moral virtue, Greuze and Chardin produced genre paintings that dignified the lives and work of ordinary people.

At the same time, eighteenth-century archeological investigations encouraged interest in the Greco-Roman past. The neoclassical works of David, as well as those of other artists, swept away the rococo in the same way that the French Revolution swept away the Old Regime. The neoclassical style spread from Paris to England to America and symbolized the Enlightenment ideals of reason and liberty. In music, the rococo style gave way after mid-century to the classical style, as composers like Haydn and Mozart sought clarity of design in instrumental forms, such as the symphony, string quartet, sonata, and concerto.

Outline	Pronunciation Guide

A. Rococo style
  1. historical context: France
  2. in Austria and Bavaria
  3. French rococo painting
    a. Watteau
    b. Boucher
    c. Vigée-LeBrun
    d. Fragonard
  4. French rococo sculpture
B. Genre painting
  1. as reaction against rococo
  2. Greuze and Chardin
C. Neoclassicism
  1. the new archeology
  2. as expression of Enlightenment ideals
  3. architecture
    a. Soufflot
    b. Jefferson
    c. Gibbs
	Ottobeuren [ah tow boy ren]
	Boucher [boo SHAY]
	Watteau [wah TOW]
	fête galante [fet gah LANT]
	Vigée-LeBrun [vee JAY le BRUN]
	Fragonard [fra gow NAHR]
	Greuze [GROOZ]
	Chardin [shahr DAN]
	Canova [kah NOW vah]
	David [dah VEED]
	Ingres [ANG ru]
	Couperin [coo pu RAN]
	Stamitz [SHTAH mits]
	Haydn [HEYE dun]
	Mozart [MOWT tsart]
	da Ponte [dah POWN tay]

         4. sculpture
             a. Houdon
             b. Canova
             c. Wedgwood
         5. painting
             a. David
             b. Ingres
         6. neoclassicism under Napoleon
     D. Eighteenth-century music
         1. rococo music
         2. classical music
         3. birth of the orchestra
         4. classical instrumental forms
         5. the classical style: Haydn; Mozart; early
             Beethoven

Key Terms: rococo, neoclassicism, *fête galante,* symphony, string quartet, sonata form, score, *opera buffa.*

Key Images:	
Fisher, Benedictine Abbey, Ottobeuren	Soufflot, Sainte Geneviève (The Panthéon)
Watteau, *Departure from the Island of Cythera*	Adam, Marble Hall, Derbyshire
Boucher, *Venus Consoling Love*	Canova, *Pauline Borghese as Venus*
Vigée-LeBrun, *Marie Antoinette*	Houdon, *Thomas Jefferson*
Fragonard, *The Swing*	David, *Oath of the Horatii*
Chardin, *The Kitchen Maid*	Ingres, *La Grand Odalisque*; *Apotheosis of Homer*

Study Questions

Factual

1. In Figures 26.1 through 26.6 point out the features that are rococo and say why they belong to that style.
2. Describe a *fête galante.* Is there any such entertainment in contemporary society?
3. How did the paintings of Greuze and Chardin differ from those of Watteau, Boucher, and Fragonard?
4. What events inspired the neoclassical revival of the eighteenth century?
5. What events are represented in David's *Oath of the Horatii?* Why did the painting become a symbol of the French revolutionary spirit?
6. In what ways is Ingres' *Apotheosis of Homer* the quintessential statement of neoclassical ideals?
7. What are the two principal meanings of the term *classical style* in music?
8. What composers are associated with the refinement of the classical style in music?
9   What are the main groups of instruments in the classical symphony?

Challenge

1. Compare Figures 26.1 and 26.17; in which interior would you prefer to live? Why?

2. What moral values might one associate with David's neoclassical canvases? How did David's style underscore the content of his paintings?

3. To what extent was the style of eighteenth-century neoclassical buildings faithful to their models? Compare some of these (Figures 26.15–26.17; 26.22, 26.24, 26.31) with the neoclassical architecture of the Renaissance (Chapter 17). Which period represents a more sensitive appreciation of Greek and Roman architecture? Which is more accurate?

4. Find examples in American architecture and popular culture of the neoclassical heritage. Do these symbols still carry the meaning intended by the Founding Fathers?

5. Canova's contemporaries found the marble likeness of Pauline Borghese extremely erotic. The statue was not on public view but was seen by private invitation and often inspected by candlelight. Was there a sensual dimension to neoclassical paintings? If you think so, offer examples.

6. Mozart has been called "the most gifted of all human beings." What aspects of his music do you personally enjoy? What differences do you hear between the music of Haydn and that of Mozart (Music Listening Selections II–9 and II–10)?

7. In what contexts and for what specific occasions did instrumental music serve during the eighteenth century? Did all social classes demand instrumental music? If so, how?

8. How do the paintings of Watteau, Boucher, and Fragonard reflect the "pursuit of pleasure"?

9. Which architectural monuments are most representative of the neoclassical style in France, England, and the United States?

Strategies for Discussion/Lecture

1. This chapter gives the instructor a good opportunity to stress interiors and workmanship of materials in a slide lecture, or using text illustrations.

   If students have done tracing and studies of proportion of exteriors in previous chapters, the present one allows them to add meaning to the scale and distribution of interior spaces in similar buildings, and to appreciate how luxurious items of practical use could be in the age immediately preceding machine production.

   A slide presentation could focus on the contrast between rococo and neoclassical in the interiors of the Benedictine Abbey (Figure 26.4), where structure is hidden behind the frosting, and the Pantheon (Figures 26.15 and 26.16), where the interior reflects the exterior structure, but where religious sentiment is almost nonexistent. Quite likely most students would not recognize the Pantheon as a place of worship.

2. If painting is the lecturer's choice of focus, a good preparatory assignment would be Factual question 3, which contrasts two major trends, to which David and neoclassicism can be added.

3. Comparing illustrations/slides from Chapter 21 (aristocratic style) with those of interiors in Chapters 25 and 26, the instructor can display living spaces of the ruling class, city middle class (Hogarth), village (Greuze), and servant class (Chardin). Ask students to comment on the presence or absence of "luxuries" like windows and mirrors and the mere quantity of space occupied.

4. The rococo taste for ornament is strongly felt in music. Play the Couperin selection (Music Listening Selection II–8) as background music to viewing Figures 26.1 and 26.4, asking students to comment on the nature of the musical line.

5. Urge students to attend a live performance or listen to a complete symphony by Mozart or Haydn. Open class discussion as to whether there is in this country today such a thing as upper-class music, middle-class music, lower-class music.

Chapter 26 Audiovisuals

Video/CD-ROM Sources

AN AGE OF REASON: Art of The Western World Series 30 min., color **CPB**

AMADEUS
DIRECTOR: MILOS FORMAN (1984) 158 min., color **AZ**

CIVILISATION—Vol. #09: The Pursuit of Happiness (1970)
DIRECTOR: CLARK, SIR KENNETH 53 min., color **PBS**

CIVILISATION—Vol. #10: The Smile of Reason (1970)
DIRECTOR: CLARK, SIR KENNETH 53 min., color **PBS**

MOZART
Series of four sections each on works for violin and piano set in an Italian drawing room. (1991)
120 min. **AE**

Music Resources

Haydn, *Quartets (6) for Strings, Op. 50*, Juilliard String Quartet, CBS M2K-42154, CD.
Haydn, *Symphonies (104)*, Marriner, St. Martin's Academy, Philips 6768003 PSI.
Mozart, *Piano Music*, Barenboim, Angel CDC–47384, CD.

Web Resources

Neoclassic art—http://www.artcyclopedia.com/history/neoclassicism.html

Biographical information about Mozart—http://www.mozartproject.org/

Biographical information about Mozart, including selections of music—
http://mozart.composers.net/index.html

Resources related to Beethoven—http://w3.rz-berlin.mpg.de/cmp/beethoven.html

Information about Haydn—http://home.wxs.nl/~cmr/haydn/

Rococo art—http://www.artcyclopedia.com/history/rococo.html

Rococo and Classical composers—http://www.geocities.com/vienna/5879/main.html

McGraw-Hill Resources

Music Listening Selections: CD II
II–8 Couperin, *Order,* No. 22, "Le Croc-en-jambe"
II–9 Haydn, *Symphony* No. 94
II–10 Mozart, Serenade in G Major, "Ein Kleine Nachtmusik"
II–11 Mozart, *Marriage of Figaro*, "Dave Sono"

Transparencies: M.14 Sonata Form (classical)
　　　　　　　 MA.8 Middle Modern World 1789–1914
　　　　　　　 MA.14 Music-Art-European Map (Nineteenth Century)

Sample Test Questions for Chapter 26

Select the letter of the choice that BEST answers the question:

1. All of the following are true of the rococo style of painting EXCEPT
   a. such art did not generally convey any noble message.
   b. artists focused on themes of sensuality and pleasure.
   c. artists employed delicate colors and fragile forms.
   d. artists favored stark contrasts of light and dark.
   Ans: d

2. Rococo art took as its subject matter
   a. the preoccupation with fashion and the material world.
   b. the dignity of everyday work.
   c. dramatic political events.
   d. the histories of Greece and Rome.
   Ans: a

3. Genre painting depicted scenes of
   a. military strife.
   b. extreme sensuality.
   c. ordinary life.
   d. religious ecstasy.
   Ans: c

4. The Enlightenment emphasis on reason, clarity, and order was most closely associated with
   _____ art.
   a. genre
   b. rococo
   c. neoclassical
   d. pastel
   Ans: c

5. The style of Thomas Jefferson's rotunda at the University of Virginia shows the influence on early America of
   a. rococo taste.
   b. the spirit that animated the *genre* painters in France.
   c. Baroque taste.
   d. Enlightenment neoclassicism.
   Ans: d

6. The sonata form included ALL BUT which one of the following elements?
   a. three or four divisions or movements
   b. designation of specific tempos
   c. encouragement of improvisation
   d. contrasting groups of instruments
   Ans: c

7. The French artist, Ingres, argued that _____ is the most important element of art.
   a. color
   b. contrast
   c. perspective
   d. line
   Ans: d

8. Nowadays, one of the musical forms Haydn developed and excelled at is no longer performed in the space for which it was intended, namely
   a. liturgical music.
   b. operas.
   c. symphonies.
   d. chamber music.
   Ans: d

9. The most important instrumental musical ensemble grouping that emerged in the eighteenth century was
   a. the string trio.
   b. the orchestra.
   c. the operatic quartet.
   d. the wind quintet.
   Ans: b

10. *Exposition, development,* and *recapitulation* are names of the elements of which one of the following eighteenth-century musical genres?
    a. the sarabande
    b. the minuet
    c. the opera
    d. the sonata form
    Ans: d

11. The younger contemporary of Franz Joseph Haydn, who composed *The Marriage of Figaro,* was
    a. Mozart.
    b. Stamitz.
    c. Couperin.
    d. da Ponte.
    Ans: a

Answer the following with a word or phrase:

12. Governmental buildings constructed at the end of the eighteenth century in England and America were most likely to be designed in the _____ style, a symbol of power and prestige.
   Ans: neoclassical

13. Jean-Jacques Soufflot, one of the leading French architects, designed a national memorial to revolutionary heroes known as the _____.
   Ans: Pantheon

14. The designer of the Virginia State Capitol, as well as many neoclassically styled buildings on the University of Virginia campus, was _____.
   Ans: Thomas Jefferson

15. The fusion of politics and art, which exalted the ideal of service and sacrifice to one's country, is seen in the painting *Oath of the Horatii,* by _____.
   Ans: David

Open Book

16. Fiero, Figure 24.14: The collection illustrated in this drawing shows that the taste of the period was centered PRIMARILY on
   a. Roman art and architecture.
   b. Christian art and architecture.
   c. Greek art and architecture.
   d. Greek and Christian art and architecture.
   Ans: a

17. Fiero, Figures 26.15, 26.20, and 26.22. Of these three structures, the one that treats the space inside the pediment most like Greek temples such as the Parthenon is
   a. Church of Saint Geneviève.
   b. Saint Martin-in-the-Fields.
   c. University of Virginia, Rotunda.
   Ans: a

18. Fiero, Figure 26.24. In his presentation of George Washington, Houdon places at the figure's left side
   a. the symbol of the office of the president.
   b. a Greek column with fluting.
   c. a Roman symbol of authority.
   d. a symbol associated with an English gentleman's sports interest.
   Ans: c

19. If we review all the paintings in Chapter 26, we see a clear trend in the subject matter of the eighteenth century, namely,
    a. from the depiction of aristocratic life to the representation of the lives of working people.
    b. from the depiction of women to the depiction of men.
    c. from the representation of historical figures to religious subjects.
    d. from aristocratic life to the life of commoners, as well as historical allegories.
    Ans: d

20. Comparing Figure 20.19, a ceiling in Borromini's San Carlo with 26.16, a ceiling in Soufflot's Pantheon: The Pantheon's neoclassical rejection of baroque exuberance is apparent first of all in the preference for the circle over the visually and conceptually more complicated oval.
    Ans: T

21. Although not far removed in time, Clodion's *The Intoxication of Wine*, Figure 26.10 and Canova's *Pauline Borghese as Venus*, Figure 26.18 seem to belong to different stylistic worlds. This transition is called the change in style from
    a. Baroque to romantic
    b. liberal to conservative
    c. rococo to neoclassical
    d. Gothic to classical
    Ans: c

22. Figure 26.25, *The Oath of the Horatii*. The degree of accuracy in depicting ancient scenes characteristic of eighteenth-century neoclassicism can be seen in David's choice of architectural orders in the background of this painting, namely
    a. Roman Doric.
    b. Greek Doric.
    c. pure Ionic.
    d. Corinthian.
    Ans: a

23. The musical form that features one or more solo instruments and an orchestra is known as a
    a. chamber piece.
    b. sonata.
    c. concerto.
    d. symphony.
    Ans: c

24. An Austrian by birth, Haydn made his reputation in the performance of symphonies in
    a. Paris.
    b. London.
    c. New York.
    d. Vienna.
    Ans: b

BOOK 5

Romanticism, Realism, and the Nineteenth-Century World

PART I   The Romantic Era

Chapter **27** **The Romantic View of Nature**

Summary

Nature and the natural landscape were central to nineteenth-century romanticism. While the nature poets Wordsworth and Shelley viewed the landscape as a refuge from the evils of industrialism and a source of sublime understanding, Keats rejoiced that nature's fleeting beauty might forever dwell in art. As in Europe, America's romantics, such as Walt Whitman, exalted robust individualism, the life of the imagination, and the cultivation of a more natural language of poetic expression. Emerson and Thoreau sought the union of self with nature through the movement called transcendentalism. Such themes found their counterparts in the landscape paintings of Constable and Turner in England, Friedrich in Germany, Corot in France, and Cole, Bierstadt, and Church in America. The romantic embrace of nature manifested itself intellectually, as well, in the pantheism of Schopenhauer and the evolutionary dialectic of Hegel. It found its most far-reaching implications, however, in Darwin's theory of natural selection, which, ironically, toppled human beings from their lofty place in nature.

Outline	**Pronunciation Guide**

A. Historical context
    1. economic and social conditions
    2. birth of European romanticism
B. Nature and the natural in European literature
    1. Wordsworth
    2. Shelley
    3. Keats
C. Nature and the natural in Asian literature
    1. Chinese nature poetry and landscape art
    2. Shen Fu and Chinese prose
D. Romantic landscape painting
    1. Constable
    2. Turner
    3. Friedrich
    4. Corot
	Keats [KEETS]
	Corot [kow ROW]
	Ville d'Avray [VEEL dav RAY]
	Bierstadt [BIR stat]
	Fichte [FIK tu]
	Hegel [HAY gul]
	Schopenhauer [SHOW pen hou er]
	Novalis [now VAL es]

E. Romanticism in America
   1. transcendentalism
      a. Emerson
      b. Thoreau
   2. Walt Whitman
   3. moralizing landscapes
   4. Native American arts and nature
F. Nature and intellectual thought
   1. Schopenhauer
   2. romantic mysticism
   3. Hegel
   4. Darwin and evolution

Pronunciation Key: apple, play, **ah** (altar), **e**gg, k**ee**p, **i**nch, **eye**, gl**ow**, b**oo**ze, **ou**tfit, b**u**lk, **u** in b**oo**k, s**i**ngle, **sh**in, **ch**apter, **j**ust, **z**ebra, **zh**ivago, can**y**on.

Key Terms: industrial revolution, nationalism, landscape, romanticism, painting out of doors, transcendentalism, romantic individualism, nostalgia, exoticism, mysticism, dialectic, evolution, natural selection, "survival of the fittest."

Key Images	
Turner, *Interior of Tintern Abbey* Constable, *Wivenhoe Park, Essex* Turner, *Snowstorm: Steamboat Off Harbour's Mouth* Catlin, *The White Cloud, Head Chief*	Bierstadt, *The Rocky Mountains* Friedrich, *Two Men Looking at the Moon* Corot, *Ville d'Avray* Cole, *The Oxbow*

Study Questions

Factual
1. Nature is a key motif in romantic poetry. How does Wordsworth's "Tintern Abbey" (Reading 5.1) illustrate this fact?
2. What does the wind represent in Shelley's "Ode to the West Wind"?
3. Who were the American transcendentalists? How did they regard the role of nature in human life?
4. What did Thoreau mean by "the indescribable innocence" of nature?
5. What is free verse? Cite an example from Chapter 27.
6. How did Hegel explain the operation of nature? Did he believe that the dialectic operated in an absolute manner?
7. Explain in your own words the phrase "evolution by natural selection."
8. What does "survival of the fittest" mean? Was Darwin's primary meaning that fit individuals survive?
9. How did American landscapes differ generally from those of European artists?
10. Can you see what Thoreau calls "the indescribable innocence" of nature in Shen Fu's *Six Chapters from a Floating Life* (Reading 5.4)?

Challenge
1. Explain what Wordsworth means when he calls nature "The anchor of my purest thoughts, the nurse,/The guide, the guardian of my heart, and soul/Of all my moral being." Compare your own responses to nature and the natural landscape.

2. Is Keats' view that beauty and truth are one an exclusively romantic point of view? How, for instance, did Winckelmann (Chapter 26) define beauty?

3. The text calls attention to Shelley's use of literary tone color: the sounds of words that make an appeal to the senses. Find other examples of such in the poetry in Chapters 27 and 28.

4. In what way was Thoreau's life at Walden Pond an adventure in practical survival? In what ways was it a mystical experience? Are these two kinds of experience compatible?

5. Compare neoclassicism and romanticism as stylistic and intellectual modes of approaching reality.

6. What do each of the following statements reveal about the nineteenth-century romantic?
   a. I fall upon the thorns of life! I bleed! (Shelley)
   b. I see all; the currents of the Universal Being circulate through me. (Emerson)
   c. I want to live deep and suck out all the marrow of life. (Thoreau)
   d. Feeling is all. (Goethe)
   e. I have no love for reasonable painting. (Delacroix)

7. Compare Constable's paintings with the poetry of Wordsworth. In your view, do they show the reflectiveness and spirituality of Wordsworth's poetry? What of the other landscape painters of the period?

8. In what ways does Darwin's theory of natural selection challenge traditional views? Is this theory compatible with a belief in a supreme being? If so, how so?

9. In what ways did the cultural contributions of China and India influence nineteenth-century intellectuals? Do you see any parallels between Chinese lyric poetry (Chapter 14) and the poetry of the romantics?

10. Compare the landscapes of Turner, Constable, and Bierstadt. In what ways are they similar? How do they differ in sensibility and mood?

Strategies for Discussion/Lecture

1. The organization of the chapter is perfect for asking students to come to class with the poets matched to a landscape painting, giving written reasons for their choices. The variety of matches will go right to their understanding of the poets, the painters, and romanticism. The lecturer may wish to concentrate on landscape (ideally with slides), then treat poetry in more detailed discussion, using one or more of the following suggestions as a focus.

2. The beginnings of poems are so important that comparisons of first lines will almost always yield interesting results. Here Wordsworth is mostly past, Shelley present, and Keats future. Do the respective time frames fit the sense of nature's cycles in each poet?

3. Keats' "Ode on a Grecian Urn" (Reading 5.3) can be confusing if the class is not prepared beforehand for what is going on. A painted Greek vase is provided for illustration, but one might do well to have students look first at something simpler and more directly affecting, such as Fiero, Chapter 6, Figure 6.26, Berlin Painter, "Woman with a Kithera." Use it like pictures in thematic apperception tests, asking students to tell the story behind the picture: "What is she thinking about as she sings?" Keats' "Ode on a Grecian Urn," they will see, is a series of questions of that kind.

4. In his "Ode on a Grecian Urn" (Reading 5.3), Keats suggests that the lovers will be forever happy without the possibility of physical contact (lines 17–20). Do you think human lovers would accept this arrangement? Would you accept this arrangement?

5. Imagine Darwin reading Emerson, Thoreau, and Whitman. What would he like or dislike about their views of nature?

Chapter 27 Audiovisuals

Video/CD-ROM Sources

AMERICAN QUILTS
From the days of the earliest settlers to the most modern times, quilts with their kaleidoscope of colors have adorned homes everywhere. Now you can follow the footsteps of their history and learn more about their unique symbolism in the family and the arts. Discover how the artists who create them are as varied as the patterns they produce. Find out the secrets each one holds and visit popular American quilt shows in Paducah, Kentucky and Houston, Texas. 80 min. **PBS**

ASCENT OF MAN: The Ladder of Creation 52 min., color **TLF**

CIVILISATION—Vol. #11: The Worship of Nature (1970)
DIRECTOR: CLARK, SIR KENNETH 53 min., color **PBS**

EUGENE DELACROIX: THE RESTLESS EYE.
Written and narrated by Colin Nears 60 min. **PH**

ENGLISH LITERATURE: The Early Romantic Age (1990) 24 min., color **CORONET**

ENGLISH LITERATURE: Romantic Period 14 min., color **CORONET**

THE SPIRIT OF ROMANTICISM 27 min., color **EBEC**

J.M.W. TURNER: THE SUN IS GOD
The life and artistic development of this great painter. 63 min. **FFH**

WALT WHITMAN—Voices and Visions Series (1987) 60 min., color **CPB**

Web Resources

Information about Wordsworth—http://www.wordsworth.org.uk/

Biographical information and resources related to Percy Bysshe Shelley—
http://www.spartacus.schoolnet.co.uk/prshelley.htm

Biographical information and selected works by John Keats—http://hem.passagen.se/jonnyl/keats/

Information about Transcendentalism—http://www.transcendentalists.com

Resources related to Ralph Waldo Emerson—http://www.transcendentalists.com/1emerson.html

Resources related to Henry David Thoreau—http://www.walden.org/thoreau/Default.asp

Resources related to Henry David Thoreau—http://www.eserver.org/thoreau/

Information related to Walt Whitman—http://jefferson.village.virginia.edu/whitman/

Biographical information related to Charles Darwin—http://emporium.turnpike.net/~mscott/darwin.htm

McGraw-Hill Resources

Transparencies: MA.8 Middle Modern World 1789–1914

Sample Test Questions for Chapter 27

Select the letter of the choice that BEST answers the question.

1. Among the developments that transformed nineteenth-century Europe were
    a. a shift from farming to industry.
    b. a decline in nationalism.
    c. the outbreak of the plague.
    d. the development of new artillery.
    Ans: a

2. Romanticism was a rebellion against all the following EXCEPT
    a. religious authority.
    b. reason.
    c. industrialization.
    d. national identity.
    Ans: d

3. The poet _____ argues in his "Ode on a Grecian Urn" that pleasure is fleeting and that art alone records the pleasure of past experiences.
    a. Shelley
    b. Wordsworth
    c. Keats
    d. Byron
    Ans: c

4. Emerson's statement (from the essay *Nature*), "There [in the woods] I feel that nothing can befall me in life—no disgrace, no calamity. . . , which nature cannot repair" is most reminiscent of
    a. Wordsworth.
    b. Keats.
    c. Shelley.
    d. Darwin.
    Ans: a

5. The author who retreated to isolated Walden Pond in Massachusetts to write what he called "a handbook for living" was
    a. Emerson.
    b. Cooper.
    c. Alcott.
    d. Thoreau.
    Ans: d

6. The form of poetry that breaks with traditional meters and is based on irregular rhythmic patterns is called
   a. iambic pentameter.
   b. free verse.
   c. dactylic hexameter.
   d. alliteration.
   Ans: b

7. Hegel's notion of dialectical principles greatly influenced the theories of
   a. Karl Marx.
   b. Charles Darwin.
   c. Ralph Waldo Emerson.
   d. Bronson Alcott.
   Ans: a

8. Darwin's conception of evolution cannot work without presuming one of the following.
   a. Hegel's dialectic
   b. zero population growth
   c. transcendentalism
   d. vast stretches of time
   Ans: d

9. Darwin's theories met with strong opposition because of ALL BUT ONE of the following reasons
   a. They seemed to undermine traditional morality.
   b. They appeared to displace humans from their central position in the animal world.
   c. They suggested that humans were related to lower forms of animal life.
   d. They challenged the existence of God.
   Ans: d

10. The misinterpretation of Darwin by which the "survival of the fittest" is applied to social groups instead of to species is called
    a. transcendentalism.
    b. evolutionary process.
    c. Hegelian dialectic.
    d. social Darwinism.
    Ans: d

11. Emerson's experience of nature includes the phrases "all mean egotism vanishes. I become a transparent eyeball; I am nothing"; This sentiment does NOT seem to be present in Walt Whitman.
    Ans: T

12. Hegel's conception of freedom finds its ultimate perfection in the individual and not in the state.
    Ans: F

13. Social Darwinists used the theory of evolution to justify imperialism and economic exploitation.
    Ans: T

Answer the following with a word or phrase.

14. The feeling of loyalty to a specific territory, whose inhabitants shared a common language and culture, is called _____.
Ans: nationalism

15. The poet whose "Tintern Abbey" exalts the beneficent value of nature is _____.
Ans: Wordsworth

16. The American romantics who believed that knowledge gained through intuition surpassed knowledge gained through reasoning were called _____.
Ans: Transcendentalists

17. The American romantic who developed the notion of passive resistance later adopted by Gandhi and Martin Luther King was _____.
Ans: Thoreau

18. The process by which a condition (thesis) generates an opposite condition (antithesis) to produce a synthesis is called _____.
Ans: the dialectic

19. The idea that species flourish because they are able to preserve certain traits that enable them to survive is called _____.
Ans: natural selection

Open Book

20. Fiero, Figure 27.8, Turner, *Snowstorm: Steamboat Off Harbour's Mouth*. The view of nature held by the writers in this chapter that we might most closely associate with this painting is that of
   a. Keats.
   b. Wordsworth.
   c. Emerson.
   d. Shelley.
   Ans: d

21. Fiero, Figure 27.1, Turner, *Interior of Tintern Abbey*. Turner's interest in this topic probably reflects romantic
   a. love of vegetation.
   b. nostalgia for cultures past.
   c. idealism.
   d. nationalism.
   Ans: b

22. Fiero, Reading 5.1, Wordsworth, "Tintern Abbey." The "Dorothy episode" of this poem serves to underscore
    a. the poet's feeling that women are closer to nature.
    b. that the poet must share his feelings about nature with someone his own age.
    c. that the poet finds his youthful self in his sister.
    d. that the poet's connection to people is more important than his connection with the natural world.
    Ans: c

23. Fiero, Reading 5.2, Shelley's "Ode to the West Wind." In the fifth stanza, the speaker locates his own time of life in a comparison with the cycle of nature's seasons, namely,
    a. Spring.
    b. Summer.
    c. Fall.
    d. Winter.
    Ans: c

24. Fiero, Reading 5.6, Thoreau, *Walden,* lines 50–55. Thoreau states how *other people* view the goal of human life. That other view most closely resembles the view of human destiny of
    a. the ancient Greeks.
    b. the Hindus.
    c. the Christian Middle Ages.
    d. the European Enlightenment.
    Ans: c

25. Fiero, Reading 5.6, Thoreau, *Walden.* Thoreau's very last question might have special appeal to which one of the following?
    a. Hegel
    b. Emerson
    c. Keats
    d. Darwin
    Ans: d

26. Fiero, Figure 27.12, Thomas Cole, *The Oxbow.* The relationship of the human figures in this painting to the rest of the natural world is reminiscent of the attitude of Chinese landscape painters.
    Ans: F

27. Fiero, Figure 27.3, *Poet on a Mountain Top* by Shen Zhou. Part of the charm of landscapes at this scale comes from the effect of miniatures—here a fingernail-size poet in a miniature landscape. In this chapter, a similar effect is made in words alone by
    a. Walt Whitman.
    b. Thoreau.
    c. Wordsworth.
    d. Shen Fu.
    Ans: d

28. An aspect of romantic fascination with unspoiled nature and "natural man" in America was the portrayal of Native Americans by the painter
    a. George Catlin.
    b. Thomas Cole.
    c. Albert Bierstadt.
    d. Thomas Eakins.
    Ans: a

29. Fiero, Figure 27.18, Quilt. The dominant images in this artifact are
    a. Animals.
    b. Human beings.
    c. Flowers.
    d. Ships.
    Ans: c

Chapter **28** **The Romantic Hero**

Summary

Among nineteenth-century romantics, the hero was an expression of expansive subjectivity, national sentiment, and the creative imagination. Characterized by superhuman ambition and talent, the romantic hero, whether a historical figure or a fictional personality, experienced life with passionate intensity. Romantic writers—Byron in England, Pushkin in Russia, and Goethe in Germany—portrayed real-life figures (Napoleon) and literary heroes (Prometheus and Faust) who symbolized the quest for knowledge and power. Human liberty, a concept central to the heroic spirit, dominated abolitionist literature in America. The romantic heroine and romantic love and longing assumed a special importance in the arts of the nineteenth century. While many artists tended to stereotype the female as either angelic or demonic, female writers, such as George Sand, created heroines who enjoyed self-direction and sexual freedom.

Outline	Pronunciation Guide

A. Nationalism and the romantic hero
  1. liberty and nationalistic sentiment
  2. nineteenth-century hero worship
  3. Rousseau's influence
B. The romantic hero
  1. Napoleon
  2. Prometheus
    a. Mary Shelley
    b. Byron
    c. Pushkin
  3. American abolitionism
    a. Douglass
    b. Sojourner Truth
    c. slave songs and spirituals
  4. Goethe's *Faust*
C. The romantic heroine
  1. popular stereotypes
  2. Sand and other female writers
	Promethean [prow MEE thee un]
	Goethe [GUR te]
	Mephistopheles [me fi STAHF u leez]
	Delacroix [de lah KWAH]
	Heine [HEYE ne]
	Bizet [bee SAY]
	femme fatale [fam fu TAHL]

Key Terms: nationalism, Byronic egotism, Promethean, "feeling is all," abolitionists, spirituals, stereotype, *femme fatale*.

Study Questions

Factual
1. Why did Napoleon become a symbol of the romantic hero?
2. How did the Promethean hero differ from real-life heroes such as Napoleon and Byron?
3. Why may Faust be considered the quintessential romantic hero?
4. According to Pushkin (Reading 5.11), what did Napoleon fail to recognize in Russia?
5. In Frederick Douglass' *My Bondage and My Freedom* (Reading 5.12), the writer appeals to two principles that confer rights on the slave. What are these and how did Douglass arrive at them.
6. What does Goethe achieve by setting the first scene of *Faust* in heaven?
7. Does Goethe's Mephistopheles have a sense of humor? Find examples.
8. What stereotype is created by the simile in Heine's poem "You Are Just Like a Flower" (Reading 5.14)?
9. George Sand shocked many of her contemporaries. What in her writings and her life contradicted the stereotype offered by romantic poets like Heine?
10. In what ways did nineteenth-century spirituals express the condition of the African-American?
11. Who was Frankenstein and what role did he play in the imagination of the period?

Challenge
1. "The defect of our modern institutions," wrote Napoleon, "is that they do not speak to the imagination." To what extent do you find this observation valid for our own time?
2. Compare Faust with those heroes that you have encountered in the epics and other works of literature included in this text, such as Gilgamesh, Achilles, Roland, Lancelot, and Othello.
3. Proud, bored, solitary, cynical, self-pitying, passionate, melancholy, violent, adventuresome, alienated; these are some of the adjectives one associates with the romantics but also with modern teenagers. Comment or discuss.
4. How would you stage Goethe's *Faust* if you were given unlimited funds and the choice of any medium (stage, film, television, etc.)?
5. Do today's romance novels, television soap operas, or other forms of popular entertainment still feature the stereotype of the *femme fatale,* the clinging female, any other stereotypes? How might such stereotypes affect women's perceptions of themselves and men's perceptions of women?
6. Do a research project on either Frankenstein or Don Juan. Why did these characters capture the nineteenth-century romantic imagination? Do they still do so? If so, why?
7. Do a short research project on female stereotypes in history and myth. Look especially at the image of the "suitor-slaughtering virago" that figures in mythology and literature (Tiamat, Atlanta, Medea, Turandot, La Belle Dame sans Merci, *et al.*).
8. The Byronic hero, like Prometheus, defies the gods and (metaphorically) all symbols of established authority. Discuss.
9. *Faust* was more than a character in a German play; he became the inspiration for some of the greatest artists of the nineteenth century. For many he is the symbol of Western man. Discuss, focusing on the personality of *Faust* and its inspirational value in nineteenth-century culture.
10. Do a research project on slave songs and spirituals, outlining the range of subjects and themes.

Strategies for Discussion/Lecture

1. Students might be asked to write a preparatory essay on their choice of heroic personages from the chapter. The lecturer may wish to treat these larger-than-life characters as a type or concentrate on a single figure from among Napoleon, Frankenstein, Faust, Prometheus, Frederick Douglass, and Sojourner Truth.

    The Factual and Challenge questions allow for wide-ranging discussion of heroes over time, while the following suggestions offer techniques for individual treatment.

2. Project a slide of David's *Napoleon Crossing the Great Saint Bernard Pass* at full scale. Ask students to comment on the relative scale of other human beings in the painting, as well as the scale of nature. Discussion could take the form of comparison with Bierstadt's *The Rocky Mountains* (Fiero, Figure 27.13).

3. Arrange a showing of one of the more recent Frankenstein films; how does Mary Shelley's compare: Why and how has this literary work captured the modern imagination?

4. Reading 5.12. The depiction of the details of slave life has its purpose in Douglass' writing, but a discussion of this text can also bring out the author's links to the ideals of the American Revolution and the Enlightenment (lines 75–83, 19–23). One "Promethean" aspect of Douglass' action and his lengthy justifications is his revolt against the pulpit (Prometheus against Zeus). Students are inclined to debate hotly whether or not circumstances authorize the breaking of laws. How absolute is "You shall not steal?" What is the difference between an ethical hero and a scoff-law?

5. Have students enact part of Goethe's *Faust* (Fiero Reading 5.14). The personalities of each figure tend to come alive when the lines are read aloud. How do the personalities of Faust and Mephistopheles differ? Do either have a sense of humor?

Chapter 28 Audiovisuals

Video/CD-ROM Sources

JANE AUSTEN COLLECTION: HER LIFE, HER WORKS, HER SOCIETY

Why did this quiet, gentle eighteenth-century Englishwoman become so incredibly popular in today's worlds of film, TV, and literature? This fascinating series begins by recounting her life in the little village of Steventon, her move to Bath, her budding career and the scenes and events that inspired her writing. You'll explore her six published novels, thrilled by her sparkling wit and penetrating insights as Jane's talent is brought to life. Finally, learn about the extraordinary period she lived in—its social and political conventions—and the changes that were dramatically shaping England for the future. Titles are: "Her Life," "Her Works," and "Her Society." 180 minutes on 3 tapes **PBS**

CIVILISATION—Vol. #12: The Fallacies of Hope (1970)
DIRECTOR: CLARK, SIR KENNETH 53 min., color **PBS**

FRANKENSTEIN, THE MAKING OF THE MONSTER

In 1816, at age 18, Mary Wollstonecraft Shelley had a waking dream. An evening of ghost story-telling contests with Byron and Shelley produced a vision of a lonely, artificially created monster that retains a place in our cultural consciousness. This program gives full treatment to the magic of the novel and the baroque and maudlin comics and movies it spurred. Why is the story so compelling? Its themes—the sovereignty of science vs. religion, the alien who aches to belong, a creation destroying its creator—are eternally juicy. Authors Anne Rice and Ann Mellor comment on the impact Frankenstein has had on all monster stories thereafter. This blend of popular culture fodder and serious historic context makes this video a fun tool for inspiring literary analysis. (1993) 50 min. **HTG**

FRANKENSTEIN (1931)
  DIRECTOR: JAMES WHALE **AZ**

NAPOLEON: AN EMPIRES SPECIAL

For nearly two decades he strode the world stage like a colossus—loved and despised, venerated and feared. From his birth on the rugged island of Corsica to his final exile on the godforsaken island of St. Helena, NAPOLEON brings this extraordinary figure to life. NAPOLEON bears passionate witness to a man whose charisma swayed an empire and sparked his exalted belief in his own destiny. He is a figure riddled with contradictions that are the essence of his glory and undoing: his youthful enthusiasm for the ideals of the French Revolution did not prevent him from crowning himself Emperor. His passionate love of Josephine did not prevent him from divorcing her to marry the 18-year-old Archduchess of Austria. His military genius did not save him from the disastrous invasion of Russia. His love of France was so compromised by his notions of personal glory that he repeatedly plunged his beloved country into war. Framed by the grand sweep of history, woven from intimate accounts of and by the man himself, NAPOLEON is a tale as grand as any novel, a story of passion, vaunting ambition, and pride ending in exile and loss. 216 minutes on 2 tapes **PBS**

NATIONALISM 20 min., B&W **EBEC**

MARY SHELLEY'S FRANKENSTEIN (1994)
  DIRECTOR: KENNETH BRANAGH **AZ**

SPIRIT OF ROMANTICISM 27 min., color **EBEC**

TYRANTS AND HEROES: NINETEENTH CENTURY CZARS

In Russia, the nineteenth century was an era of wrenching violence and artistic progress. During turbulent times, Russian royalty continued to collect resplendent paintings and sculpture. From the French influence after 1812 and Alexander III's bloody reign, the Hermitage was further shaped. **HTG**

Web Resources

Mary Shelley—http://www.ucalgary.ca/UofC/Others/CIH/writinglives/WLMslinks.html

Resources related to Lord Byron—http://www.lordbyron.cjb.com

Resources related to Lord Byron—http://englishhistory.net/byron.html

Resources related to Napoleon—http://www.napoleonbonaparte.nl/

Biographical information and resources related to Pushkin—http://falcon.jum.edu/~gouldsl/pushkin/

Frederick Douglass National Historic Site—http://www.nps.gov/frdo/freddoug.html

Biographical information about Sojourner Truth—http://www.nisto.com/wct/who/sojourn.html

The history of the American Abolitionist movement—http://www.loc.gov/exhibits/african/abol.html

Biographical information about Goethe—http://www.serve.com/shea/germausa/goethe.htm

Biographical information about George Sand—http://virtual.park.uga.edu/232/sand.html

McGraw-Hill Resources

Transparencies: MA.8 Middle Modern World 1789–1914

Sample Test Questions on Chapter 28

Select the letter of the choice that BEST answers the question:

1. In his *Diary,* Napoleon states that his power comes ultimately from
   a. the *Napoleonic Code.*
   b. his victories in battle.
   c. his fame.
   d. the support of his soldiers.
   Ans: b

2. In his poem "Prometheus," Byron says that the crime of Prometheus was
   a. his opposition to Zeus.
   b. stealing the wife of Zeus.
   c. making men like gods.
   d. lessening the wretchedness of humans.
   Ans: d

3. In his poem "Napoleon," Pushkin's final evaluation of the French general is
   a. that he should be pitied as a tragic hero.
   b. that he should be praised for his effect on the Russian people.
   c. that he should be condemned for destroying the Russian countryside.
   d. that he was "the greatest man that ever existed."
   Ans: b

4. Byron analyzed Napoleon's defeat as being the product of
   a. an international conspiracy.
   b. destiny.
   c. his unbridled passions.
   d. his inability to command.
   Ans: c

5. In *My Bondage and My Freedom,* Frederick Douglass tells us he stole food
   a. on the grounds of morality.
   b. as an act of revenge against his master.
   c. because every other slave did so.
   d. impulsively, without thinking of the consequences.
   Ans: a

6. In *My Bondage and My Freedom,* Frederick Douglass implicitly compares the slave master to
   a. the tyrannical kings killed by revolutionaries.
   b. capitalist exploiters of the working class.
   c. fathers who restrict the freedom of their children.
   d. the Greek god Zeus.
   Ans: a

7. In *My Bondage and My Freedom,* Douglass says that the moral basis of his action was
   a. racial equality.
   b. private property and self- preservation.
   c. the biblical principle that the fruits of the earth belong to all.
   d. an eye for an eye, a tooth for a tooth.
   Ans: b

8. The scene of the "bet" between the Lord and Mephistopheles near the start of *Faust* is reminiscent of
   a. the *Epic of Gilgamesh.*
   b. the *Book of Job.*
   c. the *Song of Roland.*
   d. *Candide* by Voltaire.
   Ans: b

9. According to the text, Doctor Faustus is symbolic of the Western
   a. veneration of class.
   b. quest for control over nature.
   c. preoccupation with the material.
   d. reverence for monotheism.
   Ans: b

10. Romantics frequently modeled themselves after
    a. reforming politicians.
    b. wealthy aristocrats.
    c. heroes from "exotic" cultures.
    d. mystical religious leaders.
    Ans: c

11. The *philosophe* considered the "prophet of romanticism" is
    a. Rousseau.
    b. Voltaire.
    c. Montesquieu.
    d. Beccaria.
    Ans: a

12. Sojourner Truth condemns as non-Christian the practice of
    a. mock marriages between slaves.
    b. slave-holding in general.
    c. punishing slaves.
    d. restricting slaves from religious worship.
    Ans: a

13. While the *philosophes* tended to examine individuals from a social perspective, romantics generally studied their emotions and senses.
    Ans: T

14. The English poet Byron died defending Greek independence against the Turks.
    Ans: T

15. In *Faust,* the central character sells his soul to the devil in return for boundless love.
    Ans: F

16. George Sand defied social conventions by creating characters in her novels who engaged in free love, much as the author herself did.
    Ans: F

Answer the following with a word or phrase.

17. The French political leader whose egotism and individualism led many romantics to label him as a hero was _____.
    Ans: Napoleon

18. The mythical Greek hero who stole fire and thus brought humankind civilization was _____.
    Ans: Prometheus

19. The romantic author who made the sixteenth-century story of Doctor Faustus into a nineteenth-century allegory was _____.
    Ans: Goethe

20. In the romantic poem *Faust,* the devil or Satan of the Christian religion is called _____.
    Ans: Mephistopheles

21. In 1843, the African-American reformer, Isabella Bomefree, adopted the name _____.
    Ans: Sojourner Truth

Summary

Like their literary counterparts, romantic painters, sculptors, and composers favored dramatic subjects that gave free rein to the imagination and the heart. Increasingly independent of official patronage, artists tended to turn inward and to explore new possibilities in composition and technique. Landscapes (see Chapter 27), heroic and exotic stories, medieval legends, and contemporary subjects related to liberty and national identity were among the favorite themes of the painters Gros, Goya, Géricault, and Delacroix. A neo-Gothic revival in architecture was challenged by early experiments in prefabricated cast iron. As in the visual arts, so in music and dance, themes of nature, heroism, and love prevailed. In style, romantic composers abandoned classical models to fit their feelings. They enlarged the symphony orchestra and extended the lyrical and tonal possibilities of music. Two of the most popular musical forms of this era were ballet and opera.

Outline	Pronunciation Guide
A. The romantic style	**Gros** [GROW]
B. Heroic themes	**Géricault** [zhe ree KOW]
1. in painting: Gros, Goya, Géricault, Delacroix	**Delacroix** [de lah CWAH]
2. in sculpture: Bartholdi, Rude, Cordier	**Cordier** [kor dee AY]
C. Trends in nineteenth-century architecture	*lied* [LEED]
1. neomedievalism	*idée fixe* [ee DAY FEEKS]
2. exoticism in Western architecture	*scherzo* [SKER tsow]
D. The romantic style in music	*leitmotif* [LEYET moh teef]
1. instrumental and vocal composition	*arpeggio* [ahr PEJ ee oh]
a. Beethoven	*impromptu* [im PROM too]
b. German art songs	**La Marseillaise** [lah mahr say EZ]
c. Berlioz	**Berlioz** [ber lee OWZ]
d. Chopin	**Wagner** [VAHG nur]
2. ballet	**Garnier** [gahr nee AY]
3. romantic opera	**Carpeaux** [kahr POW]
a. Verdi	**Taglioni** [tal YOW nay]
b. Wagner	**Goya** [GOW yah]
	Chopin [show PAN]

Key Terms: irrationality, heroic allegory, "medievalism" in architecture, cast iron construction, romantic symphony and concerto, art song, dynamic contrast, *leitmotif, scherzo, tremolo, lieder, idée fixe,* programmatic music, prelude, nocturne, impromptu, *etude, prima ballerina,* music-drama.

Key Images	
Gros, *Napoleon Visiting the Plague Victims at Jaffa*	Bartholdi, *Statue of Liberty*
Goya, *The Third of May 1808: The Execution of the Defenders of Madrid*	Rude, *La Marseillaise*
	Barry and Pugin, *Houses of Parliament*
	Eiffel, *Eiffel Tower*
Géricault, *The Raft of Medusa*	Garnier, *Paris Opera*
Delacroix, *Liberty Leading the People*	Carpeaux, *The Dance*

Study Questions

Factual
1. What visual devices did Gros use to cast Napoleon in the role of a hero?
2. What events are depicted in Goya's *The Third of May, 1808?*
3. Name some of the violent themes represented in the works of romantic artists.
4. How do Goya's depictions of Napoleon's occupation differ from French representations of this figure?
5. Give the factual background of Géricault's *The Raft of the Medusa.*
6. Regarding figures 29.2 through 29.6, what features do these works hold in common?
7. What are the principal features of the romantic style in music?
8. What is the style of Pugin's Houses of Parliament? Of Nash's Royal Pavilion?
9. Which musical instrument became most popular in the nineteenth century? Why?

Challenge
1. "The key to romanticism is feeling and intense experience." Discuss in relation to any aspects of the art and music of the nineteenth century.
2. What aspects of heroism can be found in the art and music of the nineteenth century? Cite specific examples from the chapter.
3. Was romanticism an exclusively Western phenomenon? What aspects of Chinese, Indian, or African culture might be called romantic?
4. Some say that ballet was the ultimate expression of the romantic imagination. Others would argue that grand opera more fully captures that imagination. Discuss and/or debate.
5. Listen carefully to Music Listening Selections II–12 through 15. To what extent is the personality and mood of romantic composers reflected in the music?
6. With reference to his monumental opera, *The Ring,* Wagner once assured a fellow composer: "The thing shall *sound* in such a fashion that people shall hear what they cannot see." In what ways does this point of view typify the spirit of romanticism and the attitude of the romantic composer?

Strategies for Discussion/Lecture

1. An effective way to bring out the specifically romantic qualities of nineteenth-century art and music is to contrast them with selected slides/illustrations and musical selections from Chapters 23 and 26. Play in sequence Couperin and Chopin, or Haydn and Berlioz. Parallel this contrast with pastoral images by Poussin, David, and Ingres followed by Géricault, Goya, and Delacroix. The class should be able to detect an increased intensity and range of emotion and color in the romantic musical

selections, and relate it to the turbulence, exoticism, and emotional expansiveness of the paintings. Changes in musical structure and pictorial composition (classical versus romantic) might also be addressed here.

2. The lecturer might also continue the treatment of Napoleon begun in the previous chapter and take up the theme of "the army of occupation as seen by the occupiers and the occupied," using Gros and Goya, and perhaps recalling Pushkin's ambivalence toward the liberator of Russia. Does either painter give an accurate and complete view of the events? Suppose we knew the facts from only one of these painters?

3. If the lecturer wishes to continue the theme of heroic individualism first taken up in the previous chapter, he or she may wish to devote some time to listening to romantic concertos, especially for the piano, the virtuoso instrument par excellence of the romantic period. Arthur Loesser's *Men, Women & Pianos* is a mine of lore on the high emotional impact of nineteenth-century superstars (Liszt, Chopin, etc.) on their audiences, as well as a thorough analysis of why the piano was well adapted to the role it came to play. The lecturer might include Rachmaninoff's 3rd Concerto and ask if romanticism is not still very much with us today.

4. Ask the class to compare the sentiments expressed in Delacroix's *Liberty Leading the People*, Rude's *Marseillaise*, and Edmonia Lewis' s *Forever Free*. General discussion concerning freedom as a theme in the arts should follow.

Chapter 29 Audiovisuals

Video/CD-ROM Sources

THE AGE OF PASSION Art of The Western World Series 50 min., color **CPB**

BEETHOVEN: The Age of Revolution Man and Music Series 53 min., color **FFH**

BERNSTEIN ON BEETHOVEN: Ode to Joy from the Ninth Symphony 27 min., color **BFA Educational Media**

EUGÈNE DELACROIX Alain Jaubert interprets the symbols and analyzes the composition of Delacroix's *Liberty Leading the People*. 29 min. **FFH**

GOYA: THE AUDACITY OF FREEDOM FFH

GOYA: HIS LIFE AND ART
An introduction to Goya's work and his period in Spanish history. An RTVE production. 44 min. **FFH**

FAVORITE TCHAIKOVSKY BALLETS
Three of Peter Ilyich Tchaikovsky's most enduring, most popular ballets are brilliantly performed by Russia's leading companies in this dazzling collection. The composer's beloved *The Sleeping Beauty* is given a command performance by the Kirov Ballet in St. Petersburg, featuring famed Kirov stars Altyna Asylmuratova and Konstantin Zaklinsky. *Swan Lake*, the timeless tale of redemption through love, receives a spectacular production with prima ballerina Galina Mezentseva in the leading role. The world's most famous Christmas ballet, *The Nutcracker*, comes to colorful, sparkling life through the many talents of the Russian State Theater Academy of Classical Ballet. 406 minutes on 3 tapes **PBS**

Music Resources

Beethoven, *Symphony No. 3 in E Flat, Op. 55, "Eroica,"* Mehta, New York Philharmonic, CBS IM–
    35883 digital; MK–35883 CD.
Beethoven, *"Leonore" Overture No. 3 and Symphony No. 5*, Boult, London Promenade Orchestra,
    Vanguard CSRV–190 cassette.
Beethoven, *Beethoven's Greatest Hits*, Various orchestras and performers, CBS MLK– 39434 CD.
Berlioz, *Symphonie Fantastique, Op. 14*, Muti, Philadelphia Orchestra, Angel DS–38210 digital; CDC–
    47278 CD; 4DS–32810 cassette.
Berlioz, *Requiem, Op. 5*, Burrows, Bernstein, French National Radio Orchestra, CBS M2-34202.
Berlioz, *Harold in Italy, for viola and orchestra, Op. 16*, Christ, Maazel, Berlin Philharmonic and
    Chorus, DG 415109–2 GH CD.
Schubert, *Songs*, Ameling, W. Baldwin, Etcetera ETC–1009; ARN–268006 CD.

Web Resources

Ludwig von Beethoven—http://w3.rz-berlin.mpg.de/cmp/beethoven.html

The Berlioz Society Home Page—http://www.standrews.u-net.com/BerliozSociety.html

Information about Chopin—http://www.geocities.com/Vienna/4279/

Information about Chopin—http://www.prs.net/chopin.html

Information about Verdi—http://www.classical.net/music/comp.lst/verdi.html

Resources related to Wagner—http://users.utu.fi/hansalmi/wagner.spml

Resources related to Wagner—http://home.no.net/wagner/links.html

A virtual tour of Goya's works at the National Portrait Gallery—
    http://www.nga.gov/collection/gallery/gg52/gg52-mainl.html

Romantic music links—http://classicalmus.hispeed.com/romantic.html

McGraw-Hill Resources

Music Listening Selection: CD II
    II–12 Beethoven, *Symphony No. 3, in E-flat Major, Eroica*
    II–13 Schubert, *Gretchen am Spinnrade*
    II–14 Berlioz, *Symphonie fantastique*, Op. 14, "March to the Scaffold"
    II–15 Chopin, *Etude in G-flat Major, Op. 10, No. 5*
Transparencies: MA.8 Middle Modern World 1789–1914

Sample Test Questions for Chapter 29

Select the letter of the choice that BEST answers the question:

1. Whereas neoclassicists emphasized symmetry, line, and sober colors, romantics sought all of the following EXCEPT
   a. irregular composition.
   b. modeling through color.
   c. restrained tonalities.
   d. visible brushstrokes.
   Ans: c

2. In an effort to capture the experience as accurately as possible, Géricault prepared for his painting *The Raft of the Medusa* by
   a. interviewing the survivors.
   b. traveling by raft on the same route.
   c. reading the same story in both Greek and Roman mythologies.
   d. selecting as models local seamen.
   Ans: a

3. In his painting *Liberty Leading the People,* Delacroix showed by their clothing whom he considered the heroes of the revolutionary action in France, namely,
   a. the common people.
   b. the military.
   c. the middle class, the working class, and racial minorities.
   d. aristocrats sympathetic to the revolutionary cause and the common people.
   Ans: c

4. The style of the facade of Charles Garnier's Paris Opera can be most closely compared to
   a. classical Roman.
   b. classical Greek.
   c. gothic.
   d. Baroque Roman.
   Ans: d

5. Joseph Paxton's Crystal Palace was designed to house
   a. the largest horticultural exhibit ever assembled.
   b. the World's Fair of 1851.
   c. plants and trees from all over the British Empire.
   d. an exhibition or art, including the first cast iron sculpture.
   Ans: b

6. A new medium of construction that transformed architectural design in the mid-nineteenth century was
   a. reinforced steel.
   b. cast iron.
   c. reinforced concrete.
   d. stucco faced with marble.
   Ans: b

7. The hallmarks of romantic music included all the following EXCEPT
   a. individualized expression.
   b. abandonment of precise forms.
   c. lyric melodies.
   d. use of the sonata form.
   Ans: d

8. The nineteenth-century musical form that best mirrors the romantic notion of the hero's solitary "encounter" with the symphonic ensemble is
   a. the opera.
   b. the *lied.*
   c. the concerto.
   d. the nocturne.
   Ans: c

9. The independent art song that united music and poetry was called the
   a. oratorio.
   b. concerto.
   c. *lied.*
   d. scherzo.
   Ans: c

10. The composer of program music who created specific moods by using an *idée fixe* (as in his *Symphonie fantastique*) was
    a. Beethoven.
    b. Vivaldi.
    c. Berlioz.
    d. Schubert.
    Ans: c

11. The works of the Polish composer Chopin include compositions focusing on the technical ability of performers. These are called
    a. sonatas.
    b. preludes.
    c. nocturnes.
    d. études.
    Ans: d

12. Most romantic ballets derived their plot lines from
    a. novels.
    b. poems.
    c. fairy tales.
    d. art songs.
    Ans: c

13. Bartholdi's celebrated *Statue of Liberty* was the largest marble sculpture produced in the nineteenth century.
    Ans: F

14. The Spanish master, Francisco Goya, painted European nobility with flattering romanticism.
    Ans: F

15. In their nostalgia for the medieval period, romantic architects frequently exalted the Romanesque style of the past.
    Ans: F

16. Cordier's African and Nash's Royal Pavilion were expressions of nineteenth-century
    a. medievalism.
    b. exoticism.
    c. nationalism.
    d. all of these.
    Ans: b

Chapter **30** Industry, Empire, and the Realist Style

Summary

As the social consequences of expanding industrialism became increasingly evident, realism came to rival romanticism both as a style and as an attitude of mind. Liberalism, conservatism, utilitarianism, socialism, and communism offered varying solutions to the realities of social injustice and inequality. In the arts, realism emerged as a style concerned with recording contemporary subject matter in true-to-life terms. Western novelists—Dickens, Dostoevsky, Flaubert, and Zola—described social conditions in sympathetic and faithful detail. Mill, Ibsen, and Chopin championed women's social and psychological independence. The new technologies of photography and lithography encouraged artists to provide objective visual records of their surroundings. Leading the realist movement in the visual arts, Courbet and Daumier in France and Eakins and Homer in America produced unembellished depictions of familiar, everyday activities and pastimes. Manet shocked critics by recasting traditional subjects in contemporary visual terms, while Puccini brought *verismo* to operatic subjects.

Outline	**Pronunciation Guide**
A. The historical context	**Lin Zexu** [lin see zhoo]
1. advancing industrialism	**Proudhon** [proo DOHN]
2. colonialism	**von Menzel** [fon MEN zul]
3. China and the West	**Dostoevsky** [dahs toy EV skee]
4. social and economic realities	**Karamazov** [ka rah MAHD zof]
B. Social theory	**Flaubert** [flow BEHR]
1. conservatism, liberalism, utilitarianism,	**K. Chopin** [SHOW pan]
socialism	**Daguerre** [dah GEHR]
2. Marx and Engels	**Courbet** [coor BAY]
3. Mill and women's rights	**Millet** [mee LAY]
C. Realism in literature	**Daumier** [dow mee AY]
1. Dickens and Twain	**Manet** [ma NAY]
2. Dostoevsky and Tolstoy	**Puccini** [poo CHEE nee]
3. Flaubert and Kate Chopin	**La Bohème** [lah bow EM]
4. Ibsen and realist drama	*verismo* [ver EEZ mow]
D. Realism in the visual arts	*salon des refusés*
1. the birth of photography	[sah LON day reh foo SAY]
2. Courbet	
3. Daumier	
4. Manet	
5. American realist painting	
E. Late nineteenth-century architecture	
1. cast iron: Paxton and Eiffel	
2. Sullivan and the skyscraper	
F. realism in music	

Key Terms: industrialism, colonialism, manifest destiny, "the white man's burden," opium wars, capitalism, entrepreneurs, utilitarianism, bourgeois, socialism/communism, proletariat, realism, lithography, photography, naturalism, *verismo*.

Key Images	
Courbet, *The Stone-breakers*	Tanner, *The Banjo Lesson*
Millet, *The Gleaners*	Eakins, *The Agnew Clinic*
Daumier, *The Third-Class Carriage*	Homer, *The Gulf Stream*
Manet, *Déjeuner sur l'herbe; Olympia*	

Study Questions

Factual

1. What were some of the main features of advancing industrialism in the West?
2. Where did European nations establish colonies during the nineteenth century? What immediate effects did nineteenth-century colonialism have on Europe and the rest of the world?
3. In Kipling's "The White Man's Burden," who are the people called "Half-devil and half-child"?
4. What was the Chinese punishment for importing or smoking opium? (See Reading 5.16.)
5. Briefly explain the positions of the following European social theorists: conservatives, liberals, utilitarians, socialists, communists, anarchists.
6. How did Marx and Engels seek to revolutionize Western society?
7. How, in Mill's view, does the relationship between male and female differ from that of master and slave?
8. What were the principal subjects and themes of realist painters? How did they differ from those of the romantics?
9. What were the principal subjects and themes of realist writers? How did they differ from those of the romantics?
10. What material holds up the Guaranty Building, Figure 30.28? Is it visible in the photograph?
11. Who were the pioneers in the development of photography/lithography?

Challenge

1. What aspects of realism ran counter to the perceptions and beliefs of the romantics? How did the realist credo manifest itself in the paintings of von Menzel, Kollwitz, and Courbet, and the novels of Dickens and Flaubert?
2. According to the text author, the varieties of realism in nineteenth-century cultural expression reflect "a profound concern for social and economic inequities and offer a critical reassessment of traditional Western values." Do you agree or disagree? Discuss, offering specific examples to defend your point of view.
3. How did journalism, lithography, and photography serve nineteenth-century European society? Use specific examples to make your case.
4. Offer an assessment of the ideas set forth in the *Communist Manifesto*; why, in your view, has communism collapsed in such countries as the former Soviet Union?
5. Try to see a staged performance (or video) of Ibsen's *A Doll's House*. How does the heroine break with romantic stereotypes? How does Nora compare with Antigone (Chapter 4)?
6. Marx argues that the Western bourgeoisie has created "a world after its own image." Do recent developments in the former Soviet Union, especially the collapse of the communist regime, seem to support this observation?

7. Flaubert is said to have been a master of close observation, concrete detail, and objectivity. Are these qualities clearly reflected in Reading 5.20? Are they equally apparent in the prose of Dickens (Reading 5.19), Twain (Reading 5.21), Dostoevsky (Reading 5.22), and Kate Chopin (Reading 5.24)?

8. Survey the visual art in this chapter; choose the best examples to illustrate (a) the description of realistic style as "portraying men and women in actual, everyday, and often demoralizing situations"; and (b) the notion that "realism did not totally displace romanticism." Do you find "romantic" features in some realist visual depictions? If so, where?

Strategies for Discussion/Lecture

1. If only one class meeting is devoted to the chapter, the lecturer might wish to assign ahead student response to Factual Questions 8 and 9 and employ responses as the basis for class discussion. Slides will be helpful here as well.

2. A class meeting might be centered on Ibsen's play, with Challenge question 5 assigned as a preliminary theme; *A Doll's House* can be combined with Mill, Flaubert, and Chopin in a class that follows the thread of women's struggles in the century.

   If possible, students should be given the opportunity to see Ibsen's play in one of the versions currently available on video, excerpts of which might be shown in class. Although the playwright's sympathies are clearly with Nora, he is also interested in portraying Helmer's entanglement in work and in his reputation in the community. This social dimension gives the final scene a broader meaning and magnifies the courage of Nora's decision. What reasons does Nora give Helmer for leaving him; does Helmer offer to persuade her to stay?

   A similar comparison of film and story may be employed with Kate Chopin's "The Story of An Hour" (Reading 5.24), which is available in a video recording entitled *The Joy that Kills* (1990). See Audiovisuals.

3. The lecturer may wish to gather the various texts and illustrations around the theme of industrialization and work, with added importance given to Marx, iron construction, photography, and Dickens. In this case, Factual question 5 would be the appropriate written assignment for the class.

4. The realism of Courbet, Daumier, and Manet do not look shocking or "scandalous" to twentieth-century eyes, but such was the case for nineteenth-century viewers. Compare the works of these artists with those illustrated in Chapter 27. How do the realist works differ? What did the public find shocking about the subject matter and the style of these artists?

Chapter 30 Audiovisuals

Video/CD-ROM Sources

AGE OF UNCERTAINTY Thirteen parts (1977) **FI**

MADAME BOVARY

Gustave Flaubert's classic fills the screen in this unforgettable production. Francesca Annis stars as the beautiful Emma Bovary, whose loveless marriage to a kind widower (Tom Conti) leads to reckless extravagance and illicit passion. In the nineteenth-century French world of class struggle, manners, and expectations, her relentless search for happiness propels her toward one last attempt to break free from the nightmare her life has become. 195 minutes on 4 tapes **PBS**

CIVILISATION—Vol. #13: Heroic Materialism (1970)
DIRECTOR: CLARK, SIR KENNETH 53 min., color **PBS**

DICKENS: GREAT EXPECTATIONS
With John Mills, Alec Guinness, Valerie Hobson, and Martita Hunt. 118 min., B&W **FFH**

A DOLL'S HOUSE (1973)
DIRECTOR: PATRICK GARLAND color **AZ**

EARLY VICTORIAN ENGLAND & CHARLES DICKENS 30 min., color **EBEC**

HISTORY OF SOCIAL CLASSES, A
DIRECTOR: LEDUC, LOUIS-ROLAND
Marx divided the industrial world into two antagonistic classes: the bourgeois and the proletariat. In today's society, this simple dichotomy fails to capture the many segments of a global marketplace. From the communal hunter/gatherers and agrarian cultures; to ancient empires and medieval fiefdoms; to the technocrats, executives, laborers, and others of the stratified modern world, this program examines how each era has organized its members into social classes. Although the opportunistic meritocracy of the global marketplace has displaced earlier societal models, do older patterns of privilege still linger? (1999) 53 min., color **FFH**

IMPERIALISM AND EUROPEAN EXPANSION 13 min., B&W **CORONET**

INDUSTRIAL REVOLUTION, THE (Series)
This series is a basic survey of the Industrial Revolution where it began and where it has had the most striking effects: Britain. The programs follow a case study approach to industry, transportation, and settlement. Their purpose is to provide a basic understanding of the chronology of the main events and the relationships between them. 5-part series, 20 minutes each, color (1992) **FFH**

THE INDUSTRIAL REVOLUTION IN ENGLAND 26 min, B&W **EBEC**

A LITTLE BIT OF MAGIC REALIZED: WILLIAM FOX TALBOT'S DISCOVERY
Fox Talbot's discovery of the negative-positive process and his skill as an artist. Recommended: Video Rating Guide for Libraries Gold Medal, New York Film and TV Festival 26 min. **FFH**

MAGIC OF THE IMAGE: PHOTOGRAPHY REVEALED
This elegant program artistically unfolds the history of photography, including the contributions of Joseph Niépce, Louis Daguerre, Fox Talbot, and the Lumières. **FFH**

KARL MARX AND MARXISM (1993)
52 min. **CREES**

LES MISÉRABLES 54 min., B&W **IU**

SHOCK OF THE NEW: VOL 1: The Mechanical Paradise (1980) 52 min., color
available through Joan @ Videofinders at 1-800-343-4727

Web Resources

Karl Marx and Fredrick Engels internet archive—
    http://csf.colorado.edu/mirrors/marxists.org/archive/marx

Information about Charles Dickens—http://humwww.ucsc.edu/dickens/index/html

Information about Charles Dickens—http://www.helsinki.fi/kasv/nokol/dickens.html

Resources related to Mark Twain—http://www.geocities.com/paris/tower/6326/

Quotations and selected writings of Mark Twain—http://www.twainquotes.com/

Resources related to Leo Tolstoy—http://www.ltolstoy.com/

Resources related to Dostoevsky—http://www.kiosek.com/dostoevsky/

Biographical information about Edouard Manet—http://www.mystudios.com/manet/manet.html

Resources related to Kate Chopin—http://www.womenwriters.net/domesticgoddess/chopinl.htm

History of photography—http://www.rleggat.com/photohistory/

The Eiffel Tower web page—http://www.endex.com/gf/buildings/eiffel/eiffel.html

McGraw-Hill Resources

Transparencies: MA.8 Middle Modern World 1789–1914

Sample Test Questions for Chapter 30

Select the letter of the choice that BEST answers the question:

1. Colonization of the Third World in the nineteenth century was linked to all of the following
    EXCEPT
    a. Industrialism.
    b. Nationalism.
    c. Social Darwinism.
    d. All of the above.
    Ans: d

2. Colonialism had as its motivating force the
    a. need for materials and markets.
    b. suppression of native uprisings.
    c. search for exotic cultures.
    d. fear of communism.
    Ans: a

3. The doctrine of utilitarianism articulated by Jeremy Bentham argued that governments should
   a. defend religious authorities.
   b. ensure the well-being of the greatest number of people.
   c. maintain power and order in their traditional forms.
   d. maintain governmental structures that had no economic impact.
   Ans: b

4. The author of the *Communist Manifesto* argued that the "history of all existing society is the history of
   a. corrupt rulers."
   b. manipulative religions."
   c. class struggles."
   d. conflicting ideologies."
   Ans: c

5. John Stuart Mill wrote that men do not simply want obedience from women (as men might demand from slaves) but women's _____ as well.
   a. money
   b. sentiments
   c. improvement
   d. submission
   Ans: b

6. In Flaubert's novel, Emma Bovary meets with disaster as she
   a. struggles against the conditions of industrialization.
   b. tries to inject romance into her everyday life.
   c. confronts an intolerant aristocracy.
   d. deals with an overbearing and unfaithful husband.
   Ans: b

7. In "The Story of an Hour" by Kate Chopin, Mrs. Mallard discovers in her mourning what is "the strongest impulse of her being," namely,
   a. self-preservation.
   b. her love for her husband.
   c. her freedom to choose.
   d. her Christian faith.
   Ans: c

8. Unlike realistic novels, naturalistic works like those by Zola were grounded in the belief that human beings were
   a. products of their environment.
   b. in control of their own destinies.
   c. happiest in natural surroundings.
   d. equal, whether male or female.
   Ans: a

9. The "doll" whom Ibsen described in his play was Nora, who had been
   a. without personality or imagination.
   b. under the authority of first her father, then her husband.
   c. smitten with an obsession for material acquisitions.
   d. without any sensual feeling.
   Ans: b

10. Daumier's lithographs satirized all the following except
    a. modern technology.
    b. monarchy.
    c. profiteering.
    d. the working class.
    Ans: d

11. The "white man's burden" referred to the grim conditions in industrial factories.
    Ans: F

12. The *Communist Manifesto* confidently predicted that a "classless" society would result when workers seized all property and divided it among themselves.
    Ans: F

13. According to Karl Marx, the class of people he calls the bourgeoisie has played a revolutionary role in human history.
    Ans: T

Answer the following with a word or phrase.

14. The radical socialist who advocated violent revolution as a means of seizing power was _____.
    Ans: Karl Marx

15. The panoramic novel by Leo Tolstoy that follows the fortunes of five families during Napoleon's invasion of Russia is _____.
    Ans: *War and Peace*

16. The technological invention that began with Talbot and Daguerre and would later revolutionize the world of art was _____.
    Ans: photography

17. The French painter who scandalized the public by presenting traditional themes in unconventional ways (as in his *Olympia*) was _____.
    Ans: Manet

18. The Italian composer who took contemporary East–West cultures as a theme for an opera was

    _____.

    Ans: Puccini

19. The expression used to justify unlimited expansion into the American West was _____.
    Ans: manifest destiny

20. The river traveled by Huck and Jim was the _____.
    Ans: Mississippi

Open Book

21. Fiero, Figure 30.1, *Westerners Through Chinese Eyes*. This representations illustrates a fact emphasized in Lin Zexu's *Letter to Queen Victoria*, namely that only Western visitors to China smoked opium.
    Ans: F

22. Fiero, Figure 30.3, *March of the Weavers*. The social background for appreciating this etching includes the fact that
    a. worker revolts were rare in the nineteenth century.
    b. women were not included among proletarian workers.
    c. between 1855 and 1861 there were almost 500 peasant uprisings across Europe.
    d. protests like the one illustrated led to the early formation of labor unions.
    Ans: c

23. Fiero, Figures 30.5 and 30.6. Comparing the photographs by Thomas Annan and Julia Margaret Cameron, we can say that, from a stylistic point of view,
    a. They are identical.
    b. Cameron, coming earlier than Annan, could not yet focus her camera accurately.
    c. Annan's style is more romantic than realistic.
    d. Compared to Annan, Cameron's photograph tries to imitate romantic painting.
    Ans: d

24. Compare Manet's *Olympia* (Figure 30.18) with Titian's *Pastoral Concert*. The conventions of art are such that in a delicate genre like the female nude, the distance is not far from artistic nude to a slightly pornographic atmosphere. In *Olympia,* the major departure from convention is
    a. the fact that she is reclining.
    b. the presence of a servant.
    c. the fact that she is wearing slippers and a ribbon at her throat.
    d. the presence of an animal in the scene.
    Ans: c

25. Fiero, Figure 30.26. Joseph Paxton's Crystal Palace was designed to house
    a. the largest horticultural exhibit ever assembled.
    b. the Great Exhibition of London, 1851.
    c. plants and trees from all over the British empire.
    d. an exhibition of art, including the first use of cast iron.
    Ans: b

Summary

The move toward modernism that occupied the last quarter of the nineteenth century witnessed the collapse of romantic illusionism and the flowering of an art-for-art's-sake sensibility. Nietzsche, Bergson, and the symbolist poets offered alternate, if not iconoclastic, reassessments of the social and aesthetic order. Amidst new theories of sensation and perception, and new theories of light and motion, symbolists and impressionists tried to record an instantaneous, intuitive vision of the world that sacrificed naturalistic detail in favor of elusive feelings and fleeting atmospheric effects. While Monet, Renoir, and Pissarro brought these concerns to painting (and Debussy to music), Degas and Rodin shared the sculptor's interest in figural gesture and movement. In the last decades of the century, Western Europe came under the sway of Japanese art and design in the form of woodblock prints. The postimpressionists Gauguin and van Gogh used color as a means of achieving visionary expressionism, while Seurat and Cézanne invested form with new, more abstract, architectural stability.

Outline	Pronunciation Guide
A. Historical context: the late nineteenth century	**Nietzsche** [NEET che]
1. Paris as cultural mecca	**Zarathustra** [za rah THOOS trah]
2. scientific and technological advances	**Übermensch** [OO ber mench]
B. Philosophy and literature	**Bergson** [berg SOWN]
1. Nietzsche	**Mallarmé** [mal ahr MAY]
2. Bergson	**Debussy** [deb yoo SEE]
3. Mallarmé and the symbolists	**Monet** [mow NAY]
C. Impressionism	**Rouen** [roo AHN]
1. Music: Debussy	**Degas** [de GAH]
2. Painting at the end of the century	**Renoir** [ren WAHR]
a. Monet	**Morisot** [mow ree SOW]
b. Renoir, Pissarro, and Degas	**Muybridge** [MEYE brig]
D. The Arts of Africa and Oceania	**Hokusai** [how koo SEYE]
E. The Arts at the end of the century	**Cassatt** [ke SAHT]
1. the influence of Japanese prints	**Toulouse-Lautrec** [too LOOZ low TREK]
2. *art nouveau*	***art nouveau*** [AHR noo VOW]
3. sculpture: Degas and Rodin	**Rodin** [row DAN]
4. Mary Cassatt and Toulouse-Lautrec	**Gauguin** [gow GAN]
5. Postimpressionism	**Seurat** [se RAHT]
a. van Gogh and Gauguin	**Cézanne** [say ZAHN]
b. Seurat and Cézanne	***ukiyo-e*** [yoo KEE yoh ay]

Key Terms: art for art's sake, morality of the superior individual, intuitionism, symbolism, Impressionism, slice of life, woodblocks, "floating" world, poster art, *art nouveau,* japonisme, Postimpressionism, pointillism, *cloisonné.*

<table>
<tr><td colspan="2">Key Images</td></tr>
<tr>
<td>
Monet, Impression: Sunrise; Rouen Cathedral
Renoir, Le Moulin de la Galette
Degas, Before the Ballet
Cassatt, The Bath
Toulouse-Lautrec, At the Moulin-Rouge
Hokusai, Mount Fuji Seen Below a Wave at Kanagowa
</td>
<td>
Rodin, The Age of Bronze
van Gogh, The Starry Night
Gauguin, The Day of God
Seurat, Sunday Afternoon on the Island of La Grande Jatte
Cézanne, Mont Sainte-Victoire
</td>
</tr>
</table>

Study Questions

Factual

1. Did Nietzsche believe that the nineteenth century and its art were an improvement on the past?
2. Who were the symbolist poets? What were they trying to achieve?
3. What is a faun? A nymph? What role does each play in Mallarmé's "Afternoon of a Faun"?
4. What were the favorite subjects (subject matter) of late nineteenth-century artists?
5. How were the theories of Henri Bergson reflected in the arts of the late nineteenth century?
6. What were the unique features of African art in the late nineteenth century?
7. In what ways did Parisian urban life influence the art of the impressionists and postimpressionists?
8. How did the subject matter and style of Gauguin differ from that of the impressionists and other postimpressionists?

Challenge

1. What qualities in Debussy's music (Music Listening Selection II–16) resemble Mallarmé's poetry and Monet's paintings?
2. "Impressionism was never a single, uniform style." How do the works of Degas and Cassatt differ from those of other impressionists?
3. Describe the influence of Japanese art on the visual artists of the late nineteenth century.
4. What role did dance and dancers play in the works of Rodin?
5. Is Mallarmé's poetry more difficult to understand than Wordsworth's or Whitman's? If so, why? What effects was such poetry aiming to achieve?
6. In what aspects of European life were the impressionists interested? Is it accurate to say that these artists were more concerned with paint than with what was painted? If so, why? If not, why?
7. A Parisian critic of 1891 observed of the paintings of Toulouse-Lautrec that there was nobody like him "for depicting the mugs of decrepit capitalists sitting at tables in the company of whores." Make a survey of this artist's paintings and drawings to discover the kinds of works that prompted this biting observation.
8. Why do you think that the canvases of the postimpressionists were so strongly attacked in their time, but have become so enormously popular in our own time?
9. In what ways might Mallarmé, Debussy, Monet, and Cézanne be called "the last of the romantics"?
10. Examine the role of color in the paintings of the late nineteenth century. How did the invention of synthetic paint affect art? Is it fair to suggest that technology had a major impact on pictorial style?
11. Could Nietzsche be considered the philosopher of the "romantic hero"? If so, how so?
12. Why has Vincent van Gogh become such a "culture hero" in our own time?

Strategies for Discussion/Lecture

1. The chapter illustrations are well suited to a slide-based lecture focused on developments in painting leading to twentieth-century abstraction. From Monet's "Impression" through the later Cézanne, students can observe tendencies toward abstraction in the treatment of subject matter and an interest in art that is no longer based on the representation of an external reality. Here one might deal with Nietzsche's query, "How could one understand it [art] as purposeless, as aimless, as *l'art pour l'art*?" (Reading 5.26).

2. This chapter provides the lecturer with an opportunity to inquire into what may eventually be seen as the beginnings of "globalization." Whereas the term mainly refers to world markets in today's speech, the longest tradition in trade with Asia seems to be in art, starting with the porcelain ware that eventually gave us the word "china," and including the objects presented in this chapter. The strength of this eastern influence should not be underestimated: students should be reminded that while photography was making significant advances, western artists were increasingly moving *away from* photographic realism under the influence of Japanese artists like those represented in this chapter. Hokusai's "Thirty-six Views of Mount Fuji" might be profitably juxtaposed to Monet's twenty-five views of Rouen cathedral, if only on the level of conceptions of art: such repetitions inevitably underscore the primacy of the rendering over the subject matter. Further parallels might be drawn between the art of Gauguin and the arts of both Africa and Oceania.

3. A micro project based on the first strategy would be to consider the facade of medieval cathedrals (illustrated in Fiero, Chapter 13), contrasted with Monet's series of twenty views of the facade of the cathedral of Rouen. The medieval churches are such solidly anchored monuments, virtual encyclopedias of the Middle Ages, with their aspirations toward the heavenly city. Monet's churches, by contrast, are passing moments in time, and hardly three-dimensional. The comparison can also raise most of the important questions about the artist, the nature of artistic work, the community it addresses, and the ownership of art works. Nietzsche's parable (Reading 5.25) could also be brought in: "What are these churches now . . . ?"

4. A program of modern dance, if available, would provide the opportunity to prompt students to compare modern dance with classical ballet (discussed in Chapter 29).

Chapter 31 Audiovisuals

Video/CD-ROM Sources

ART OF THE WESTERN WORLD
    Program 7: Realism and Impressionism & Post-Impressionism **HTG**

CÉZANNE: The Man and His Mountain MMA

PAUL CÉZANNE—ON CD-ROM
    Experience the master's understanding of color and form, and embrace the rich tradition of Impressionism at its zenith in this completely interactive CD-ROM. Included are 33 of Cézanne's greatest works, details and scholarly analysis of each work, studies of the paintings' compositions, and comparisons with other works, periods, and artistic styles. Biography presents a chronology of key events in Cézanne's life. The CD-ROM can be used with either Windows or Macintosh. **FFH**

PAUL CÉZANNE: A Life in Provence 26 min., color **FFH**

A FRESH VIEW: Impressionism and Post-Impressionism 60 min., color **CPB**

A FRESH VIEW: Realism and Impressionism 30 min., color **CPB**

A FRESH VIEW: Post-Impressionism 30 min., color **CPB**

PAUL GAUGIN: The Savage Dream MMA

IMPRESSIONISM and NEO-IMPRESSIONISM IFB

THE IMPRESSIONIST SURFACE: PERCEPTIONS IN PAINT FFH

THE POST-IMPRESSIONISTS 25 min., color **IFB**

GEORGES SEURAT
In this program, video graphics are used to focus on key elements of Seurat's *A Sunday Afternoon on the Island of La Grande Jatte* and to analyze its structure and composition. 32 min. **FFH**

HENRI DE TOULOUSE-LAUTREC
The canvases *Décoration pour la baraque de La Goulue* and their extraordinary destiny are the subject of this program. 32 min. **FFH**

VINCENT VAN GOGH REVISITED—ON CD-ROM
An interactive sojourn through the life and works of one of the world's greatest impressionist painters. In French. Cindy Award Winner Recommended: PC Review, Home PC **FFH**

Music Resources

Debussy, *La mer (1903–1905)*, Ashkenazy, Cleveland Orchestra, London 417488-1 LH digital; 417488-2 LH, CD.
Debussy, *Prélude à l'après-midi d'un faune (1892–1894)*, Rubinstein, RCA 5670–2–RC, CD.

Web Resources

The Rodin museum—http://www.rodinmuseum.org/

Musee Rodin in Paris—http://www.mussee-rodin.fr/welcom.htm

Paris in the 19th Century—http://www.bohemiabooks.com.au/eblinks/spirboho/paris1830/index.html

Biographical information about Friedrich Nietzsche—http://plato.stanford..edu/entries/nietzsche/

Biographical information about Claude Debussy—http://www.music.indiana.edu/~u520/biography.html

Debussy, biographical information and select pieces —
http://classicalmus.hispeed.com/articles/debussy.html

The Impressionists, Biography.com's companion site—http://www.biography.com/impressionists/

Resources related to Art Nouveau—http://www.encyclopedia.com/articles/00782.html

The Vincent van Gogh gallery—http://www.vangoghgallery.com/

McGraw-Hill Resources

Music Listening Selection: CD II
   II–16 Debussy, *"Prélude à l'après-midi d'un faune"*

Sample Test Questions for Chapter 31

Select the letter of the choice that BEST answers the question.

1. Discoveries in the physics of _____ profoundly influenced the late nineteenth-century cultural community.
   a. sound
   b. light
   c. waves
   d. time
   Ans: b

2. The French artist whose painting gave a name to the impressionist school was
   a. Manet.
   b. Mallarmé.
   c. Monet.
   d. Maeterlinck.
   Ans: c

3. Impressionist painters believed that paint should be applied in
   a. clear lines.
   b. pure brush strokes of color.
   c. shadings of clashing impastoes.
   d. invisible brush strokes.
   Ans: b

4. Which of the following pairs, linking artist with subject matter, is INCORRECT?
   a. Monet—haystacks
   b. Renoir—Parisian society
   c. Degas—ballerinas
   d. van Gogh—birds
   Ans: d

5. Late nineteenth-century painters looked to Japanese woodblock prints for all the following EXCEPT
   a. flat, bold colors.
   b. startling perspectives.
   c. forceful calligraphy.
   d. heroic subject matter.
   Ans: d

6. The American impressionist whose work did much to popularize that artistic style in North America was
   a. Berthe Morisot.
   b. Nora Torvald.
   c. Mary Cassatt.
   d. Mary Shelley.
   Ans: c

7. The Dutch postimpressionist who expressed his reaction to a subject rather than to its physical appearance was
   a. Maurice Maeterlinck.
   b. Stéphane Mallarmé.
   c. Vincent van Gogh.
   d. Paul Claudel.
   Ans: c

8. The French artist who became entranced with unspoiled nature, especially as it existed in Tahiti, was
   a. Paul Verlaine.
   b. Vincent Rimbaud.
   c. Paul Gauguin.
   d. Stéphane Mallarmé.
   Ans: c

Answer the following with a word or phrase.

9. The French philosopher of the late nineteenth century who argued that all reality is constantly in the process of evolving and can only be understood intuitively was _____.
   Ans: Bergson

10. The impressionist composer who was inspired by the five-tone scale of East Asian music was _____.
    Ans: Debussy

11. The artist most closely associated with the colorist style known as pointillism is _____.
    Ans: Seurat

12. The "father of modern painting," who was more concerned with the composition and technique of a painting than its content, was _____.
    Ans: Cézanne

13. Fiero, Figure 31.10, Hokusai, *Mount Fuji Seen Below a Wave at Kanagawa*. If Hokusai had wanted to portray the elements in this scene in their respective scales, the element that would have predominated would be
    a. the men in the boats.
    b. the mountain in the distance.
    c. the boats themselves.
    d. the waves.
    Ans: b

14. Fiero, Figure 31.11, *Actor as a Monkey Showman* by Torii Kiyonobu. One departure from realism in this print that points to abstraction is the flattening of the garments to the extent that a body behind them is scarcely apparent.
    Ans: T

15. The media employed in the two illustrations from nineteenth-century African cultures are
    a. Gold and silver.
    b. Glass beads and brass.
    c. Ceramic pottery and wood.
    d. Bronze and marble.
    Ans: b

16. African art and artifacts came to the attention of western artists through
    a. European expansion and colonialism.
    b. promotion of African artists in Mediterranean port cities.
    c. religious missions to Africa.
    d. safaris.
    Ans: a

Essay Question

17. Fiero, Figure 31.11, *Mount Fuji Seen Below a Wave at Kanagawa*. When we learn that Fuji is a sacred mountain, the home of the gods, it changes our view of relative values in this picture. In a short essay, first list the things represented in this picture, then give their relative scale, and lastly, try to give an interpretation of the relationship between these things as seen through the eyes of Hokusai.

18. Fiero, Figure 31.31. Make a schematic drawing of Cézanne's still life, using only circles, rectangles, squares, and triangles. What do you discover about the structure of this painting?

BOOK 6

The Global Village of the Twentieth Century

Chapter **32** **The Modernist Assault on Tradition**

Summary

The modernist assault on tradition involved a conscious rejection of centuries-old values and norms. Atomic physicists provided a new model of the universe that explained matter as a form of energy, and space and time as relative to the position of the observer. Disjunction and uncertainty, the cosmic facts of the new physics, were also the quintessential features of early modernism. Early twentieth-century artists challenged the established ways of perceiving and interpreting experience. Imagist poets (led by Ezra Pound) and cubist painters (led by Pablo Picasso) fragmented form and juxtaposed motifs in ways that lacked smooth and predictable transitions. Cubists, futurists, and fauves anticipated the radical elimination of recognizable imagery by nonobjective artists like Brancusi, Kandinsky, Malevich, and Mondrian. Abstraction and formalism characterized the modern aesthetic in the architecture of Frank Lloyd Wright and Walter Gropius, and in the birth of the international style. In music, Schoenberg and Stravinsky produced compositions characterized by dissonance and rhythmic disjunction. Just as these composers rejected the time-honored traditions of tonality and fixed meter, so modern choreographers abandoned the rules of conventional dance and classical ballet.

Outline	**Pronunciation Guide**
A. Historical context	**Les Demoiselles d'Avignon**
1. global village	[LAY dem wah ZEL dah vee NYOWN]
2. the new physics	**Braque** [BRAHK]
B. Modernist poetry	**Boccioni** [bow CHOW nee]
1. imagists	**Duchamp** [doo SHAHM]
2. Frost	**Mondrian** [mown dree AHN]
C. Modernist art	*De Stijl* [de STEYEL]
1. cubism	**Malevich** [MAL ev itch]
2. futurism	**Popova** [POP ow vah]
3. the birth of film	**Bauhaus** [BAHW hahws]
4. the fauvism	**Le Corbusier** [le kowr boo ZEEAY]
5. abstract sculpture	*pilotis* [pee low TEES]
6. nonobjective art	**Schoenberg** [SHURN berg]
7. constructivism	**Nijinsky** [ni ZHIN skee]
D. Modernist architecture	
1. Wright	
2. the Bauhaus	
3. Le Corbusier	

E. Modernist music and dance
1. Schoenberg
2. Stravinsky
3. dance

Key Terms: relativity theory, uncertainty principle, imagist poetry, cubism, futurism, fauvism, nonobjective art, international style, constructivism, ferroconcrete cantilever, atonal music.

Key Images	
Picasso, *Les Demoiselles d'Avignon*	Kandinsky, *Painting for Edwin Campbell*
Boccioni, *Unique Forms of Continuity in Space*	Mondrian, *Composition in Red, Yellow, Blue, and Black*
Duchamp, *Nude Descending a Staircase #2*	Malevich, *Suprematist Composition: White on White*
Matisse, *The Dance*	Wright, *Robie House*
Brancusi, *Bird in Space*	Gropius, *Bauhaus*
	Le Corbusier, *Villa Savoye*

Study Questions

Factual

1. Who were the imagists; what were they trying to achieve?
2. What is the subject matter of *Les Demoiselles d'Avignon*? What influences were at work on Picasso when he executed the painting?
3. What is the difference between analytic cubism and synthetic cubism?
4. What modern technological achievements did the futurists celebrate in their art?
5. What is nonobjective art? Are there distinct differences in the styles of the three nonobjective artists mentioned in this chapter?
6. What individuals were responsible for the birth of motion pictures?
7. What are the principal features of the architecture of Frank Lloyd Wright and Le Corbusier?
8. What radical features did Arnold Schoenberg and Igor Stravinsky introduce into early twentieth-century music?

Challenge

1. Use the words *relativity* and *uncertainty* in a paragraph that describes the revolution in modern physics that took place in the early twentieth century.
2. It is often said that tradition, like history, is continually being recreated and remodeled. To what extent did writers, painters, and composers of the early twentieth century deliberately break with tradition? How did they accomplish that goal?
3. Between 1900 and 1925, traditional norms were violated or abandoned in art, music, and literature. What factors might have brought about this situation? Offer specific examples to illustrate your general statements.
4. The American painter Robert Motherwell wrote:
   > The function of abstraction is to get rid of a lot of reality. You start with as much richness as you want, and subtract, and then you arrive at the residue of essences that you're interested in.

   How might you apply these words to the art of Picasso, Matisse, Brancusi, and Mondrian?

5. Do you agree that creative expression at the beginning of the twentieth century represents the "dehumanization of art"? If so, why? If not, why not?
6. Compare the poems of Pound and Frost for economy of expression. How do these poems compare with those from Tang China that appear in Chapter 14?
7. Based on a survey of the domestic and commercial architecture of your university, town, or city, how would you evaluate the influence of Frank Lloyd Wright, Le Corbusier, and the international style?
8. What similarities do you detect between Picasso's *Les Demoiselles d'Avignon* and Stravinsky's *The Rite of Spring?*
9. People often find the music of Schoenberg and Stravinsky (Music Listening Selection II–17 and II–18) difficult to listen to. Why might this be the case? Are acid rock, rap, or any of the popular forms of contemporary music easier to listen to? What similarities and differences do you find between these kinds of music?
10. How did the media of photography and film respond to the modernist aesthetic?

Strategies for Discussion/Lecture

1. The chapter is well-suited to a slide lecture, or a lecture in conjunction with part of a video presentation. As preparation, students can be asked to write on Challenge questions 2 or 4. The following suggestions highlight specific approaches to more focused topics.
2. Architecture. Robie House (Figure 32.21) and Apartment block in Marseilles (Figure 32.25). From S. Giedion, *Space, Time and Architecture,* enlarge and copy the floor plans of these structures. For F. L. Wright, ask, "Does the exterior of the house reveal how the owners live in the interior spaces?" "What did Wright learn from East Asian art and architecture?" For Le Corbusier ask, "Can this building be considered, in the architect's words, 'a machine for living'"?
3. If non-Western themes are being emphasized through the course, the instructor might examine the influence of Japanese poetry on the imagists, and of various non-Western art forms on Picasso.
4. If the instructor has been following the progress of poetry, this would be a good opportunity to integrate slides of oriental artworks with the imagist poets, especially Pound.
5. The words *disjunction, discontinuity,* and *uncertainty* are very effective for use with various artworks in this chapter. The word *abstraction* should also be defined as part of the lecture or discussion of this chapter. The phrase *make it new* also provides a theme for general lecture and discussion.

Chapter 32 Audiovisuals

Video/CD-ROM Sources

AIR, LIGHT, AND UTOPIA: THE MODERN MOVEMENT IN ARCHITECTURE
Combining interviews with leading architects, historians, and conservationists with location footage from all over Europe, this timeless program examines the Modern Movement in architecture. **FFH**

ART OF THE WESTERN WORLD
Program 8: Into the Twentieth Century & Between the Wars **HTG**

ASCENT OF MAN: Knowledge or Certainty 52 min. color **TLF**

BAUHAUS: The Face of the 20th Century (1996)

This stunning program looks at the development of the Bauhaus and at the key figures involved in it—including Walter Gropius, Mies van der Rohe, Laslo Moholy-Nagy, and Josef Albers. 50 min., color **FFH**

CUBISM 21 min., color **IFB**

FROM CZARS TO COMMISSARS: A MUSEUM SURVIVES

As the royalty lived gilded lives within the Hermitage, serfs suffered in the fields. Revolution and war are set against the background of works by Picasso and Matisse. The Hermitage barely survived Stalinism and Nazi sieges. **HTG**

INTO THE TWENTIETH CENTURY 30 min., color **CPB**

MEANING IN ABSTRACT ART **FFH**

PIET MONDRIAN: A Film Essay (1980) **IFB**

PARIS: 1900

It is the fin de siècle. This program captures that magical period in all of its glory on archival film by the renowned Lumière brothers. **FFH**

PICASSO: A Painter's Diary—Formative Years 36 min., color **TLF**

PICASSO AND BRAQUE: New Ways of Seeing **MMA**

PICASSO AND HIS TIME

A superb documentary covering the long and extraordinary life of Picasso. 34 min. Recommended: School Arts, *School Library Journal* **FFH**

PIONEERS OF MODERN PAINTING 40 min., color **IFB**

EZRA POUND Voices and Visions Series 60 min., color **CPB**

SHOCK OF THE NEW—Vol. #1: The Mechanical Paradise (1980)
DIRECTOR: HUGHES, ROBERT 52 min., color
available through Joan @ Videofinders at 1-800-343-4727

SHOCK OF THE NEW—Vol. #3: Landscape of Pleasure (1980)
DIRECTOR: HUGHES, ROBERT 52 min., color
available through Joan @ Videofinders at 1-800-343-4727

SHOCK OF THE NEW—Vol. #5: Trouble in Utopia (1980)
DIRECTOR: HUGHES, ROBERT 52 min., color
available through Joan @ Videofinders at 1-800-343-4727

STRAVINSKY CRM

IGOR STRAVINSKY 42 min., B&W **CAROUSEL**

UNITY OF PICASSO MMA

Music Resources

Schoenberg, *Verklärte Nacht, Op. 4 (1899)*, Boulez, Ensemble Intercontemporain, CBS IM-39566 digital; MK–39566 CD; IMT–39566 cassette.

Schoenberg, *Pierrot Lunaire, Op. 21 (1912)*, DeGaetani, Weisberg, Contemporary Chamber Ensemble, Elektra/Nonesuch H–71309; 71251–4 cassette.

Schoenberg, *Quartet No. 2 in F sharp for Soprano and Strings, Op. 10 (1907–1908)*, Beardslee, Sequoia Quartet, Elektra Nonesuch D–79005; D1–79005 cassette.

Web Resources

An examination of Picasso's career—http://www.tamu.edu/mocl/picasso/

Resources related to Frank Lloyd Wright—http://marin2.marin.org/mc/pos/flw/

Biographical information and selected works of Robert Frost—The Vincent van Gogh gallery—http://www.poets.org/poets/poets.cfm?prmld=196&cfid=3973192&cftoken=44572748

The Robert Frost web site—http://www.robertfrost.org/indexgood.html

Resources related to Cubism—http://www.artcyclopedia.com/history/cubism.html

Resources related to the history of film—http://www.cln.org/themes/history_film.html

Resources related to Bauhaus architecture—http://www.cd.umb.edu/~alilley/bauhaus.html

Resources related to Le Corbusier—http://www.encyclopedia.com/articles/07311.html

Schoenberg Archives at University of Southern California—http://www.usc.edu/isd/archives/schoenberg

Resources related to Igor Stravinsky—http://www.geocities.com/vienna/1807/strav.html

McGraw-Hill Resources

Fiero Music Listening Selections: CD II
    II–17 Schoenberg, *Pierrot Lunaire*
    II–18 Stravinsky, *The Rite of Spring*, "Sacrificial Dance"

Sample Test Questions for Chapter 32

Select the letter of the choice that BEST answers the question:

1. Einstein's theory of relativity asserted that
   a. in studying subatomic particles, time and space were relative.
   b. planetary movement could not be accurately calculated.
   c. the earth's rotational speed depended on the time year.
   d. all of Galileo's theories were inaccurate.
   Ans: a

2. One of the early poets of twentieth-century America who explored literature from China and Japan and who exhorted colleagues to "make it new" was
   a. Ezra Pound.
   b. Hans Heisenberg.
   c. Amy Lowell.
   d. Hilda Doolittle.
   Ans: a

3. The American poet who exalted individualism in his lyric works by affirming that he took the road "less traveled" was
   a. Ezra Pound.
   b. Carl Sandburg.
   c. Robert Frost.
   d. Walt Whitman.
   Ans: c

4. The celebrated *Les Demoiselles d'Avignon* shocked observers because
   a. it depicted women with unprecedented brutality.
   b. it portrayed nudity in exceptional detail.
   c. its subjects wore Japanese warrior masks.
   d. it featured unusual colors for skin tones.
   Ans: a

5. The Italian art movement that emphasized the close relationship between science and art was
   a. cubism.
   b. pointillism.
   c. futurism.
   d. scientism.
   Ans: c

6. The fauves, led by Matisse, made _____ the most important feature of their canvases.
   a. line
   b. composition
   c. texture
   d. color
   Ans: d

7. Nonobjective art as practiced by Malevich, Kandinsky, and Mondrian eliminated _____ from art.
   a. nudity
   b. color
   c. subject matter
   d. brushstrokes
   Ans: c

8. Early movies generally were of two genres: the western and
   a. war stories.
   b. science fiction.
   c. historical romances.
   d. adventure stories.
   Ans: b

9. In general, twentieth-century music rejected all except which of the following elements?
   a. lyric melody
   b. traditional tonality
   c. free use of meter
   d. traditional harmonies
   Ans: c

10. Unlike Newtonian physics, modern science persuaded many that the operations of the universe could not be predicted with any certainty.
    Ans: T

Answer the following with a word or phrase.

11. The early group of twentieth-century poets who sought simplicity, directness in speech, and concentration of effect was called the _____.
    Ans: imagists

12. The Japanese poetic form that has three lines and seventeen syllables is called _____.
    Ans: haiku

13. *Les Demoiselles d'Avignon,* which inaugurated the cubist impulse, was painted by _____.
    Ans: Picasso

14. The German architectural school founded by Walter Gropius, which emphasized functionalism, was known as the _____.
    Ans: Bauhaus

15. The twentieth-century composer who startled audiences through his use of "serial" music or the twelve-tone scale was _____.
    Ans: Schoenberg

16. The creator of *The Rite of Spring,* which would later be recognized as the "birth certificate of modern music," was _____.
    Ans: Stravinsky

17. In the text, the French artist and theorist, Maurice Denis, defines painting as "a flat surface covered with shapes, lines and colors assembled in a particular order."
Using the letters A, B, and C as a scale going from *close* to the spirit of this definition to *far from* the definition, rank the following four paintings:

Figure 32.3, Picasso, *des Demoiselles d'Avignon*
Ans: b

18. Figure 32.13, Matisse, *The Dance*
Ans: b

19. Figure 32.19, Mondrian, *Composition in Red, Yellow, Blue, and Black*
Ans: a

20. Figure 32.18, Mondrian, *Horizontal Tree*
Ans: b

21. "Form and Function." The exterior of the Robie House (Figure 32.22) suggests that what holds the building up is
    a. the principle of the Roman arch.
    b. post and lintel brick construction.
    c. steel girder construction.
    d. a combination of b and c.
    Ans: d

22. The exterior of Falling Water (Figure 32.23) suggests that the construction method includes
    a. Roman arch.
    b. cantilever.
    c. gothic arch.
    d. moorish arch.
    Ans: b

23. Le Corbusier (Figure 32.). The apartment block in Marseilles is an example of this building method.
    a. cantilever steel beam
    b. reinforced concrete
    c. post and lintel
    d. steel cage
    Ans: b

24. The Villa Savoye (Figure 32.) includes this feature of Le Corbusier's building style.
    a. elaborate brickwork
    b. pilotis or posts
    c. modular construction
    d. glass curtain wall
    Ans: b

25. Of the following, the one artwork that stands apart from the others in style is
    a. Mondrian's *Horizontal Tree.*
    b. Weston's *Two Shells.*
    c. Brancusi's *Bird in Flight.*
    d. Malevich's *White on White.*
    Ans: d

26. The most controversial ballet of the first half of the twentieth century was Stravinsky's 1918 creation,
    a. *Pierrot lunaire.*
    b. *Bluebeard's Castle.*
    c. *The Rite of Spring.*
    d. *Salome.*
    Ans: c

Summary

The theories of Sigmund Freud had a revolutionary effect on the beliefs and morals of modern society, as well as on the arts. In literature, the works of Proust, Kafka, and Joyce illustrate the new preoccupation with the subconscious mind and with the forces of memory and desire. The methods of Freudian psychoanalysis had their counterparts in stream-of-consciousness prose and free association. Parallel with these developments, visual artists explored the realms of fantasy and dreams. In the wake of a brutal war that seemed to confirm Freud's negative view of civilization, dada artists (led by Marcel Duchamp) spread the gospel of irrationality; but the movement that best mirrors Freud's influence on the arts was surrealism, which sought to liberate the life of the subconscious from the restrictive bonds of consciousness. In music, the expressionistic monodramas of Schoenberg and the sexually charged operas of Strauss, Bartók, and Berg clearly reflect the impact of Freud.

Outline	**Pronunciation Guide**

A. Freudian revolution
  1. theories and techniques
  2. model of the psyche: id, ego, superego
  3. Jung's archetypal subconscious
B. Impact of new psychology on literature
  1. Proust
  2. Kafka
  3. Joyce
  4. e.e. cummings
C. Impact of new psychology on the visual arts and music
  1. expressionism: Munch and Kirchner
  2. metaphysical art and fantasy: de Chirico and Chagall
  3. dadaism
  4. surrealism
    a. Picasso, Miro, and Klee
    b. Magritte, Dali
    c. O'Keefe and Kahlo
  4. still photography and film
  5. early twentieth-century music
	Jung [YUNG]
	Munch [MOONK]
	Kirchner [KIRK ner]
	de Chirico [de KI ree kow]
	Magritte [mah GREET]
	Klee [KLAY]
	Höch [HOWK]
	Giacometti [jah kow MET tee]
	Kahlo [KAH low]
	sprechtstimme [SHPREK shti mu]

Key Terms: psychoanalysis, id, ego, superego, libido, archetype, stream of consciousness, interior monologue, concrete poem, magic realism, ready-made sculpture, "found objects," method acting, photomontage, *sprechtstimme.*

<table>
<tr><td colspan="2">Key Images</td></tr>
<tr>
<td>

Munch, *The Scream*
De Chirico, *The Nostalgia of the Infinite*
Chagall, *I and the Village*
Miró, *Person Throwing a Stone at a Bird*
Duchamp, *Fountain (Urinal)*

</td>
<td>

Klee, *Fish Magic*
Magritte, *The False Mirror*
Dali, *The Persistence of Memory*
Kahlo, *The Broken Column*
Oppenheim, *Object*

</td>
</tr>
</table>

Study Questions

Factual

1. How did each of the parts of Freud's three-part psyche (id, ego, and superego) function, according to Freud?
2. What, according to Freud (Reading 6.3), are some of civilization's "discontents"?
3. What experiences trigger the narrator's memory in *Swann's Way* (Reading 6.4)?
4. What images in Kafka's short story *The Metamorphosis* (Reading 6.5) create a mood of apprehension in the reader?
5. What is the subject of cummings' "[she being Brand]" (Reading 6.6)?
6. What parts of Europe were most active in the birth of expressionism in art?
7. To what specific event or events were the proponents of Dada responding? Why so?
8. What were the aims of the surrealists, as defined by Breton in the first "Surrealist Manifesto"?
9. What musical compositions expressed the aesthetic of surrealism?

Challenge

1. How did Sigmund Freud respond to the precept, "Thou shalt love thy neighbor as thyself"? Assess the validity of Freud's theory of human nature in the twentieth century. Use specific historical and cultural examples to illustrate your arguments.
2. Freud held that religion was a "universal obsessional neurosis of humanity." What did he mean? Evaluate this assertion from your own point of view.
3. What symbols of the collective unconscious seem to you both universal and eternal? Give examples of their appearances in religion, art, literature, etc.
4. Create a stream-of-consciousness diary entry of your experiences since you awoke this morning. Does your entry capture these experiences more effectively than a narrative description of them might?
5. It has been said that James Joyce is "the Shakespeare of modernism." Read more of *Ulysses* and offer your own assessment of this statement.
6. Which of the surrealist artists (Picasso, Dali, Magritte, Miró, Kahlo, et al.) "speaks" to your own subconscious life most directly? Why and how so?
7. Find specific examples in contemporary advertising (magazines, television, etc.) in which the influence of surrealism is apparent.
8. How and why does music that is written for film often "work" better in the cinematic context than in the concert hall? Find examples that illustrate this phenomenon.

Strategies for Discussion/Lecture

1. The chapter is about evenly divided between literary and visual documents, and the lecturer may wish to concentrate on one aspect and use the other for illustration and background. A preparatory written theme on Freud (Factual question 1) or Proust (Factual question 3) would set the stage for a discussion of wide range. One user of the text begins by showing Luis Buñuel's film, *Andalusian Dog* (20 minutes), and develops a lecture on the basis of its images.
The following suggestions are intended to bring out the emphasis on the irrational and the irreverent in works inspired by research on the subconscious.

2. The discussion of happiness in Aristotle (Chapter 4) makes a worthy benchmark for appreciating Freud's reduction of human experience to pain and pleasure. Is there any proof in Freud that happiness can be reduced to these two poles? Class discussion of *Civilization and Its Discontents* should follow.

3. A close in-class reading of the Proust passage (Reading 6.4) may take the discussion of the subconscious farther than the Freud reading. Each step in the liberation of suppressed memory will call on the Freudian analysis in a more familiar way than theory could. Factual question 3 provides an excellent focus.

4. Students can be asked to rewrite e.e. cummings' "[she being Brand]" as a prose paragraph, noting as they go along how many conventions the poet breaks. Is the resulting rewrite a poem? How does the original produce its effects?

5. The surrealists used a variety of techniques for freeing the subconscious in the act of writing. These include asking students to write automatically or producing "found poems" (in class) by using the list of Key Images to the chapter: arranging these titles in a number of ways may produce some interesting results and commentary. Another method is to type a familiar poem onto the screen of a word processor, then use "search and replace" to generate random variants. This method was used long before computers became widely known, by the surrealist poet Raymond Queneau in his sonnet sequence written on moveable strips, capable of generating billions of poems. Similar techniques can be applied in the visual arts by assembling random images and dropping them on a surface.

6. The instructor will find it hard to get an open-minded hearing for some twentieth-century music. It may help to take advantage of the one genre most young listeners know: MTV. Instead of playing the Stravinsky selection on the cassette, try playing the sequence in Walt Disney's *Fantasia* (death of the dinosaurs!) that uses it as background music. After reading the Proust selection, try playing the Satie *Gymnopédies* without announcing composer and title. It goes remarkably well with the mood of reflective, inwardly turned literature. Satie is also one of the sources of the various strains of less accomplished New-Age, wallpaper music now enjoying some popularity. Try playing the John Cage selection from the CD II-20 without revealing the instrument, for the sake of the pleasant shock of discovery.

Chapter 33 Audiovisuals

Video/CD-ROM Sources

SERGEI EISENSTEIN This richly personal documentary uses first-person narration, artwork, film clips, and photographs to trace the life and achievements of this legendary artist and filmmaker. 56 min. **FFH**

EXPRESSIONISM 26 min., color **IFB**

GERMAN DADA 55 min., color **MMS**

FRIDA KAHLO: PORTRAIT OF A WOMAN A look at the life and work of this first-rate painter. Recommended: School Arts Films for the Humanities & Sciences 20 min., color **FFH**

FRIDA KAHLO
Kahlo is the artist who brought surrealism to Mexico. Her paintings—literal interpretations of dreams, desires, and loss—haunt us still. Her art reflects her constant struggle with her ravaged body (the result of a terrible accident as a teenager), and a culture with an ambivalent attitude toward a woman with a mind of her own. Her marriage to Diego Rivera also influenced her work. (Some of Kahlo's work contains explicit imagery...please preview prior to public exhibition). (1988) 62 min. **HTG**

MIRÓ: THE CATALAN MASTER Joán Miró talks about his life and the various influences on his work. RTVE. Int'l Emmy Award Nominee Recommended: School Library Journal (Spanish) 55 min. **FFH**

JOÁN MIRÓ: CONSTELLATIONS
The work of Joán Miró (1893–1983) sparkles with surreal cartoons, primary colors, and the power of simple, whimsical lines. His emblematic vocabulary consisted of stars, eyes, women, and birds, done in a tone of dark playfulness. These liberal, wacky paintings are said to have facilitated the 1950s post-dictatorship spirit in his native Spain. Miró's approach to life was as bold as his approach to art. He and his surrealist cohorts delighted in Freudian symbols and anti-bourgeois politics. This video takes a new approach to outlining Miró: dancers in elaborate costumes designed by Miró himself bring his drawings to life. Teens in particular should be able to relate to Miro's rebelliousness and angst. As the video states: "Miró was on the side of freedom and offers freedom to all who see his work." (1992) 53 min. **HTG**

EDVARD MUNCH
This program covers Edvard Munch's most productive years in Germany, including those in Weimar and Berlin. A Deutsche Welle Production. 30 min. **FFH**

SHOCK OF THE NEW—Vol. #2: The Powers That Be (1980)
DIRECTOR: HUGHES, ROBERT 52 min., color
available through Joan @ Videofinders at 1-800-343-4727

SHOCK OF THE NEW—Vol. #5: Threshold of Liberty (1980)
DIRECTOR: HUGHES, ROBERT 52 min., color
available through Joan @ Videofinders at 1-800-343-4727

STRAUSS: Salome, Vol. 3 of the Covet Garden Opera (1992) 105 min., color **VC**

SURREALISM 24 min., color **IFB**

Music Resources

Fiero Music Listening Selections CD II
II-17 Schoenberg: *Pierrot Lunaire*, Op. 21, Part 3, No. 15, "Heimweh"

Web Resources

Resources related to Richard Strauss—http://www.richard-strauss.com/

Resources related to Richard Strauss—http://people.unt.edu/ ~ dmeek/rstrauss.html

Resources related to Sigmund Freud—http://www.freudpage.com/en-us/freud/index.html

Resources related to Sigmund Freud—http://www.freud.org.uk/

A study of Marcel Proust and his times—http://www.library.uiuc.edu/kolbp/

Biographical information about Franz Kafka—http://info.pitt.edu/ ~ kafka/intro.html

Biographical information and selected works of Salvador Dali—http://www.salvadordalimuseum.org/

Biographical information and selected works of Salvador Dali—http://daligallery.com

Biographical information about Rene Magritte—http://www.magritte.com/

Surrealism—http://www.surrealomania.co.uk/

Biographical information about Marcel Duchamp—www.marcelduchamp.net/

Biographical information about Marcel Duchamp—http://www.marcelduchamp.org/

Biographical information about Marcel Duchamp—
    http://www.franceweb.fr/zumba/Duchamp/index.html

Georgia O'Keefe Museum—http://www.okeefe.org/indexflash.html

Georgia O'Keefe online gallery—http://www.happyshadows.com/okeefe/

McGraw-Hill Resources

Transparencies: MA.9 The Twentieth Century 1900–Present
                MA.15 Music-Art-European Map (Twentieth Century 1900–1990)

Sample Test Questions for Chapter 33

Select the letter of the choice that BEST answers the question:

1. The principal tools of Freud's psychoanalysis were dream analysis and
    a. the identification of complexes.
    b. free association.
    c. hypnosis.
    d. behavioral experiment.
    Ans: b

2. Freud considered his work on _____ to be his most valuable contribution.
   a. the Oedipus complex
   b. dreams
   c. sexual preference
   d. early childhood
   Ans: b

3. According to Freud, the greatest block to civilization was
   a aggression.
   b. class division.
   c. totalitarianism.
   d. ignorance.
   Ans: a

4. Included in the collective unconscious of Jungian theory were ALL BUT which one of these archetypes?
   a. earth mother
   b. wise old man
   c. the garden
   d. older sister
   Ans: d

5. Marcel Proust's primary objective was to
   a. depict an old man's dreams.
   b. analyze a mother–son relationship.
   c. rediscover a sense of the past.
   d. assess the influence of the superego.
   Ans: c

6. Influenced by Freudian theories, James Joyce employed a _____ technique in his novel *Ulysses.*
   a. dream analysis
   b. hypnosis
   c. stream of consciousness
   d. symbolist
   Ans: c

7. The American poet e. e. cummings sought to sharpen the focus of his poems by
   a. convoluting syntax and word placement.
   b. limiting the subject matter of his poetry.
   c. accompanying his written work with drawings.
   d. snipping words out of magazines and newspapers.
   Ans: a

8. Expressionist artists created a style that featured
   a. pastel colors.
   b. huge patches of white.
   c. collage.
   d. distorted forms.
   Ans: d

9. According to Marcel Duchamp, the modern artist should be the
   a. conscience of a society.
   b. destroyer of tradition.
   c. eyes of the people.
   d. advocate for peace.
   Ans: b

Answer the following with a word or phrase.

10. In the excerpt from *Swann's Way,* Proust uses the technique of _____ to bring up memories related to *petites madeleines,* or cookies.
    Ans: free association

11. Freud divided the psyche into three parts, _____, _____, and _____.
    Ans: id, ego, superego

12. The Swiss physician who affirmed the existence of a universal layer of unconscious life was

    _____.
    Ans: Jung

13. The painter of *The Scream,* who explored the psychic life of the individual, was _____.
    Ans: Edvard Munch

14. The first world war convinced artists of the _____ movement that the world had gone mad.
    Ans: dada

15. Literature in the wake of Freud took a sharp turn inward. An early twentieth-century French novelist interested in recapturing the past was a precursor to this movement: _____.
    Ans: Proust

16. Founded in Zurich, Switzerland in 1916, this movement set about challenging the very nature of art:
    Ans: Dada

17. The artistic movement largely inspired by Freud and interested mainly in exploring the material of dreams was _____.
    Ans: Surrealism

18. Give the name of the artistic movement that corresponds to this definition: "Psychic automatism, in its pure state...exempt from any aesthetic or moral concern."
    Ans: Surrealism

19. This American painter is called the "high priestess" of early modernism:
    Ans: Georgia O'Keefe

20. Of the human senses, the one Proust finds most powerful for unlocking long-lost memories is
    a. sight
    b. smell/taste
    c. hearing
    d. touch.
    Ans: b

21. The pioneer in the technique of photographic collage was
    a. Köch.
    b. Magritte.
    c. Dali.
    d. Miro.
    Ans: a

22. This fragment from James Joyce's *Ulysses*: "Night sky moon, violet, color of Molly's new garters" is reminiscent of the early twentieth-century school of poetry known as the
    a. dadaists.
    b. romantics.
    c. imagists.
    d. surrealists.
    Ans: c

23. The artistic movement in Dresden and Munich that came to be called German Expressionism was heavily influenced by the art of
    a. Africa and Oceania.
    b. the United States.
    c. the classical eighteenth century.
    d. ancient Greece.
    Ans: a

24. The key figure in the development of operatic recitation known as Sprechstimme was
    a. Stravinsky.
    b. Cocteau.
    c. Satie.
    d. Schoenberg.
    Ans: d

Summary

The twentieth century has been molded in the crucible of two world wars and numerous totalitarian dictatorships. Searing indictments of World War I are sounded in the poetry of Owen and Yeats, the novels of Remarque, and the art of Ernst and Grosz. Second World War literature emphasized the dehumanizing effects of war and the brutality of atomic warfare. The Russian Revolution of 1917, the Stalinist gulags of the 1940s, the Nazi policy of militant racism in Germany, and the totalitarian purges in Communist China were traumatic episodes that inspired moving responses in all of the arts. Throughout the world, photographs and films documented the shocking facts of twentieth-century warfare, while paintings (such as Picasso's *Guernica*) and musical compositions (such as Britten's *War Requiem*) gave unique expression to the harsh realities of modern aggression.

Outline	**Pronunciation Guide**

A. Total war
  1. literary responses to World War I
  2. art of Ernst, Grosz, and Leger
B. The Russian Revolution
  1. Lenin and Stalin
  2. socialist realism
C. Great Depression in America
  1. literature
  2. Benton and mural painting
  3. photography
D. Totalitarianism and World War II
  1. Hitler and Nazi totalitarianism
  2. nature of the war
  3. poetry: Jarrell and Shuson
  4. prose: Jeller and Wiesel
  5. film and photojournalism
E. The arts in the war era
  1. Picasso's *Guernica*
  2. music
    a. Shostakovich and Prokofiev
    b. Britten and Penderecki
	Ernst [ERNST]
	Grosz [GROWS]
	Remarque [re MAHRK]
	Yeats [YAYTS]
	Guernica [GWER ni kah]
	Rivera [ri VE rah]
	Orozco [ow ROWS kow]
	Tamayo [tah MEYE ow]
	Riefenstahl [REE fen shtahl]
	Penderecki [pen de RETS kee]
	Shostakovich [shahs tah KOW vich]
	Wiesel [VEE zel]

Key Terms: total war, totalitarianism, Russian Revolution, montage, Great Depression, mural art, Holocaust, *gulag*, tone cluster, documentary photography, gallows humor.

Key Images	
Grosz, *Fit for Active Service*	Benton, *City Activities*
Rivera, *The Liberation of the Peon*	Lange, *Migrant Mother*
S. Eisenstein, *The Battleship Potemkin*	Picasso, *Guernica*
Leger, *Three Women*	

Study Questions

Factual

1. Why are World Wars I and II called "total wars"?
2. What images in the poems by Owen, Yeats, Jarrell, and Shuson best capture the sense of despair and rage felt by the poets?
3. What is the difference between "social realism" and "socialist realism"? Cite examples of each.
4. Define gallows humor and give examples. Why was this genre particularly appropriate to the subject of modern warfare?
5. What event prompted Picasso to paint *Guernica?* Did the artist represent the actual event in the painting?
6. How did Britten and Penderecki translate the horrors of war into music?
7. How does Copland's music compare with that of the Europeans of the war era?
8. In what ways did film makers throughout the world respond to total war and totalitarianism?

Challenge

1. Would Remarque's *All Quiet on the Western Front* (Reading 127) be equally effective if it were narrated in the past tense?
2. What role did Lenin play in creating a new social order in Russia? What ideals did he hope to achieve? What aspects of human nature did he fail to consider when he drafted his reforms for an all-embracing world communism?
3. Is violence inherent in the human condition? Can violence be controlled? Instigated? Do twentieth-century modes of telecommunication actually work to foster violence? Or do they work to foster peace?
4. How did film and photojournalism serve in the war era?
5. Give examples of totalitarianism from various periods in history. Does the totalitarianism of the twentieth century seem more virulent to you? If so, why? Do recent events in China and in the former Soviet Union suggest a growing global intolerance of totalitarianism?
6. Research the art of the revolutionary Latin American mural painters. How did Diego Rivera, Jose Clemente Orozco, and Rufino Tamayo use art as a vehicle of social protest?
7. How did Eisenstein in Russia and Riefenstahl in Germany use film to serve the state? Did American film makers use film in the same manner? Give examples.
8. In what ways does Picasso's *Guernica* constitute a universal indictment of war when the painting itself includes no objects that are directly associated with modern warfare?
9. Read Heller's *Catch–22* in its entirety. What is the "catch" that inspires the title of the novel?
10. Listen to recordings of Britten's *War Requiem* and Penderecki's *Threnody.* Are they more "difficult" to appreciate and enjoy than Shostakovich's *Leningrad Symphony?* How so?

Strategies for Discussion/Lecture

1. Presentation of the chapter seems to call for a brief lecture overview of the central historical events of the era, then the focus on the nature of modern warfare and the central theme of violence. Challenge question 3 is a natural choice for a preparatory written theme that would carry over into discussion.
2. One user of the text begins by showing the "Odessa steps" portion of Eisenstein's *The Battleship Potemkin,* and stresses the artistic interpretation of events rather than the events themselves—an effective prelude to the "war on TV" and to newsreel footage of current hotspots, such as Israel and Ireland.
3. A discussion on smaller-scale works may suit some classes better. Comparison of the short lyrics, for instance, will bring out distinctive artistic strategies for dealing with violence. What do Owen, Yeats, and Jarrell want you to see and feel? Do the haikus of Shuson present a distinct cultural alternative to expressing violent themes?
4. The visual material in the chapter shows a split between realistic and abstract styles. A comparison of Dorothea Lange, Rivera's murals, and Picasso's *Guernica* can be used to probe the issue of art for its own sake versus narrative art for the sake of social change. Social versus socialist realism may be clarified here.
5. If possible, make use of such films as *All Quiet on the Western Front, From Here to Eternity, The Great Dictator, The Triumph of the Will, Catch 22, Schindler's List*, and *Saving Private Ryan.*

Chapter 34 Audiovisuals

Video/CD-ROM Sources

THOMAS HART BENTON: TOM BENTON'S MISSOURI

An examination of Thomas Hart Benton's "Social History of the State of Missouri." 28 min. CINE Golden Eagle; Red Ribbon, American Film & Video Festival Recommended: Booklist, Video Rating Guide for Libraries, School Library Journal, School Arts **FFH**

THE CHINESE REVOLUTION 24 min., color **FFH**

DEGENERATE ART

In the early 20th century, a struggling artist named Adolf Hitler was painting landscapes in a realistic style. Hitler soon abandoned art for politics, but he always acknowledged art's power and championed the aesthetics of classicism. In 1933, the Nazi party organized the best-attended art exhibit in history. It was called "Entarte Kunst," or "degenerate art." Organized to call public attention to the German expressionist movement—a style Hitler considered subhuman, filthy, and insane—the exhibit showcased the surrealistic works only to deride them. Attempting to visualize interior experience, the new style presented war in a nightmarish light and abstracted the human form. The banning of this art had dire consequences for the artists and for art history itself. Narrated by David McCollough, this documentary provides insight into the power of art, the hell of war, and the tyranny of censorship. (1993) 52 min. **HTG**

THE FRESCOES OF DIEGO RIVERA

An artist must be the conscience of his age. So said Diego Rivera, leader of the Mexican mural movement of the 1920s and 30s. This program explores Rivera's art and politics and their inextricability, capturing the largesse of his attitude toward life and art. (1988) 35 min. **HTG**

FROM BITTER EARTH: ARTISTS OF THE HOLOCAUST

Throughout the Holocaust, Jewish artists created work that vividly documented the horror of Hitler's reign. This program pays tribute to these artists, to the politics of their art, and to the tenacity of their creative spirit. A BBC Production. 50 min. **FFH**

GLOBAL WAR 1939–1945 3PK

Relive the world's deadliest war with this remarkable set. Archival combat footage and newsreels re-create in THE GROWTH OF FASCISM Hitler's ascent and Japan's attack on Pearl Harbor. The Allies turn back Axis forces in the Pacific and North Africa in RESTORING THE BALANCE. In LIBERATION OF THE PEOPLE, Allied troops invade Europe and force Japan's surrender with atomic bombs. In b/w. 150 minutes on 3 tapes **PBS**

THE GREAT WAR: Fifty Years After 25 min., color NBC

JUDGMENT AT NUREMBERG (1961)

DIRECTOR: KRAMER, STANLEY 187 min., B&W, sound **AZ**

DOROTHEA LANGE: A VISUAL LIFE

This film captures the spirit of Dorothea Lange (1895–1965), a great American photographer. Lange's images of the Great Depression are etched in history, and her compassion for the downtrodden conveys itself clearly in her collected works. Lange shot breadlines, migrant camps, ex-slaves in the South, and interned Japanese-Americans in California. A VISUAL LIFE brings to life five decades of American history with photographs and narration by Lange, revealing her passion for the medium of photography and her commitment to record the rapidly changing face of America. A quiet portrait of a generous artist. (1994) 48 min. **HTG**

LENIN AND TROTSKY 27 min., B&W CBS

MUSIC BOX (1989)

DIRECTOR: COSTA-GAVRAS, CONSTANTINE 126 min., color **AZ**

NAZI CONCENTRATION CAMPS 59 min., B&W NAVC

NIGHT AND FOG (1955)

DIRECTOR: RESNAIS, ALAIN 34 min., color **AZ**

PAWNBROKER, THE (1965)

DIRECTOR: LUMET, SIDNEY 116 min., B&W **AZ**

PICASSO: A Painter's Diary—from Cubism to Guernica 36 min., color TLF

DIEGO RIVERA: ART AND REVOLUTION

NewsHour correspondent Jeffrey Kaye surveys the life and artwork of Diego Rivera, a larger-than-life figure and one of the twentieth century's truly revolutionary artists—both creatively and politically. 11 min. **FFH**

RUSSIA: Czar to Lenin CRM

SCHINDLER'S LIST (1994)
     DIRECTOR: SPIELBERG, STEVEN 197 min., B&W **AZ**

THE SPANISH TURMOIL 64 min., B&W **TLF**

TRIUMPH OF THE WILL (1934)
     DIRECTOR: RIEFENSTAHL, LENI 107 min., B&W **AZ**

TWISTED CROSS: The Rise of Nazism 55 min., B&W **MGHF**

VIETNAM: A TELEVISION HISTORY (Series) (1987)
     DIRECTOR: ELLISON, R. & SMITH, M. color **AZ**

WHO SHALL LIVE AND WHO SHALL DIE? (1982)
     DIRECTOR: JARVIK, LAURENCE 90 min., B&W **AZ**

Web Resources

Resources related to Elie Wiesel—http://www.kirjasto.sci.fi/wiesel.htm

Resources related to Dmitri Shostakovich—http://www.shostakovich.org/

Information about Mao-Tse-tung and the Chinese Communist Revolution—http://www.maoism.org/

Resources related to World War I—http://www.pbs.org/greatwar/

Resources related to the Russian Revolution—http://aj.encyclopedia.com/printable/11250.html

Resources related to the Great Depression—http://www.amatecon.com/greatdepression.html

Resources related to World War II—http://www.cfcsc.dnd.ca/links/milhist/wwii.html

Resources related to World War II—http://www.lib.muohio.edu/inet/subj/history/wwii/

Biographical information about Adolf Hitler—http://remember.org/facts.root.hitler.html

Resources related to Dmitri Shostakovich—http://www.shostakovich.org/

McGraw-Hill Resources

Fiero Music Listening Selections CD-II
    II-19 Copland: *Appalachian Spring*, section 7, theme and variations on "Simple Gifts."
Transparencies: MA.9 The Twentieth Century 1900–Present

Sample Test Questions for Chapter 34

Select the letter of the choice that BEST answers the question:

1. World War I, or the Great War of 1914, began in part because of
   a. rivalry between France and England.
   b. a system of defensive alliances among European states.
   c. a rebellion in Eastern Europe.
   d. African demands for independence.
   Ans: b

2. Like Hemingway and Owen, the German novelist _____ was deeply affected by his personal war experience.
   a. Heisenberg
   b. Remarque
   c. Fichte
   d. Schoenberg
   Ans: b

3. The artistic style that portrayed social problems in an objective manner was called social
   a. objectivity.
   b. realism.
   c. determinism.
   d. relativism.
   Ans: b

4. The bull and horse in Picasso's *Guernica* may be regarded as a metaphor for
   a totalitarianism.
   b. violent combat.
   c. advanced technology.
   d. bureaucratic incompetence.
   Ans: b

5. One of the earliest satirical films, which mocked Hitler and Stalin, was *The Great Dictator*, starring
   a Trevor Howard.
   b. Douglas Fairbanks.
   c. Charlie Chaplin.
   d. Abbott and Costello.
   Ans: c

6. To depict the brutality of war, Picasso crafted *Guernica* with bright and jarring colors.
   Ans: F

7. World War I undermined the shaky regime of the Russian czar, leading to the 1917 Revolution.
   Ans: T

8. Mao's reforms tried to replace the Confucian emphasis on filial piety and family with loyalty to the state and the economic unit.
   Ans: T

9. In opposition to the modernists, American social realist painters during the Depression, like Thomas Hart Benton, painted recognizable images.
Ans: T

10. The American who photographed the *Migrant Mother*, sometimes called the "Madonna of the Dustbowl," was _____.
Ans: Dorothea Lange

Answer the following with a word or phrase.

11. Known as the "dean of American music," _____ joined regional themes with lyric harmonies.
Ans: Copland

12. One of the most moving testimonies to the Holocaust is the autobiographical *Night* by _____.
Ans: Wiesel

13. As crafted by Thomas Hart Benton, the public _____ became a major form of public art during America's Great Depression.
Ans: mural

14. The Irish poet who despaired that the world was falling apart, "the center cannot hold," was

_____.
Ans: Yeats

15. According to Lenin, the highest stage of capitalism is _____.
Ans: imperialism

16. The "bible" of the Chinese Revolution was
    a. *Quotations from Chairman Mao*
    b. Li Hua's *Roar!*
    c. Lenin's *State and Revolution*
    d. Stalin's *Diary*
    Ans: a

17. For much of his music, Copland drew on
    a. American folk songs.
    b. Stravinksy's ballets.
    c. the twelve-tone system.
    d. wartime themes.
    Ans: a

Essay Question

18. After re-reading Wiesel's *Night*, write an essay on why you think the episode described by the author calls for the question asked by "someone behind me," and why the response is found in the speaker's own mind?

Chapter *35* The Quest for Meaning

Summary

Alienation and anxiety were the unique conditions of the modern world at mid-century. The quest for meaning in modern life led Sartre to shape existentialism, a humanistic philosophy that asserts the importance of individual choice exercised in the absence of moral and religious absolutes. The literary works of T. S. Eliot and Samuel Beckett, which feature memorable antiheroes, are representative of the existentialist search for freedom and identity in an absurd and meaningless world. In the visual arts, abstract expressionists and action painters explored the balance between choice and chance. New, more personalized directions in sculpture and architecture challenged the austerity of the international style. At mid-century, the composer John Cage experimented with random methods of integrating sound and silence. His colleague, Merce Cunningham, revolutionized modern dance by rejecting thematic and musical associations in favor of gesture, random movement, and form.

Outline	Pronunciation Guide

A. The postwar condition
   1. alienation and anxiety
   2. utopias and dystopias
B. Existentialism and freedom
   1. Sartre's humanistic existentialism
   2. Christian existentialism
   3. existentialism and literature
      a. Camus and other prose masters
      b. theater of the absurd: Beckett
C. The quest for meaning in modern poetry
      a. Eliot and Thomas
      b. Tagore
      c. Islamic poetry: Iqbal and Anwar
D. Film at mid-century
E. The visual arts at mid-century
   1. painting
      a. abstract expressionism
      b. color field painting
      c. regional realism
   3. sculpture
      a. constructed sculpture
      b. mobiles
   4. architecture
      a. international style
      b. Saarinen
      c. Wright
F. Music and dance at mid-century
   1. Cage and aleatory music
   2. Cunningham's radical choreography
	Sartre [SAHRT]
	Niebuhr [NEE ber]
	Tillich [TI lik]
	Malamud [MAL ah mud]
	Giacometti [jah kow MET tee]
	Mies van der Rohe [MEES VAN der row]
	Saarinen [SA ri nun]
	Tagore [tah GOOR]
	Iqbal [IK bahl]
	Anwar [AHN vahr]
	Kurasawa [koo rah SAH wah]
	Kyokai [kee OH keye]

Key Terms: Existentialism, antihero, the absurd, bad faith, action painting, color field, abstract expressionism, color field, mobile, film *noir*, international style, aleatory music, Islamic nationalism.

Key Images	
De Kooning, *Woman*	Giacometti, *City Square*
Pollock, *Convergence*	Segal, *Bus Riders*
Rothko, *Untitled*	Smith, *Cubi XIX*
Frankenthaler, *Before the Canes*	Calder, *Mobile*
Hopper, *Nighthawks*	Mies van der Rohe, Seagram Building
Wright, Guggenheim Museum, NYC	Saarinen, TWA World Flight Center, NYC

Study Questions

Factual

1. Explain the following: "existence precedes essence," "existential anguish," "bad faith."
2. What does Sartre mean when he says we are all "condemned to be free"?(page 86)
3. Describe the personality of Eliot's J. Alfred Prufrock. In what sense is he an antihero?
4. In Tagore's "The Man Had No Useful Work," do you find the conception of heaven familiar?
5. What absurd things occur in Beckett's play *Waiting for Godot* (Reading 6.12)?
6. What is abstract expressionism and who were its major proponents?
7. How did Jackson Pollock create *Convergence?* Describe the medium, size, technique, etc.
8. How did industrial techniques influence the sculpture of the postwar era?
9. What is the style of Hopper's *Nighthawks*? How does he achieve mood and meaning?
10. Film at mid-century: Describe the basic characteristics of film noir; of neorealism.
11. What was revolutionary about the music of John Cage? The choreography of Merce Cunningham?

Challenge

1. What are the defining characteristics of the modern antihero? In what ways does Eliot's Prufrock (Reading 6.13) fit your definition?
2. How does the theater of the absurd differ from traditional kinds of drama? Use Sophocles' *Antigone* (Chapter 4), Shakespeare's *Othello* (Chapter 19), Molière's *Le Bourgeois Gentilhomme* (Chapter 21), or Ibsen's *A Doll's House* (Chapter 30) for comparison.
3. Robert Motherwell said that in the history of all art "there was never a movement as hated as abstract expressionism." Why might this movement have incurred such criticism and wrath?
4. "You don't have to paint a figure to express human feelings." Apply this statement to international art at mid-century. What "human" feelings are conveyed by, for instance, the action paintings of Jackson Pollock or the sculptures of David Smith?
5. Read Beckett's *Waiting for Godot* in its entirety. Does the excerpt capture the spirit of the play? If so, how so?
6. With a guitar, drum, or some other musical instrument accessible to you, "prepare" or alter the instrument in order to enlarge its sound potential; then improvise your own "musical" composition on the instrument.
7. Analyze the role of chance versus choice in the paintings of Pollock, the music of John Cage, and the choreography of Merce Cunningham. Did these artists achieve a balance between freedom and control and between meaninglessness and purposeful action?

8. In what ways did the choreography of Merce Cunningham break with that of such predecessors as Martha Graham?
9. Investigate and discuss the reciprocal relationship between literature, the visual arts, and film at mid-century? In what ways, for instance, was Hopper influenced by the cinema?
10. See the film *Pollock* (2000); to what extent does the personality of artists shape the kind of art they create?

Strategies for Discussion/Lecture

1. A lecture and discussion on the fundamentals of Sartrean existentialism is a good beginning; students might welcome clarification on the differences between Sartre's secular view and those of the Christian existentialists. Central to this lecture would be Reading 5.11 and a previously assigned mini-theme answering Factual question #1.
2. One user of the text begins by playing Musical Listening Selection II–20 by John Cage, and uses student reactions as a springboard into discussing the material.
3. Challenge question #4 will cover a good part of the painted work. Try asking if the Pollock *Convergence* is really a product of chance. To what degree does chance enter into it? To what extent choice? Is it as random as, say, Pollock's drop cloth?
4. Despite Motherwell's statement (Challenge question #3), the persistence of some degree of figural realism (Giacometti, Segal, Hopper, Bacon) seems to stand as a challenge. Are there human feelings that abstract expressionism is unable to capture?
5. The motif of the scream appears in a number of major modernist artworks, the most famous of which is probably Edvard Munch's canvas of 1893 (Figure 33.1). Discuss the use of this motif in the following: Eisenstein's *Battleship Potemkin* (Figure 34.8, page 79), Picasso's *Guernica* (Figure 34.11), and in Bacon's *Study* (Figure 35.9). :

Chapter 35 Audiovisuals

Video/CD-ROM Sources

FRANCIS BACON
Francis Bacon (1909–92) is often regarded as the greatest and most controversial British painter of the later twentieth century. This film, made on the occasion of Bacon's major retrospective at the Tate Gallery in 1985, combines an extended interview by Melvyn Bragg with a survey of Bacon's career. Bacon himself provides a forthright commentary on key works, stressing what, for him, makes a picture succeed or fail. In his own studio he discusses the 'ordered chaos' he finds necessary for artistic creation and explores the theme of violent (often homoerotic) physicality in his work. Picking through the torn photographs and magazine clippings that litter the studio floor, he explains the influence of particular images on his artistic process. This remarkable film captures Bacon in many moods, providing an intimate and compelling portrait of one of the towering figures of modern art. Edited and presented by Melvyn Bragg; produced and directed by David Hinton; 55 minutes **PH**

CAGE/CUNNINGHAM (1991)

Director: Elliot Caplan
Cunningham Dance Foundation
Media Department
55 Bethune Street
New York, NY 10014
(212) 255-8240 stacy@merce.org

CALDER'S CIRCUS

Sculptor Alexander Calder was part artist, part engineer, and very playful. In this short piece, he amuses his French friends with a circus of his own making, featuring tiny wire figurines who walk tightropes, lift barbells, and do acrobatics. The figures are now housed at the Whitney Museum in New York. This film introduces viewers to the talents and charm of an engineering genius with the mind of a happy child; it also indirectly celebrates the importance of play and experimentation in the learning process. (1971) 19 min. **HTG**

CAMERA THREE: A VIDEO EVENT, PARTS I and II (1974)

Cunningham Dance Foundation
Media Department
55 Bethune Street
New York, NY 10014
(212) 255-8240 stacy@merce.org

COLLABORATORS, THE: Cage, Cunningham, Rauschenberg (1987)

DIRECTOR: KETC Public TV 55 min., color
Cunningham Dance Foundation
Media Department
55 Bethune Street
New York, NY 10014
(212) 255-8240 stacy@merce.org

DOUBLE INDEMNITY (1944)

Director: Billy Wilder **AZ**

T.S. ELIOT Voices and Visions Series 60 min., color **CPB**

MASTER POETS COLLECTION: PART III

Enjoy one of the world's most intriguing collections of poetry when you bring this entertaining and enlightening video collection into your home. Literary enthusiasts around the world will appreciate the works of such masters as Walt Whitman, e.e. cummings, and Sylvia Plath. As The First Poetry Quartet takes you on a splendiferous and moving journey through excerpts of their lives, you see who and what inspired the greatest works of all times. Coupled with a lively after-dinner game in which the troupe and their guests identify movie, song, and book titles from the poetry world. Dozens of selections designed to entertain and enrich the mind. 120 minutes on 4 tapes **PBS**

OPEN CITY (1945)

Director: Roberto Rossellini **AZ**

PERSONA
Director: Ingmar Bergman **AZ**

POLLOCK (2000)
Director: Ed Harris **AZ**

JACKSON POLLOCK AND MARK ROTHKO: Icons of Abstract Expressionism FFH

RASHŌ MAN (1950)
Director: Akira Kurosawa **AZ**

REAR WINDOW (1954)
Director: Alfred Hitchcock **AZ**

THE SEVENTH SEAL (1956)
Director: Ingmar Bergman **AZ**

SHATTERING THE MYTH Art of the Western World Series 30 min., color **CPB**

SHOCK OF THE NEW - Vol. #6: View From the Edge (1980)
DIRECTOR: HUGHES, ROBERT 52 min., color
available through Joan @ Videofinders at 1-800-343-4727

WAITING FOR GODOT: Beckett Directs Beckett: A Trilogy I (1990) 137 min., color **VC**

WILD STRAWBERRIES (1957)
Director: Ingmar Bergman **AZ**

Music Resources

Cage, John, *Sonatas and Interludes for Prepared Piano (1946–1948)*, Fremy, Etcetera ETC–2001; KTC–2001 CD.

Web Resources

Resources related to Existentialism—http://www.tameri.com/csw/exist/exist.html

Biographical information about and resources related to Jean-Paul Sartre—
http://www.tameri.com/csw/exist/sartre.html

Resources related to Albert Camus—http://www.levity.com/corduroy/camus.html

Resources related to T.S. Eliot—www.virtual.jpark.uga.edu/ ~232/eliot.taken.html

The poetry of Rabindranath Tagore—http://www.indolink.com/poetry/tgorindx.html

Resources related to Dylan Thomas—http://www.users.bigpond.com/dylanthomas/

Resources related to Abstract Expressionism—http://artlex.com/artlex/a/abstractexpr.html

Resources related to John Cage—http://wings.buffalo.edu/epc/authors/cage/

Merce Cunningham—http://www.pbs.org/wnet/americanmasters/database/cunningham_m.html

McGraw-Hill Resources

Fiero, Music Listening Selection: CD II
    II–20 Cage, *Sonata V*
Transparencies: MA.9 Twentieth Century 1900–Present
                MA.15 Music-Art-European Map (Twentieth Century, 1900–1990)

Sample Test Questions for Chapter 35

Select the letter of the choice that BEST answers the question:

1. The artist who walked around the canvas while working in order to literally be "in" the painting was
   a. Jackson Pollock.
   b. Mark Rothko.
   c. Helen Frankenthaler.
   d. Edward Hopper.
   Ans: a

2. The creator of whimsical wire constructions or mobiles was
   a. Edward Albee.
   b. James Evans.
   c. Collier Smith.
   d. Alexander Calder.
   Ans: d

3. The most celebrated existentialist film maker, who directed *The Seventh Seal* and *Wild Strawberries*, was
   a. John Ford.
   b. Mark Rothko.
   c. Edward Hoffman.
   d. Ingmar Bergman.
   Ans: d

4. Beckett's *Waiting for Godot* belongs to a dramatic genre known as
   a. theater of the absurd.
   b. neorealism.
   c. science fiction.
   d. stream of consciousness.
   Ans: a

5. A symbol of corporate wealth, skyscrapers designed in the _____ style embodied the spirit of the West in the late twentieth century.
    a. functional
    b. international
    c. horizontal
    d. capitalistic
    Ans: b

6. According to composer John Cage, music has as its only common denominator
    a. melody.
    b. the twelve-tone scale.
    c. rhythm.
    d. silence.
    Ans: c

7. In writing music for twelve radios and twenty-four performers, John Cage was questioning the relationships between
    a. traditional instruments.
    b. artistic conception and execution.
    c. music education and genius.
    d. symphony and conductor.
    Ans: b

8. An existentialist hero is one who embraces a set of political ideals.
    Ans: F

9. Sartre argued that all human action takes place within a universe that is meaningless.
    Ans: T

Answer the following with a word or phrase.

10. According to Sartre, individuals are defined by the _____ that they make.
    Ans: choices

11. Existentialists affirm that the sense of total responsibility for one's destiny leads to a sense of
    _____.
    Ans: anguish

12. The American artistic movement of the 1940s and 1950s that embodied the break with traditional, representational art was called _____.
    Ans: abstract expressionism

13. The Welsh poet who exalted life-affirming action in the face of death was _____.
    Ans: Dylan Thomas

14. John Cage created _____ music, that is, music based on random choices and procedures.
    Ans: aleatory

15. One of the first choreographers to develop "abstract" movements, with no reference to a story line, was _____.
Ans: Merce Cunningham

Chapter **36** **Identity and Liberation**

Summary

The quest for liberation from poverty, oppression, and inequality is a hallmark of twentieth-century culture. In Latin America, India, Africa, and elsewhere, movements for decolonization have inspired passionate expressions of freedom in the arts. Racial and ethnic minorities throughout the world have launched crusades, both political and aesthetic, to oppose discrimination as practiced by the majority culture. In the United States, the struggle of African Americans to achieve freedom from the evils of racism is mirrored in a rich heritage of the arts. While the black contribution to literature and the visual arts is considerable, it is in music and dance that black culture has had its greatest impact. Equally important has been this century's quests for gender and sexual equality. During the postwar era, women worked to gain political, economic, and social parity. Feminist writers, such as Woolf and Beauvoir, addressed the psychological conditions of female oppression, while feminist visual artists have questioned traditional concepts of female identity. Amidst a worldwide AIDS epidemic, controversial issues of sexual orientation and sexual behavior have come to preoccupy contemporary writers, painters, and composers. More recently, issues of ethnicity and ethnic identity have come to preoccupy the creative minds of our time.

Outline	**Pronunciation Guide**

A. The quest for political equality
   1. decolonization movements
   2. Neruda and Latin America
B. The quest for racial equality
   1. Harlem renaissance
     a. Hughes and Brooks
     b. Wright
   2. The civil rights movement
     a. Martin Luther King
     b. Malcolm X
     c. Baldwin, Ellison, and Alice Walker
   3. African Americans and the visual arts
   4. African Americans and jazz
   5. African Americans and dance
	Neruda [ne ROO dah]
	misogyny [mis AH je nee]
	Beauvoir [bow VWAHR]
	Friedan [free DAN]
	de Saint-Phalle [de sayn FAL]
	LeGuin [leh GWIN]
	Mapplethorpe [MAY pul thowrp]
	apartheid [ah PAHR teyed]
	Corigliano [kor ee LYAN oh]
	Mendieta [men dee AY ta]
	Jiménez [hee MAY nays]
	Cisneros [sees NEHR os]
	Osorio [o SO ree o]
	chicana [chee KAH na]

C. The quest for gender equality
   1. feminist protest: Woolf and de Beauvoir
   2. feminist poetry: Sexton, Sanchez, Rich
   3. feminist art
     a. de Saint Phalle, Marisol, Menendez
     b. Judy Chicago's *Dinner Party*
     c. gender stereotypes: Sherman, Kruger, Neshat
   4. sexual orientation and sexual freedom
     a. Mapplethorpe, Le Guin, Kushner
     b. AIDS arts projects
D. Ethnicity and identity
   1. ethnic literature: Cisneros
   2. ethnicity an the visual arts

Key Terms: decolonization, Harlem Renaissance, Civil Rights Act, black nationalism, apartheid, bebop, ragtime, scat, blues, swing, jazz, hip-hop, suffragette, misogyny, feminism, AIDS, ethnicity, identity politics.

Key Images	
Lawrence, *"Race riots were numerous..."*	Basquiat, *Horn Players*
Colescott, *Les Demoiselles d'Alabama*	Saint-Phalle, *Black Venus*
Betye Saar, *The Liberation of Aunt Jemima*	Escobar, *Women and Dog*
Jiménez, *Border Crossing,*	Chicago, *The Dinner Party*
Mapplethorpe, *Lisa Lyon*	Cindy Sherman, *Untitled*

Study Questions

Factual

1. What is the United Fruit Company (Reading 6.17)? What part does it play in Pablo Neruda's poem of the same name?
2. Who were the central figures of the Harlem renaissance, and what did they achieve?
3. What is the message of Martin Luther King's *Letter from a Birmingham Jail* (Reading 6.20)?
4. How did the anthropological research of Dunham and Primus influence their contributions to modern dance?
5. When, where, and why did the civil rights movement take place?
6. What does Ellison's protagonist (Reading 6.23) mean when he says that he is "an invisible man"?
7. Who are the central figures in the beginnings of jazz history?
8. What reason does Simone de Beauvoir give (Reading 6.25) for woman's traditional subordination to men?
9. How did Malcolm X's position and views on the status of blacks differ from those of Martin Luther King?
10. What is the message of Alice Walker's short story, "Elethia" (Reading 6.23)?
11. Define these words: gender, ethnicity, misogyny.

Challenge

1. When you read "Harlem" by Langston Hughes, one line *already* sounds familiar, doesn't it? Why do you think some writers' expressions enjoy widespread popular circulation over generations?

2. What differences in spirit and sentiment do you detect between the literary contributions of Richard Wright (Reading 6.19), Martin Luther King (Reading 6.20), Ralph Ellison (Reading 6.22), and Alice Walker (6.23)? Can you name any significant African-American writers who are pressing any similar issues today?

3. Critics have noted that jazz is the most daring of musical forms and the most perfect metaphor for the process of creativity. Explain and discuss. Do you detect any similarities between jazz and abstract expressionism?

4. Describe the character, Pease, in Richard Wright's *The Ethics of Living Jim Crow* (Reading 6.19). Is he a believable character?

5. Why, according to Woolf (Reading 6.24), did Shakespeare's imaginary sister fail to achieve greatness?

6. Woolf observed that chastity in her own day and in former times had "a religious importance in a woman's life." How might these circumstances have affected the roles and destinies of women and men?

7. What reason does Simone de Beauvoir give for women's traditional subordination to men? Compare this point of view with that of either Mary Wollstonecraft (Reading 4.20), John Stuart Mill (Reading 5.18), or Virginia Woolf (Reading 6.25).

8. Characterize postwar feminism in terms of the poetry and art included in this chapter.

9. In the early 1990s, an intimate biography of Anne Sexton was published that attempted to "explain" her art on the basis of her turbulent psychic life. To what extent, in your view, is the personal life (or the sex) of the artist relevant to her creative endeavors? Does such information and understanding alter the significance or value of the work of art?

10. Compare your own ethnic background and identity to that expressed by Cisneros in the story, "*Bien Pretty.*"

Strategies for Discussion/Lecture

1. The lecturer might address the subject of stereotyping and racial prejudice at the elementary level of childhood's first images, as illustrated in Richard Wright's *The Ethics of Living Jim Crow*. Reading Wright is almost certain to perplex a majority white class, since Wright's early negative associations with white people are the very reverse of white folks' associations with those objects (e.g., trimmed hedges), just as many urban whites and blacks have stereotypically opposite images of the police. Wright's tale of his first job focuses the polarity of racial thinking on the microcosm of the small factory workplace, where his behavior is not so much attended to as subject to a racial triage: "You think you're *white*, don't you?" Ellison's *Invisible Man*, "because people refuse to see me," forms a natural sequel.

2. Written preparation for class might take the form of a short essay centered on a specific image. For example, consider Mapplethorpe's *Lisa Lyons* photograph: "Tell the story of this person; relate her story to one or more of the poems or essays in the chapter." Or assign Challenge question #10 and discuss responses in class.

3. Use the Ana Mendieta *Tree of Life* (Figure 26.10) as the basis for discussion of themes of fertility and regeneration in the history of the humanistic tradition; compare this image to the Minoan *Snake Goddess* (Chapter 4) and the *orans* figure in the Catacombs frescoes (Chapter 9).

4. Make use of the recent PBS series on the history of jazz to discuss the development of this artform and the roles of black and white composers/musicians in its success. The lecturer might open discussion on the ways in which it does and does not involve racial issues.

5. Martin Luther King Jr., *Letter from Birmingham Jail*. How does his intended audience influence his choice of themes and words? Apply to the entire chapter this sentence: "Groups are more immoral than individuals."

6. Do the feminist images in the chapter express a *human* condition or just a feminine condition? Take Marisol Escobar's *Women and Dog* (Figure 36.7); for instance, how might the artist have used the same techniques to portray *Men and Dog* or *Woman, Man and Dog?*

Chapter 36 Audiovisuals

Video/CD-ROM Sources

AFRO-AMERICAN DANCE: Establishing a Cultural Heritage 29 min., color **TLF**

BOYS in the BAND (1971)
Director: William Friedkin **AZ**

BOYZ N the HOOD (1991)
Director: John Singleton **AZ**

COLD WAR 20 min., B&W **MGHF**

DAMNED IN THE USA (1994)
DIRECTOR: YULE, PAUL 126 min., color **AZ**

DO THE RIGHT THING (1989)
Director: Spike Lee **AZ**

EUROPE THE MIGHTY CONTINENT
The concluding film in a thirteen-part series which examines the decline of Europe and European unification. 52 min., color **TLF**

LANGSTON HUGHES Voices and Visions Series 60 min., color **CPB**

KEN BURNS: JAZZ
JAZZ is a ten-part, eighteen-hour documentary series that celebrates America's greatest original art form, a music whose improvisational spirit perfectly reflects the nation that gave it birth. It is the first television series ever to tell the story of jazz. Beginning with the birth of jazz at the dawn of the twentieth century, the film incorporates the wide range of American culture and historical events that interact directly with the music: among them the harsh racial polarization of the 1890s; the artistic and political ferment of the Harlem Renaissance; the exuberance of the Jazz Age; the Great Depression and the New Deal; the Second World War; the emergence of a youth culture in the 1950s and 1960s; the hope, anger, and expectations of the civil rights movement; and the search for identity and authenticity in the 1970s, 1980s and 1990s. 1110 minutes on 10 tapes **PBS**

MALCOLM X (1972)
    Director: Arnold Perl **AZ**

MALCOLM X (1992)
    Director: Spike Lee **AZ**

MASTER POETS COLLECTION: PART III
    Enjoy one of the world's most intriguing collections of poetry when you bring this entertaining and enlightening video collection into your home. Literary enthusiasts around the world will appreciate the works of such masters as Walt Whitman, e.e. cummings, and Sylvia Plath. As The First Poetry Quartet takes you on a splendiferous and moving journey through excerpts of their lives, you see who and what inspired the greatest works of all times. Coupled with a lively after-dinner game in which the troupe and their guests identify movie, song and book titles from the poetry world. Dozens of selections designed to entertain and enrich the mind. 120 minutes on 4 tapes **PBS**

MUSIC OF AFRICA: Nigeria (1964) 59 min., color **IU**

REMARKABLE 20TH CENTURY
    If it was important and happened during the 20th century, it's in this video time capsule! Never-before-seen film footage lets you witness the great wars, devastating disasters, thrilling triumphs, and unprecedented social changes of the last 100 years. Exclusive interviews with Rosa Parks, Buzz Aldrin, Colin Powell, Henry Kissinger, Gloria Steinem, and others provide unique and illuminating perspective. ABC News anchor Howard K. Smith hosts. 600 minutes on 10 tapes **PBS**

THELMA and LOUISE (1991)
    Director: Ridley Scott **AZ**

Music Resources

Ellington, Edward K. "Duke," *Mainly Black,* Angel CDC–47621.
Black, Brown, and Beige, Bluebird 3 CD6641–3–RB.
Corigliano, John, *Symphony No. 1*, Chicago Symphony Orchestra, Erato 2292–45601–2 CD.

Web Resources

Information on the origins of Jazz—http://www.redhotjazz.com/originsarticle.html

Louis Armstrong Jazz Oral History Project—
    http://www.nypl.org/research/sc/scl/MULTIMED/jazzhist/jazzhist.html

Information about Louis Armstrong—http://independentmusician.com/louis/

Biographical information about Louis Armstrong—http://www.redhotjazz.com/louie.html

Resources related to Blues—http://mathriscl.lunet.edu/blues/blues.html

Biographical information about W.C. Handy—http://www2.una.edu/library/handy/

Resources related to Duke Ellington—http://duke.duse.net/

Resources related to Duke Ellington—http://www.dukeellington.com/

Resources related to Duke Ellington—http://www.redhotjazz.com/duke.html

Information about Richard Wright—http://www.itvs.org/richardwright/

Information about Richard Wright—http://www.olemiss.edu/depts/english/ms-writers/dir/wright_richard/

Information about Richard Wright—http://www.pbs.org/rwbb/rwtoc.html

Resources related to Ralph Ellison—http://www.centerx.gseis.ucla.edu/weblio/ellison.html

Nikki Giovanni's web site—http://athena.english.vt.edu/Giovanni/cv/biog.html

Resources related to Mohandas K. Gandhi—http://www.acusd.edu/theo/ref-gandhi.html

Negritude Internet resources—http://www.wlu.edu/~hblackme/negritude/

McGraw-Hill Resources

Fiero, Music Listening Selection: CD II
   II–21 Handy, "St. Louis Blues"
   II–22 Hardin/Armstrong, "Hotter than That"
   II–23 Ellington "Ko-Ko," Gillespie/Parker
Transparencies: MA.9 Twentieth Century 1900–Present

Sample Test Questions for Chapter 36

Select the letter of the choice that BEST answers the question:

1. In Alice Walker's short story, "Elethia", "Uncle Albert" is
   a. the owner of a restaurant.
   b. the benefactor of poor, local blacks.
   c. a totally fictional character.
   d. the stereotypical equivalent of Aunt Jemima.
   Ans: b

2. In his *Message to the Grass Roots*, Malcolm X focuses his audience's attention on their "common enemy," which is
   a. the U.S. Constitution.
   b. Jim Crow laws.
   c. the white man.
   d. disunity.
   Ans: c

3. Ralph Ellison's novel *The Invisible Man* referred to the invisibility of
   a. the individual in mass society.
   b. blacks in a white world.
   c. workers in a capitalist economy.
   d. city dwellers.
   Ans: b

4. Jazz, which began in New Orleans, had its origins in ALL BUT which of the following?
   a. African tribal dance
   b. European marching bands
   c. ragtime
   d. French art songs
   Ans: d

5. A form of jazz that is characterized by a frenzied tempo, complicated chord progressions, and complex rhythms is
   a. blues.
   b. cool.
   c. bop.
   d. swing.
   Ans: c

6. In Latin America, the United States government has traditionally supported
   a. ordinary farmers.
   b. the Church.
   c. the economic elite.
   d. dissidents.
   Ans: c

7. *Native Son,* an expression of African American's defiance and despair, was written by
   a. Langston Hughes.
   b. LeRoi Jones.
   c. Richard Wright.
   d. Toni Morrison.
   Ans: c

8. Throughout the centuries, three of the leading proponents of civil disobedience were Gandhi, Henry David Thoreau, and
   a. Martin Luther King.
   b. Malcolm X.
   c. Bloke Modisan.
   d. Franz Fanon.
   Ans: a

9. The blues began as an instrumental rather than a vocal form of music.
   Ans: F

10. In the West, the two world wars generally hindered women from attaining political and economic equality.
Ans: F

11. Virginia Woolf, a passionate feminist, argued that women must first seek political rather than economic power.
Ans: F

Answer the following with a word or phrase.

12. In her *Dances of Haiti,* _____ examined the sociological functions of dance.
Ans: Katherine Dunham

13. The exploitation of Latin America by capitalist corporations is reflected in "The United Fruit Co." by _____.
Ans: Pablo Neruda

14. The search for African-American self-identity and the demands for equality led to a flowering of creative expression in New York City known as the _____.
Ans: Harlem Renaissance

15. *The Feminine Mystique,* which argued that the media, especially advertising, had brainwashed women into subordinate positions, was written by _____.
Ans: Betty Friedan

16. In her book *The Second Sex,* _____ analyzed the biological, political, and psychological reasons for women's traditional dependence on men.
Ans: Simone de Beauvoir

17. The belief that the Church should support the drive for socialism in Latin America is called _____ theology.
Ans: liberation

18. Afro-Cuban fertility rituals inspired the performance art of _____.
Ans: Ana Mendieta

Essay

19. Are there, in your view, any features of African-American art or music that are uniquely "black"? Are there, in your view, any features of women's art that are uniquely "female"?

Chapter 37 The Information Age: Message and Meaning

Summary

Electronic mass media and computer technology have turned the last decades of the twentieth century into an Information Age. New directions in science and philosophy bring to light a wealth of information concerning both the complex nature of the universe and the genetic makeup of the human body. In the global village of the late twentieth century, the anxious subjectivity of modernism has given way to a new global consciousness and the postmodern taste for parody, whimsy, and irony. While many postmodern philosophers and poets are concerned with the self-referential function of language, others explore the ecological future of the planet, the possibilities of life in outer space, and the disjunctive aspects of contemporary urban culture, such as random violence and social dislocation. The works of Octavio Paz, Gary Snyder, Derek Walcott, Isabel Allende, Joyce Carol Oates, and Chinua Achebe are representative of these concerns.

Outline	Pronunciation Guide

A. Historical context
  1. developments in information technology
    a. television
    b. computers
  2. the birth of space exploration
  3. new directions in science and philosophy
B. Postmodernism
C. Literature in the information age
  1. postmodern poetry: Paz, Ashbery, and Walcott
  2. magic realism: Allende
  3. the literature of social conscience
    a. poetry: Snyder and Szymborska
    b. prose: Achebe and Oates
  4. science fiction and film
	Allende [eye YEN day]
	Pei [PAY]
	Paz [PAHS]
	Christo [KRIS tow]
	Wittgenstein [VIT gen shteyen]
	Foucault [foo KOW]
	Szymborska [sheem BOR skah]
	Achebe [ah CHAY bay]
	Kundera [kun DEH ra]

Key Terms: ecology, postmodernism, magic realism, deconstruction, string theory, chaos theory, genome, global paradigm, global village, multiculturalism, science fiction.

Key Images	
Paik, *George Boole*	Warhol, *Green Coca-Cola*

Study Questions

Factual

1. What are the main features of the so-called "information explosion"?
2. Briefly describe the new directions in science and philosophy since 1970.
3. Offer a brief definition of the term *postmodern*.
4. What concerns with language and communication are revealed in the three poems reproduced in Reading 6.28?
5. In what ways does Snyder's poem "Smokey the Bear Sutra" (Reading 6.30) illustrate concerns that are "holistic" and "multicultural"?
6. Where and when does the story in Allende's *Two Words* (Reading 6.29) take place?
7. Oates (Reading 6.32) gives us a distinctive perception of postmodern society. Describe it. Does it speak to you directly? Why?
8. Why is the film *2001* called a "space odyssey"?

Challenge

1. What is meant by the expression "Information Age"? How have television and computers influenced its birth and progress?
2. How have writers and artists of the last few decades worked to bring attention to the threat of ecological disaster? Can you find some examples more recent than the poetry of Gary Snyder?
3. In what ways does the literature of science fiction address contemporary concerns? Is it true to say that the science fiction hero is the hero of the future?
4. The story by Joyce Carol Oates (Reading 6.32) is representative of gratuitous violence in modern American culture. How does Oates' story compare with the kinds of information currently available in newspapers and television? Does Oates distill the experience of violence in any meaningful way? Compare Szymborska's approach (p. 134).
5. Much of postmodern literature, architecture, and art is "funny." Why do you think humor and parody are so important to postmodern expression? Would you consider postmodernism a form of satire? Give examples to defend your point of view.
6. John Ashbery and other postmodernists seem to say that experience is itself contradictory. Can you identify other contemporary works of art, literature, and music representative of this point of view.
7. Does Szymborska's "The Terrorist, He Watches" remind you of a movie? Describe how you would film it.
8. Tradition and modernity stand in constant tension in Africa. How does Achebe's short story reflect this fact? Can you think of any similar situations in your own day and time?
9. Read the short story "The Sentinel" by Arthur C. Clarke, on which the film *2001* was based. How do the two compare?
10. How has film worked to "translate" literature visually and globally? Use examples from among the writers cited in this chapter and in contemporary culture.
11. Which of the readings in this chapter reflects the influence of television? How so?

Strategies for Discussion/Lecture

1. One effective approach to the chapter materials is to assign a mini-theme or short essay comparing two types of expression found in these chapters: such as postmodern satire and magic realism, or social conscience realism and science fiction.

2. The lecturer might raise the question of a paradox of the Information Age: how is a human being, relatively unevolved compared to technology, to absorb the *quantity* and *redundancy* of information now at his or her disposal? Warhol's *Green Coca-Cola Bottles* presents the problem vividly.
3. One might open discussion with Belisa Crepusculario's discovery "that words make their way in the world without a master, and that anyone with a little cleverness can appropriate them and do business with them." Some poets, such as Snyder, decline copyright and invite the reader to copy. Is the reader a poet or a business person?
4. Contemporary critics have argued that our whole culture has become increasingly less concerned with moral responsibility. Take this point of view as a starting point for a discussion of any of the primary source readings in this chapter. Does this criticism hold up or not?

Chapter 37 Audiovisuals

Video/CD-ROM Sources

2001: A SPACE ODYSSEY (1968)
Director: Stanley Kubrick **AZ**

ISABEL ALLENDE: A Woman's Voice in Latin American Literature 56 min., color **FFH**

A BRIEF HISTORY OF TIME 84 min., color **VC**

NERDS 2.0.1: A Brief History of the Internet (Series) (1998)
Join Robert X Cringely in this much-anticipated sequel to *Triumph of the Nerds*, as he turns his well-informed and irreverent eye on the intriguing history of the Internet. Go deep into the bowels of the Pentagon to witness the birth of the Internet and follow its rapid rise to the cutting edge of the World Wide Web. On his journey, Cringely interviews the unknown nerds who laid the Internet's foundations, visits the Silicon Valley of India, and grills the founders of the networking companies who have made millions from this fascinating new technology. 180 minutes on 3 tapes **PBS**

TODAY AND TOMORROW 60 min., color **FFH**

Web Resources

History of space exploration—http://www.solarviews.com/eng/history.htm

NASA homepage—www.nasa.gov/

Defining Postmodernism—http://jefferson.village.virginia.edu/elab/hfl0242.html

The artists of magical realism—http://www.artcyclopedia.com/history/magic-realism.html

The history of magic realism—http://artcon.rutgers.edu/artists/magicrealism/magic.html

An interview with Isabel Allende—http://www.motherjones.com/mother_jones/S094/allende.html

Biographical information about Octavio Paz—http://www.kirjasto.sci.fi/opaz.htm

Biographical and critical information about Gary Snyder—
  http://www.english.uiuc.edu/maps/poets/s_z/snyder/snyder.htm

Resources related to Wislawa Szymborska—http://www.polishworld.com/wsz/

Resources related to Chinua Achebe—
  http://www.collaboratory.nunet.net/goals2000/eddy/achebe/author.html

Sample Test Questions for Chapter 37

Select the letter of the choice that BEST answers the question:

1. Jacques Ellul asserts that technology has created a "psychological collectivism" that has
   a. made the world into a global village.
   b. robbed humankind of freedom and self-esteem.
   c. allowed archetypes to emerge from the human consciousness.
   d. enabled technocrats to replace philosophers.
   Ans: b

2. Digital computers were first used widely in the
   a. 1930s.
   b. 1950s.
   c. 1970s.
   d. 1990s.
   Ans: b

3. Since the 1960s, postmodernism has featured all the following EXCEPT
   a. parody.
   b. a pastiche of styles from former eras.
   c. a taste for popular imagery.
   d. a revival of the classical heritage.
   Ans: d

4. Paz and Ashbery are representative of the postmodern poet's concern with
   a. nature.
   b. language.
   c. race.
   d. love.
   Ans: b

5. In Oates' *Ace,* the main figure is characterized as a(n)
   a. university student.
   b. inveterate gambler.
   c. disenchanted physician.
   d. overgrown boy.
   Ans: d

6. Both string theory and chaos theory are concerned with
   a. identifying the underlying patterns in nature.
   b. finding sources of electronic energy.
   c. mapping the human cellular system.
   d. uniting matter and spirit.
   Ans: a

7. Deconructivist poetry like Snyder's focuses on self and personal intuition.
   Ans: F

Answer the following with a word or phrase:

8. According to the text, _____ and _____ are two forms of technology that have altered many aspects of life in the late twentieth century.
   Ans: television, computers

9. *The Technological Society* indicts _____ as a form of totalitarian control.
   Ans: advertising

10. The process by which one takes apart discourse in order to discover the meaning of the text is called
    _____.
    Ans: deconstruction

11. The increase in carbon dioxide levels, which elevates the earth's temperatures, is known as the
    _____.
    Ans: greenhouse effect

12. In Isabel Allende's story "Two Words" the surprising insight of Belisa Crepusculario into the situation of the Colonel is
    a. that he will be the next president.
    b. that he is afraid.
    c. that he is lonely.
    d. that, like her, he is of humble origins.
    Ans: c

13. In Chinua Achebe's *Dead Man's Path,* the most important function of the footpath turns out to be
    a. that it is the path of new life.
    b. that it provides access to a source of water.
    c. that it leads to a burial ground.
    d. that it is a shortcut to a main road.
    Ans: a

14. The meaning of the African proverb, "let the hawk perch and let the eagle perch," that best suits the situation in the story "Dead Man's Path" is
    a. the headmaster and his wife should both be respected.
    b. the old ways of the village are superior to the modern ways of the headmaster.
    c. the village priest is opposed to the school regulations.
    d. old and new regulations should be allowed to coexist.
    Ans: d

15. The poet whose concerns about nature are global in reach is
    a. Paz.
    b. Snyder.
    c. Walcott.
    d. Oates.
    Ans: b

Summary

The visual arts of the postmodern era have been pluralistic, experimental, and deeply indebted to the materials and processes of high technology. The arts have felt the impact of new materials (such as fiberglass, neon, and polyester resin) and electronic technology (such as television, video, and computers). These phenomena have influenced the art and architecture of the last fifty years, even as they have worked to shape musical composition, performance, and the dissemination of music itself. Distinctions between high and low art have tended to disappear, as such styles as pop art, assemblage, and land art make use of ordinary and everyday materials and images; and as composers draw on a variety of popular musical forms (such as reggae and rock) to create new musical experiences. Distinctions *between* the arts have also tended to blur, as artist/performers integrate painting, dance, video, and other media to feed their creative designs. The postmodern infatuation with the past and ongoing artistic exchange throughout all parts of the world continue to shape the global paradigm that marks the twenty-first century.

Outline	Pronunciation Guide

A. The visual arts
  1. high-tech and electronic media
  2. pop art and assemblage
    a. Warhol, Johns, Oldenberg, Lichtenstein
    b. Rauschenberg, Chamberlain, Nevelson
  3. geometric abstraction, op, minimalism, neon, kinetic
    a. Judd, Noguchi, Riley
    b. Stella, Chryssa
  4. new realism
    a. painting: Estes, Close
    b. sculpture: Hanson
  5. new expressionism/social conscience
    a. Keinholz, Kiefer, Azaceta
    b. Abakanowicz
    c. Wang Guangyi
  6. total art
    a. performance art; happenings
    b. environmental art: Smithson, Christo
  7. video art
    a. Paik
    b. Viola
	Rauschenberg [ROU shen berg]
	Noguchi [no GOO chee]
	Christo [KRIS tow]
	Kienholz [KEYEN holtz}
	Azaceta [ah zah CHAY tah]
	Abakanowicz [ah bah KAHN oh vitz]
	Yasumasa Morimura [ya soo MAH sa mo ree MOO rah]
	Wang Gangyi [wan gan ZEE]
	Corigliano [cor ee LYAN oh]

B. Computers and the visual arts
C. The visual arts and the global paradigm
D. Architecture in the information age
E. Music in the information age
    1. microtonality: Ligeti
    2. minimalism: Glass
    3. postmodern opera: Corigliano
    4. electronic music: Babbitt; McLean
    5. rock and its spin-offs
    6. music and the global paradigm: reggae,
       new jazz
F. Dance in the information age	

Key Terms: pop art, assemblage, op art, minimalism, kinetic art, happening, performance art, environmental art, camp, global paradigm, *musique concrète,* synthesizer, rock, reggae, cyberart.

Key Images	
Warhol, *Mint Marilyn Monroe* Johns, *Painted Bronze (Beer Cans)* Oldenburg, *Soft Toilet* Rauschenberg, *Buffalo II* Stella, *Agbatana III* Judd, *Untitled* Chryssa, *Fragments for the Gates to Times Square* Smithson, *Spiral Jetty* Christo, *Running Fence*	Close, *Self-Portrait* Hanson, *Tourists* Morimura, *Portrait (Twins)* Kienholz, *The State Hospital* Azaceta, *Coke Heads VIII* Paik, *Megatron* Moriko Mori, *Pure Land* Viola, *Stations* Pei, Louvre Pyramid Gehry. Guggenheim Museum, Bilbao

Study Questions

Factual
1. Name some of the materials of the new technology that have influenced the making of art in the period between 1960 and the present.
2. Name the leading figures of the pop art movement. What do they have in common, and how is each artist's work distinctive?
3. What are some of the features of experimental film?
4. Explain the differences between the following art styles: pop art, assemblage, op art, minimalism, kinetic art, happenings, environmental art, new realism, and new expressionism.
5. What are the motives of artists who make "social conscience" art?
6. In what ways have computers influenced the visual arts?
7. How has electronic technology affected modern music?
8. What is meant by "the global paradigm" in art? Whose artworks best fit this phenomenon?
9. Describe briefly the musical contributions of Babbitt, Ligeti, and Glass.
10. Briefly describe the origins of "rock" music.
11. What are the main features of contemporary opera? Contemporary dance?

Challenge

1. How have high-technology and new industrial techniques influenced the art styles of the last fifty years? Give specific examples to support your generalizations.
2. How has commercial advertising influenced the art styles of the last fifty years? Give specific examples to support your generalizations.
3. What is the relationship between the collage techniques of Picasso and Braque, and those of the assemblage artists, such as Rauschenberg?
4. Which art styles of the last fifty years owe their greatest debt to surrealism? How so?
5. Who are the leading video artists and why is their work interesting?
6. What might land artists, those who create earth sculptures, be trying to achieve? Is the process of creating such artworks more important than the product? What other contemporary art styles share this emphasis on process?
7. The boundary between popular art and high art has become increasingly blurred since the 1960s. Is this true also of music? Consider the question with regard to jazz, as well as to the music of Ligeti, Stockhausen, Glass, and Marsalis (Music Listening Selections II–24 through II–28).
8. The boundary between process and product, and between theater and the visual arts, has also become more blurred. What roles might modern film, television, and computers have played in these developments?
9. A critic wrote that once John Cage composed *4'33"* (see chapter 35), there was nowhere to go but sideways. Using this novel statement as a starting point, outline the unique features of classical music since 1953.
10. Comment on the nature of East–West influence and interchange based on the art and music in this chapter. Offer specific examples wherever possible.

Strategies for Discussion/Lecture

1. The chapter lends itself to a two-part treatment: slide lecture, followed by the selective treatment of musical developments. Students might prepare for such by having been assigned ahead a mini-theme from Factual questions #4, 7, or 9. The influence of mass commercialism and electronic technology might be points of focus.
2. Electronic synthesizers affect all aspects of musical production. In the production of a recent Broadway musical comedy, electronic synthesizers replaced live music, saving the show's producer millions of dollars. The musicians picketed the show, claiming that the audience was being cheated. Ask students to take the positions of (1) the musician, (2) the producer, and (3) the theatergoer.
3. Revisit the question posed in Chapter 37 Strategies for Discussion: Contemporary critics have argued that our whole culture has become less concerned with moral responsibility. Based on the art and music reviewed in the chapter, is this indeed the case? If not, show evidence otherwise.
4. The global paradigm might be the focus for an entire class period. A mini-theme on Factual question #8 might be assigned ahead. The global paradigm may be understood in terms of the mass commercialism of pop art, the industrial bias of minimalism, the extensive influence of film and rock music, etc. It might also be realized in terms of the influence of *butoh* on postmodern dance, reggae and Afro-Caribbean instrumentation in popular music, and even in the remote location of the latest branch of the Guggenheim Museum.
5. Ask students: which of the art styles in this chapter might be considered "serious" and which "humorous"? How so? Why are humor and parody so important to postmodern expression?

6. Ask students to decide which of the artworks discussed in this chapter will become part of "the canon." Which might their grandchildren be studying in their humanities courses? They should be able to defend their selections and give criteria for the lasting nature of their selections.

Audiovisuals

Video/CD-ROM Sources

AMERICAN ART IN THE SIXTIES 58 min., color **Blackwood Productions**

ART OF THE WESTERN WORLD
   Program 9: In Our Own Time: Shattering the Myths & New, Newer, Newest **HTG**

ARTISTS IN WONDERLAND: Computers and Art 26 min., color **FFH**

CHRISTO: Running Fences MMA

CHRISTO: Valley Curtain MMA

COOL CATS: 25 Years of Rock 'n Roll AZ

FRANK GEHRY: ARCHITECTURE IN MOTION
   Architects, artists, critics, and Gehry himself discuss the symbolism, emotion, and spirit that invigorate Gehry's projects around the world. 45 min. **FFH**

GUGGENHEIM MUSEUM BILBAO
   Architect Frank Gehry discusses his design approach and the architectural evolution of the museum, from sketches, to computerized blueprints, to the completed project. 33 min. **FFH**

IN OUR OWN TIME (1989) 60 min., color **CPB**

IN SEARCH OF CHINA
   This documentary, in which the producers were given unprecedented access to Chinese businesses, social organizations, leaders, and average citizens, examines the social impact of China's halting experiment with a market economy. Will rising unemployment mean unrest and instability in the world's most populous nation? What will happen to those who fall behind? Will China ever become a true market economy? This program explores these and other important questions. 90 min. **PBS**

PHILIP JOHNSON: Looking Back (1999) 13 min., color **FFH**

ELLSWORTH KELLY & JASPER JOHNS: Modern Masters   FFH

NEW, NEWER, NEWEST Art of The Western World Series 30 min., color **CPB**

SHOCK OF THE NEW—Vol. #7: Culture as Nature (1980)
   DIRECTOR: HUGHES, ROBERT 52 min., color
   Videofinders at 1-800-343-4727

SHOCK OF THE NEW—Vol. #8: The Future That Was (1980)
  DIRECTOR: HUGHES, ROBERT 52 min., color
  Videofinders at 1-800-343-4727

Music Resources

Computer Music from the Outside In, Folkways 37465.
Corigliano, John. *Ghosts of Versailles*, Metropolitan Opera Company, Polygram Video, 2 VHS cassettes, 072430–3.
Glass, Philip. *Akhenaten*, CBS 2–M2K–42457.
Glass, Philip. *Einstein on the Beach*, Glass Ensemble. CBS M4–38875 CD; MXT–38875 cassette.
Glass, Philip. *Glassworks*, Glass Ensemble. CBS FM–37265; MK–37265 CD; FMT–37265.
Glass, Philip. *Satyagraha*, CBS 3 M3K–39672.

Web Resources

Resources related to Andy Warhol—http://www.warhol.dk/

The Andy Warhol Foundation—http://www.warholfoundation.org/

Biographical information about Bob Dylan—
  http://rollingstone.com/sections/artists/text/artistgen.asp?afl=googl&lookupstring=184

Resources related to Op Art—http://www.encyclopedia.com/articles/09579.html

Museum of Modern Art—http://www.moma.org/

Philip Glass—http://www.philipglass.com/

McGraw-Hill Resources

Music Listening Selection: CD II
  II–24 Ligeti, *Atmospheres*
  II–25 Babbitt, *Ensembles for Synthesizer*
  II–26 Glass, *Einstein on the Beach*, "Knee 1"
Culture 2.0: Twentieth Century
Transparencies: MA.9 Twentieth Century 1900–Present

Sample test Questions for Chapter 38

1. Pop art was born in England and flourished in the
    a. 1980s in London.
    b. 1960s in Paris.
    c. 1960s in New York.
    d. 1970s in Berlin.
    Ans: c

2. One of the principal influences on the rise of pop art was
   a. language theory.
   b. computers.
   c. mass advertising.
   d. digital imaging.
   Ans: c

3. The technique that Warhol employed to achieve the commercial image was
   a. silkscreen.
   b. lithograph.
   c. woodcut.
   d. engraving.
   Ans: a

4. Oldenburg's *Soft Toilet* looks back in spirit and in style to the works of
   a. Dali.
   b. Duchamp.
   c. Hopper.
   d. Pollock.
   Ans: b

5. Monumentalizing "the excess of the world" in assembled sculptures was the ambition of
   a. Warhol.
   b. Rauschenberg.
   c. Johns.
   d. Stella.
   Ans: b

6. Minimalist artists worked essentially out of an aesthetic inspired by
   a. machine technology.
   b. commercial advertising.
   c. computer digitization.
   d. environmental concerns.
   Ans: a

7. In the work of all "total art" it is true to say that
   a. the final product is of ultimate importance.
   b. process is more important than product.
   c. aesthetic value is purely theatrical.
   d. electronic documentation is essential.
   Ans: b

8. NOT among the neorealist artists of the late twentieth century:
   a. Close
   b. Estes
   c. Hanson
   d. Kiefer
   Ans: d

9. The Grand Castigation series of Wang Guangyi reflects the influence of
   a. Maoist reform principles.
   b. pop art.
   c. minimalist art.
   d. neoexpressionism.
   Ans: b

10. NOT among the video artists of our time:
    a. Viola
    b. Paik
    c. Mariko Mori
    d. Smithson
    Ans: d

11. The famous Bulgarian artist whose earth sculpture "fenced" terrain in California is _____.
    Ans: Christo

12. The most dramatic musical development in the area of electronic music was the invention of the

    _____.
    Ans: synthesizer

13. Musical composition since the 1960s has been characterized by ALL BUT ONE of the following:
    a. improvisation
    b. multiculturalism
    c. microtonality
    d. diatonic harmony
    Ans: d

14. The composer of the minimalist opera, *Einstein on the Beach,* is
    a. John Cage.
    b. Gyorgy Ligeti.
    c. Philip Glass.
    d. Karlheinz Stockhausen.
    Ans: c

15. A turning point in the change of rock music into a more sophisticated medium was the performance
    career of
    a. Elvis Presley.
    b. the Beatles.
    c. Bill Haley.
    d. Little Richard.
    Ans: b

16. The conceptual artist who broadcasts paradoxical and sometimes subversive messages on electronic billboards (e.g. "Lack of charisma can be fatal") is _____.
    Ans: Jenny Holzer

17. The American composer Milton Babbitt is best known for
    a. writing the first electronic music.
    b. writing an opera for voice and tape recorder.
    c. inventing the synthesizer.
    d. his ballet, *Einstein on the Beach*.
    Ans: a

18. The style of composing music that reduces the vocabulary of expression to primary components is called _____.
    Ans: minimalism

19. Contemporary composers of opera show a marked interest in
    a. a return to serialism.
    b. stories based on contemporary events and personalities.
    c. adaptations of folk and fairy tales.
    d. the integration of rock and roll in operatic music.
    Ans: b

20. Frank Gehry's spectacular new Guggenheim Museum is located in
    a. Washington, D. C.
    b. Paris, France.
    c. Bilbao, Spain.
    d. London, England.
    Ans: c